COLLECTIBLE GLASSWARE from the 40s 50s 60s...

Fourth Edition
an illustrated value guide
by Gene Florence

COLLECTOR BOOKS
A Division of Schroeder Publishing Co., Inc.

ABOUT THE AUTHOR

Gene Florence, Jr., born in Lexington in 1944, graduated from the University of Kentucky where he held a double major in mathematics and English. He taught nine years in Kentucky at the junior high and high school levels before his glass collecting "hobby" became his full-time job.

Mr. Florence has been interested in collecting since childhood, beginning with baseball cards and progressing through comic books, coins, bottles and finally, glassware. He first became interested in Depression glassware after purchasing an entire set of Sharon dinnerware for $5.00 at a garage sale.

He has written several books on glassware: *The Collector's Encyclopedia of Depression Glass*, in its thirteenth edition; *Kitchen Glassware of the Depression Years*, in its fifth edition with updated values; *Elegant Glassware of the Depression Era*, in its seventh edition; *The Collector's Encyclopedia of Akro Agate*, in its third printing; *The Collector's Encyclopedia of Occupied Japan*, Volumes I, II, III, IV, V and Price Guide Update Series 1–5; *Very Rare Glassware of the Depression Years*, Volumes I, II, III, IV and V; and the *Pocket Guide to Depression Glass*, now in its tenth edition. He also authored six editions of a baseball book that is now out of print as well as a book on Degenhart for that museum.

His Grannie Bear Antique Shop in Lexington, KY, closed in 1993, due to the death of his beloved mother, "Grannie Bear," who managed that store. However, Mr. Florence continues to sell glassware at Depression glass shows throughout the country as well as via mail order or his web page (http://www.geneflorence.com). Currently, considerable time is spent in Florida where writing is easier without the phone ringing every five minutes — and fishing is just out the office door!

If you know of unlisted or unusual pieces of glassware in the patterns shown in this book, you may write him at Box 22186, Lexington, KY 40522, or at Box 64, Astatula, FL 34705. If you expect a reply, you must enclose a SASE (self-addressed, stamped envelope) — and be patient. Very little mail is answered between Christmas and the middle of May due to his writing, research, and travel schedule. This often causes a backlog of the hundreds of letters he receives weekly. He appreciates your interest and input and spends many hours answering letters when time and circumstances permit which is often on plane trips or in motel rooms across the country. Remember that SASE! He does not open mail. Most letters without a SASE are never seen by him!

On The Cover: Fire King Swirl plate, $15.00. Fostoria Coin decanter, $195.00. Royal Ruby tumbler, $10.00. King's Crown candleholder, $125.00. Fenton Emerald Crest candle, $36.50.

Cover Design: Beth Summers
Book Design: Beth Ray

The current values in this book should be used only as a guide. They are not intended to set prices, which vary from one section of the country to another. Auction prices as well as dealer prices vary greatly and are affected by condition as well as demand. Neither the Author nor the Publisher assumes responsibility for any losses that might be incurred as a result of consulting this guide.

Additional copies of this book may be ordered from:

COLLECTOR BOOKS
P.O. Box 3009
Paducah, Kentucky 42002-3009

or

GENE FLORENCE
P.O. Box 22186   or   P.O. Box 64
Lexington, KY 40522   Astatula, FL 34705

@$19.95. Add $2.00 for postage and handling.

Printed in the U. S. A.

ACKNOWLEDGMENTS

Thanks to friends, readers, collectors, and dealers who have provided me with valuable information on patterns for this book and *The Collector's Encyclopedia of Depression Glass*! All have helped me add an additional sixteen pages of patterns and information to this fourth edition of the *Collectible Glassware from the 40s, 50s, 60s....* This book has expanded from 160 pages to 240 pages in only four editions which is a fifty percent increase in size!

Thanks, especially, to Cathy, my wife, who, over twenty-six years of writing, continues to be my chief editor and critic. She allows my words to tell you exactly what I meant to say!

Thanks, too, to Cathy's mom and dad, Sibyl and Charles, who helped sort and repack glass for days. A new system cut this job to days instead of weeks but added to the sorting chores at our annual weekly photo session. A customer at a show recently expressed his amazement at all the shelves of glass in the building to which Charles replied, "That's nothing, I've built that many shelves for him (me) over the years!" and he's right! Charles, Sibyl, and Marc kept everything under control in Kentucky while we traveled. Marc is overseeing book shipments and handling my web page (http://www.geneflorence.com) along with his electronics school courses. Chad is now married; but he's faithfully been around to load and unload photography and show glass. Revising and rewriting these books every two years requires a lot of help from both family and friends!

Glass, brochures, catalogs, and pricing information were furnished by collectors and dealers from all over the country. Among these cherished people are the following: from Illinois, Dick and Pat Spencer, and Floyd Craft; from Tennessee, Jimmy Gilbreath; from Missouri, Gary and Sue Clark, and Evelyn Rhoades; from Ohio, Dan Tucker, Lorrie Kitchen, Fred McMorrow, Sam and Becky Collings, and Ralph Leslie; from Wisconsin, Ken Fahs; from Kentucky, Calvin and Gwen Key; from Florida, Stacey VanHanswyk; from Washington, Carrie Domitz; from Oklahoma, Charles and Peggy McIntosh; and from New Jersey, René Fry. Additional information came from numerous readers across the U.S.A., Canada, England, Puerto Rico, and New Zealand! Please know I am indebted! Even information given that I cannot yet use is still much appreciated — and filed.

Photographs for the book were taken by Richard Walker of New York, and Charles R. Lynch of Kentucky, both of whom exceeded normal limits taking numerous photographs during one six day session and another seven day session that about devastated our crew from Collector Books. We decided no more seven days of shooting again! Having done five books last year, I decided to cut back some this year with two — or perhaps three!

Unwrapping, sorting, arranging, carting, and repacking glass for photography sessions was handled by Cathy Florence, Dick and Pat Spencer, Jane White, Zibby Walker, and the guys from the shipping department at Collector Books. Other Collector Books personnel kept dropping by our sessions wondering aloud if we were ever going to finish! (I think our inexhaustible candy supply seemed to encourage visitors!) Glassware brought in by collector friends filled an extra room with boxes of glass! Coordinating all these photographs in the time available is a monumental task especially since we have two photographers working four different photography stations. We shoot large groups, small groups, shelf shots, and individual shots all in the same large room. You have to see it to believe it! Richard still climbed his ladder slowly (to rest) between set-ups!

Thanks for all the measurements and the photographs confirming new discoveries (or pointing out omissions) that you readers have sent! It takes photographs to authenticate new pieces. If you have trouble photographing glass, take it outside in natural light, place the glass on a neutral surface, and forget the camera has a flash attachment. A bright cloudy day works best. If you wish photos returned, please enclose a large self addressed, stamped envelope. It has to be large enough to return your pictures.

Thanks also to Beth Ray in the Editorial Department at Collector Books who turned my e-mailed writings into actual pages of a book. It is all I can do to keep up with new software updates that come out between books without learning publishing skills! As usual, I am using new software to start this book. Little idiosyncrasies in new versions are a pain! If I've omitted someone by name who contributed, please forgive me, and know that collectors everywhere are being enlightened by your efforts.

FOREWORD

Just beginning this fourth edition has already been a nightmare! When I started the book, (early I thought) my ten-year-old Macintosh IIfx decided to give me a lesson in stress management. Who would know that a 3.6 volt lithium battery would take a week to find and install only to find out the computer had two of them instead of one? That's not mentioning the youthful computer genius who re-installed the old, dead battery the first 35 mile trip! Not to be outdone by my computer, my nine-year-old laser printer decided to die. No battery would jump start it, so it had to be put out to pasture for good. In any case, I am now writing on one new battery and hoping that the memory will stay long enough to save what I am writing until the second battery is shipped. Starting a week behind schedule means fourteen hour days to make-up time! It's a good thing the fishing here has been lousy!

This *Collectible Glassware of the 40s, 50s, 60s...* book has gone through a metamorphosis from the inaugural concept; but basically, the book covers glassware made after the Depression era that is now being bought by glass collectors. Patterns post 1940 (e.g. Holiday and Moonstone) were removed from *The Collector's Encyclopedia of Depression Glass* except for a few that overlapped both time periods. This allowed me to research newer glass being accumulated and also to expand patterns in *The Collector's Encyclopedia of Depression Glass.*

Initially, it took over five years to assemble the 50s book, but it has been so well received that some Depression glass clubs and show promoters have had to revise contracts to make allowances for glassware made during this time frame. Twenty-seven years ago when I first started writing about glass, Depression glass was found regularly at garage, estate, and rummage sales. Now, glassware made during the 40s and 50s is being encountered. Time changes all things — including collecting. Before this book, there was limited information available for collectors on this generation of glassware.

Both mass-produced and handmade glassware from this 50s era are included here since both types are being collected. A few handmade glassware patterns included were begun near the end of 1930, but their principal production was during the 1940s, 1950s, or later.

Anniversary and Fire-King patterns have always been thought of as Depression glass, but neither were introduced until after 1940. I have spent considerable time compiling available information on Fire-King lines. I have included examples of most Fire-King patterns that were mass marketed through the early 1960s. There are other Fire-King patterns made after this period that I will possibly include in subsequent editions.

Fenton had few dinnerware lines introduced before 1940. I have included several of their lines made since then.

I will continue to add company catalog pages of various patterns when available. With actual catalog pages, many pieces are precisely identified for collectors.

I asked what patterns you would like to see in this book and I received more responses for Anchor Hocking's Early American Prescut than for any other. It is now included as one of the seven new patterns in the book. I realize I am only scratching the surface of this era, but it is a start! If you have collections that you would be willing to lend for photography purposes or copies of glass company advertisements listing pieces which you received with your sets, let me hear from you. Perhaps we can use it in a book and add to the body of knowledge regarding glassware.

Collectors' requests and accumulating inclinations will establish the direction the book will take in the future. It will probably take a few more editions to make this book's format standard, but I am running out of room even now. I hope you find the learning enjoyable! Keep me apprised of your discoveries! I will endeavor to pass them along to other collectors.

ALL PRICES IN THIS BOOK ARE RETAIL PRICES FOR MINT CONDITION GLASSWARE. THIS BOOK IS INTENDED TO BE ONLY A GUIDE TO PRICES SINCE THERE ARE SOME REGIONAL PRICE DIFFERENCES WHICH CANNOT REASONABLY BE DEALT WITH HEREIN.

You may expect dealers to pay from 40% to 50% less than the prices quoted. Glass that is in less than mint condition, i.e., chipped, cracked, scratched, or poorly molded, will bring only a small percentage of the price of glass that is in mint condition. Since this book covers glassware made from 1940 onward, you may expect that dealers and collectors will be less tolerant of wear marks or imperfections than in glass made earlier.

Prices are now fairly standardized due to national advertising of glassware and dealers who market it at numerous glass shows held coast to coast. I have been attending shows in Houston, Seattle, and Chicago in the last month to study price trends. Still, there are **some regional differences in prices** due partly to glass being more readily available in some areas than in others. Many companies charged more initially for wares shipped to the West Coast, and companies distributed certain pieces in some areas that they did not in others. This happens today, also. It's called "test marketing."

Prices tend to increase dramatically on rare items. In general, they increase due to **demand** from additional collectors entering the field and from people becoming more aware of the worth of Depression and 1950s glass.

One of the most important aspects of this book is the attempt to illustrate as well as realistically price those items that are in demand. My desire is to give you the most realistic guide to collectible glass patterns available.

MEASUREMENTS

All measurements are taken from company catalogs or by actually measuring each piece if no catalog lists are available. Capacities of tumblers, stemware, and pitchers are always measured to the very top edge until nothing more can be added. Heights are measured perpendicular to the bottom of the piece, not up a slanted side. In company catalogs, plate measurements were usually rounded to the nearest inch or half inch, across the widest point; this creates problems today, when we require exactness!

CONTENTS

ANNIVERSARY JEANNETTE GLASS COMPANY, 1947 – 49; late 1960s – mid 1970s

Colors: pink, crystal and iridescent, and Shell Pink

Glassware patterns made in the 1950s have been selling extremely well. A lot of this has to do with availability. It is more fun to collect a pattern that you can find than to look for pieces of a pattern in extremely limited distribution. Many more collectors are now seeking 50s patterns. I have included an additional nine in this book. There is now a 50 percent increase in the size of this book from the first edition written only six years ago. Dealers who scoffed at the idea of a book on such relatively "new" glassware are now stocking it for their customers!

When first published, some dealers questioned the inclusion of patterns that had traditionally been considered Depression glass. Even though some patterns have been collected as Depression glass, they truthfully are not. For example, Anniversary is a pattern formerly collected by Depression glass collectors, which was never produced during that Depression era time frame.

Pink Anniversary was only recorded in Jeannette catalogs from 1947 until 1949; but crystal and iridescent could be acquired in boxed sets in "dish barn" outlets as late as 1975. You will find crystal decorated with both silver (platinum) and gold. Trimmed items presently do not sell for any more than regular pieces. Indeed, decorated pieces are often more difficult to sell unless you acquire an unbroken set. Certainly, trimmed sets are rarer and harder to find; so far, Anniversary trims are considered to be a detriment rather than an advantage.

Iridescent Anniversary is often exhibited at flea markets and antique malls; but this later color is still excluded from many Depression era glass shows since it is considered to be too recently manufactured. Considering that crystal Anniversary was made as late as the 1970s, this makes an interesting contradiction! However, iridescent is collectible and even "asked for" at shows. Iridescent Anniversary prices are actually outdistancing those of crystal in many cases; be aware that iridescent is sometimes priced as if it were carnival glass by amateur dealers. Iridescent Anniversary prices have not reached that status yet!

The Anniversary Shell Pink cake plate pictured for the first time in the third edition unfortunately has elicited no others; however, several Shell Pink Anniversary pin-up vases have now been found. Note that the Anniversary pattern is only observed from the bottom view of the cake plate! That groove around the top edge is the rest for the aluminum lid. This groove is also on the crystal cake plate. There are several styles of aluminum lids being found on this cake plate. I have now seen five square cake plates with metal lids here in Florida. Each one of these has had a different decal on the metal lid. Evidently, someone distributed them here.

Crystal Anniversary remains harder to find than pink or iridescent. It is not as enthusiastically sought by collectors, perhaps for that reason. Anniversary is a grand crystal pattern to use, and the price is reasonable when compared to other patterns of this era. The pattern itself is bold enough not to fade away on the table.

The pink Anniversary butter dish, pin-up vase, candy dish, wine glass, and sandwich plate are troublesome to find. The wine and pin-up vase are bargain priced considering how few of them are displayed at shows. That pin-up vase is a similar style to old limousine vases that collectors seek. (Fresh flowers were placed in early cars to make them more pleasant for passengers.)

The 1947 Jeannette catalog lists the open, three-legged candy as a comport and that is how I list it. Jeannette chose to use the older term "comport" rather than "compote." Terminology has simply changed over time.

	Crystal	Pink	Iridescent
Bowl, 4⅞", berry	3.50	7.50	4.00
Bowl, 7⅜", soup	8.00	17.50	6.50
Bowl, 9", fruit	10.00	25.00	12.00
Butter dish bottom	14.00	27.50	
Butter dish top	13.50	27.50	
Butter dish and cover	27.50	55.00	
Candy jar and cover	22.50	45.00	
*Cake plate, 12½"	7.00	17.50	
Cake plate w/metal cover, round	15.00		
Cake plate, 12⅜" **square** w/metal cover	22.50		
Candlestick, 4⅞" pr.	17.50		25.00
Comport, open, 3 legged	5.00	12.50	5.00
Comport, ruffled, 3 legged	6.00		
Creamer, footed	4.50	10.00	6.00

	Crystal	Pink	Iridescent
Cup	4.50	8.00	4.00
Pickle dish, 9"	5.00	12.50	7.00
Plate, 6¼", sherbet	1.75	3.00	2.00
Plate, 9", dinner	5.00	12.50	6.00
Plate, 12½", sandwich server	6.50	13.00	8.00
Relish dish, 8"	5.00	12.00	6.50
Relish, 4 part on metal base	20.00		
Saucer	1.00	2.00	1.00
Sherbet, ftd.	3.50	9.00	
Sugar	4.50	9.00	5.00
Sugar cover	6.00	11.00	3.00
Tid-bit, berry & fruit bowls w/metal hndl.	13.00		
Vase, 6½"	13.00	30.00	
**Vase, wall pin-up	15.00	30.00	
Wine glass, 2½ oz.	8.00	18.00	

*Shell Pink 195.00
**Shell Pink 175.00

Please refer to Foreword for pricing information

6

"BEADED EDGE" (PATTERN #22 MILK GLASS), WESTMORELAND GLASS COMPANY, late 1930s – 1950s

"Beaded Edge" is the collector's name for Westmoreland's Pattern #22 milk glass. The catalog sheet shown on page 13 shows a red edge which Westmoreland called a "rich coral red." According to them, "this pattern is also hand decorated in a full dinner or luncheon service in a series of eight matching fruit designs, and it is also made without decoration." Nothing is mentioned of bird decorations; that may be why only plates are found with birds! Those "chicken" sherbets shown on page 13 sell in the $20.00 range.

I enjoy trying to find pieces with decorations I do not have pictured. Like Petalware in the Depression era glass, you never know exactly what piece or decoration will be at that next show table or antique mall! On page 9 are examples of flowers and the lone bird I have been able to capture. Since I mentioned that I had found only a few birds in my travels, the price on all plates with birds have escalated. Honestly, they are available. Decorations of fruits, flowers, and birds seem to appear in sets of eight designs.

On page 10 are "Strawberries" and assorted purple fruits including "Plums," "Raspberries," and "Grapes." I tried to obtain varied pieces in each of these fruit patterns. The creamer and covered sugar shown with grapes are the same ones shown on page 11 with cherries. Rotating these to the other side reveals the other fruit, a money saving idea for Westmoreland. That sugar and creamer shown is a part of Westmoreland's Pattern #108 and not "Beaded Edge." If you collect either one of these fruit patterns, I suggest you find a set of these Pattern #108 instead of the normally found footed ones, shown in the catalog on page 14. These "patterns" were issued numbers at the company and not names that collectors are so fond of using. This was true of many companies' glassware lines.

The 12" platter, 15" torte plate, and three-part relish remain the key pieces to find in any of the decorated lines. It seems the relish is the most elusive. I was excited to find the 15" torte plate with the "Apple" design shown on page 12. So far, all of the 15" plates I have seen have that "Apple" design. Does anyone have one with a different fruit? The opposite side of that plate surprised me and is pictured at the bottom of page 12. Embossed zodiac symbols photographed better than I could have imagined! (In this book I have been promised the plate will look white and not beige!)

Note: Westmoreland pieces shown on page 14 or 15 which are not "Beaded Edge" are not priced in this book. Glass catalogs often pictured more than one pattern on a page of their catalog.

	Plain	Red Edge	Decorated
Creamer, ftd.	11.00	13.00	17.50
Creamer, ftd. w/lid #108	18.00	25.00	30.00
Cup	5.00	7.00	12.00
Nappy, 5"	4.50	6.50	16.00
Nappy, 6", crimped, oval	7.00	10.00	20.00
Plate, 6", bread and butter	5.00	7.00	9.00
Plate, 7", salad	7.00	10.00	12.00
Plate, 8½", luncheon	7.00	10.00	12.00
Plate, 10½", dinner	12.00	17.50	32.50
Plate, 15", torte	20.00	35.00	55.00
Platter, 12", oval w/tab hndls.	18.50	32.50	80.00
Relish, 3 part	22.50		
Salt and pepper, pr.	22.00	27.50	50.00
Saucer	2.00	3.00	4.00
Sherbet, ftd.	6.50	10.00	15.00
Sugar, ftd.	12.50	15.00	17.50
Sugar, ftd. w/lid #108	18.00	25.00	30.00
Tumbler, 8 oz., ftd.	8.00	12.00	18.00

Please refer to Foreword for pricing information

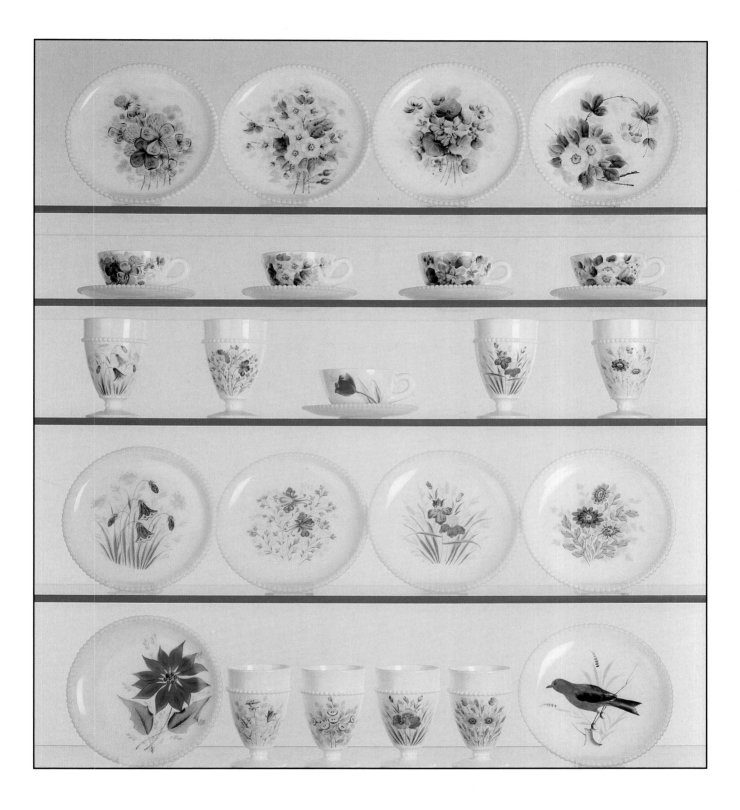

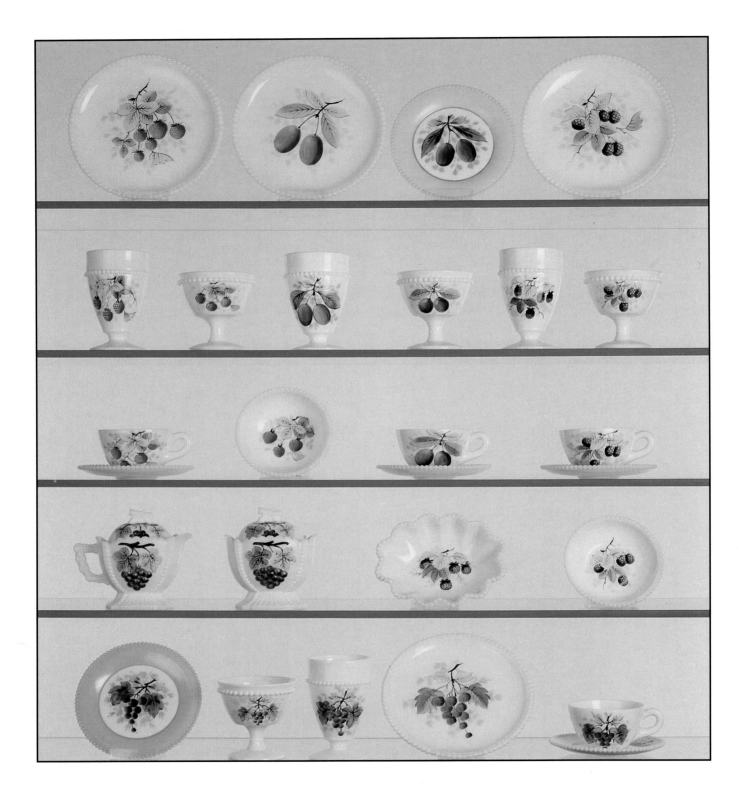

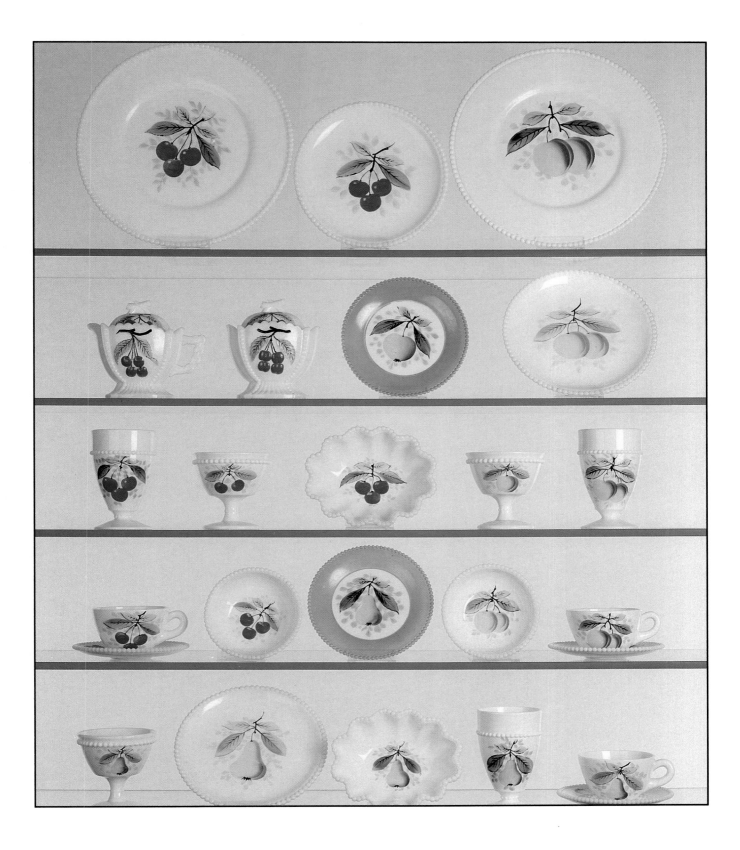

"BEADED EDGE"

America's Finest Handmade Milk Glass

The Lazy Susan breakfast, so cheerful and so companionable, is an occasion where the mood of leisure and the friendly atmosphere of informality are complemented by the sparkle and intimate loveliness of Westmoreland authentic handmade early American Milk Glass reproductions.

Illustrated in natural color is the handmade Beaded-edge pattern with the narrow row of beads hand decorated in rich coral red. This pattern is also hand decorated in a full dinner or luncheon service in a series of eight matching fruit designs, and it is made without decoration.

WESTMORELAND GLASS COMPANY

GRAPEVILLE, PENNSYLVANIA

Handmade Glassware of Quality

"BEADED EDGE"

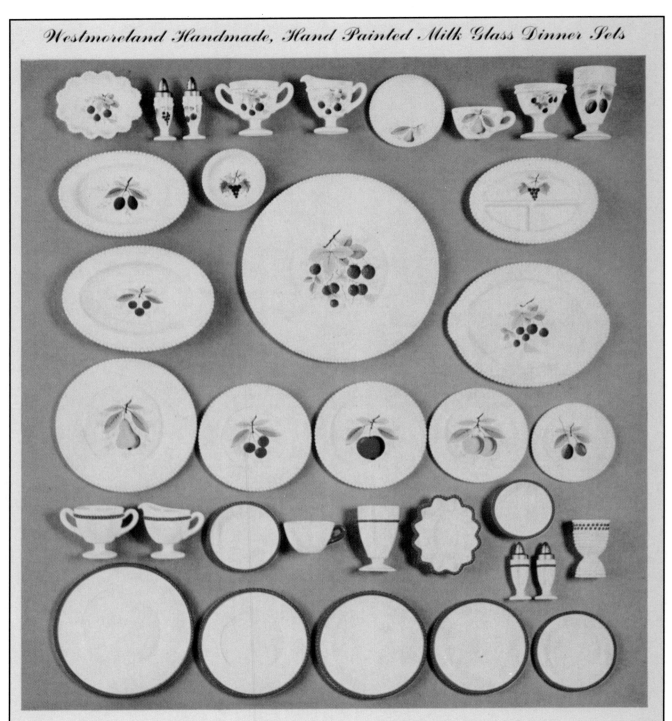

Westmoreland Handmade, Hand Painted Milk Glass Dinner Sets

Top Row: No. 22/6"/64-2. Oval crimped Nappy, "Beaded Edge." Note: all items are available in a set of eight different hand painted fruit decorations: Grape, Cherry, Pear, Plum, Apple, Blackberry, Strawberry and Peach, or in any fruit decoration specified above.
No. 22/64-2. Salt and Pepper.
No. 22/64-2. Cream and Sugar.
No. 22/64-2. Cup and Saucer.
No. 22/64-2. Sherbet, low foot.
No. 22/64-2. Tumbler, footed.

Second Row: No. 22/64-2. Celery Dish, oval.
No. 22/5"/64-2. Nappy, round.
No. 22/15"/64-2. Plate, torte.
No. 22/3part/64-2. Plate, relish, 3-part.

Third Row: 22/64-2. Dish, vegetable.
No. 22/12"/64-2. Platter, oval.

Fourth Row: 22/10½"/64-2. Plate, dinner.
No. 22/8½"/64-2. Plate, luncheon.
No. 22/1/8½"/64-2. Plate, luncheon, coupe shape.
No. 22/1/7"/64-2. Plate, salad, coupe shape.
No. 22/6"/64-2. Plate, bread and butter.

Fifth Row: No. 22/A-28. Cream and Sugar, coral red "Beaded Edge" pattern.
No. 22/A-28. Cup and Saucer.
No. 22/A-28. Tumbler, footed.
No. 22/6"/A-28. Nappy, oval, crimped.
No. 22/5"/A-28. Nappy, round.

No. 22/A-28. Salt and Pepper.

No. 77. Egg Cup, "American Hobnail" with coral red decoration.

Bottom Row: No. 22/10½"/A-28. Plate, dinner.
No. 22/8½"/A-28. Plate, luncheon.
No. 22/1/8½"/A-28. Plate, luncheon, coupe shape.
No. 22/1/7"/A-28. Plate, salad, coupe shape.
No. 22/6"/A-28. Plate, bread and butter.

(The "Red-Beaded Edge" pattern is also available in torte plate, platter, relish, vegetable dish and celery.)

Handmade, Hand Painted Fruit, Bird and Floral Plates

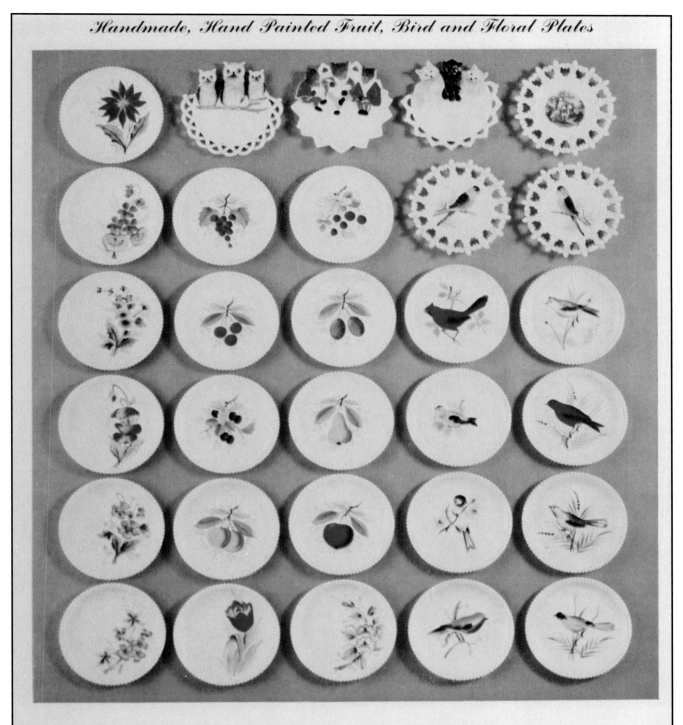

Any of the hand painted Floral, Bird, and Fruit designs shown above on "Beaded-Edge" dessert plates are available on No. 22/15" torte plate shown on opposite page. A set of eight salad plates and footed tumblers, and a 15" torte plate make an attractive luncheon or bridge set.

Top Row: *No. 22/1/7"/4. Coupe shape, dessert or salad plate, with Poinsettia decoration. One of eight hand painted floral designs as illustrated below: Violet, Yellow Daisy, Poppy, Pansy, Apple Blossom, Tulip and Morning Glory.*

No. 6/7"/4. Plate, "Three Owls" decoration.

No. 24/7"/7. Plate, "Three Bears" decoration.

No. 5/7"/1. Plate, "Three Kittens" decoration.

No. 4/7"/WFD. Plate, "Fleur-de-lis," hand applied decal, French, Watteau Scene.

Second Row, second item: No. 22/1/7"/64-2. Coupe Shape dessert or salad Plate, with Grape decoration. One of eight hand painted fruit designs as illustrated at right and below: Strawberry, Cherry, Plum, Blackberry, Pear, Peach and Apple.

No. 4/7"/76 B-R. Fleur-de-lis Plate with hand painted Parakeet (facing right).

No. 4/7"/76 B-L. Fleur-de-lis Plate with hand painted Parakeet (facing left).

Third Row, fourth item: No. 22/1/7"/70. Coupe Shape dessert or salad Plate, with Cardinal decoration. One of eight hand painted bird designs as illustrated at right and below: Titmouse, Goldfinch, Scarlet Tanager, Chickadee, Mocking Bird, Bluebird and Yellow Warbler.

—4—

15

"BUBBLE," "BULLSEYE," PROVINCIAL, ANCHOR HOCKING GLASS COMPANY, 1940 – 1965

Colors: pink, Sapphire blue, Forest Green, Royal Ruby, crystal, and any known Hocking color

"Bubble" is a pattern that is readily recognized by greenhorn collectors! This simple, orbicular design blends easily with modern decor. The vast supply of blue cups, saucers, and dinner plates makes this pattern seem readily available. However, amassing an entire set is a distinctively different subject! Despite copious basic pieces in blue, other items are in lesser supply. Creamers have always been uncommon, and the 9" flanged bowl has essentially departed from the collecting arena. A Canadian woman drove all the way to the Sanford, Florida, glass show looking for a blue "Bubble" creamer! Our Grannie Bear shop was able to accommodate her and she was thrilled. Of course, even January in Florida has to be much warmer than Canadian weather! You will look long and hard for grill plates and 4" berry bowls without inner rim damage. Grill plates are normally divided into three sections, and were used in many of the diners of the 1940s and 1950s. They kept the food separated and allowed smaller portions to fill the plate.

Original labels on crystal "Bubble" atop page 18 read "Heat Proof." A 1942 ad guaranteed this "Fire-King" tableware to be "heat-proof," indeed a "tableware that can be used in the oven, on the table, in the refrigerator." Presumably since this ad is dated 1942, they are referring to the Sapphire blue color. This added dimension is particular to "Fire-King" since most Depression glass patterns will not allow sudden changes in temperature without cracking! Forest Green or Royal Ruby "Bubble" original stickers do not proclaim these same heat-proof qualities, however; so be forewarned!

I received a light green colored saucer from New Zealand. It was very similar to our "Bubble," but was of other manufacture. Maybe the English made a look-alike pattern for "Bubble" as they did for Fostoria's American! In my fifth series *Very Rare Glassware of the Depression Years*, you can see a mottled green cup, saucer, and plate that were found in England. They are different!

Forest Green (dark) and Royal Ruby (red) dinner plates have both become difficult to find without scratches and knife marks on the surface. Observe the two green plates on the middle row of page 17. The first plate measures ⅛" larger than the normally found dinner plate. The center of this plate is smaller and there are four rows of bubbles outside the center, whereas the normally found dinner has three rings of bubbles. I point this out because there are purists who will not accept the smaller centered plate in their collection. You have to decide which style you like. The smaller center plates are harder to find. A collector recently told me that she thought the larger, small centered plates were a flour premium and distributed as a cake plate.

Many collectors use the red and green "Bubble" for their Christmas tables. Green and red water goblets (shown in green on the bottom row) were frequently used for advertising. Usually, collectors buying these pieces are intrigued by a representation of their home town or organization. Too, the first green "Bubble" sugar shown on that row has been iridized, not a common treatment for this ware. I have a creamer/sugar collector who wants my sugar when I find a creamer to go with it. The amber creamer and cup pictured are not commonly found, but I have yet to meet a collector of amber "Bubble"! Even the cover shot of amber on the last book failed to invigorate this rare color.

Pink is hard to find except for the 8⅜" bowl that sells in the $7.00 to $9.00 range. That 8⅜" berry bowl can be found in almost any color that Anchor Hocking made (including all the opaque and iridescent colors common to Hocking). Milk White was only listed in the 1959 – 60 catalog, but they must have been plenteous since so many of them still exist today. The inside depths of these bowls vary. Price all other colors as crystal. Be sure to note the plastic Bubble bowls pictured on the top of page 19. There are four colors made by S & K, but I have no other information at present.

According to one Anchor Hocking catalog, "Bubble" stemware was originally called "Early American" line. The other stemware line sold along with "Bubble" (shown bottom of page 20) has been called "Boopie" by collectors. Both of these stemware lines were manufactured after production of blue "Bubble" had ceased; so, there are no blue stems to be found. Sorry!

Royal Ruby "Boopie" is priced in the same range as Royal Ruby "Bubble" stemware; but the Forest Green "Boopie" is selling at significantly less than the Forest Green "Bubble" stemware shown on page 21. The catalog lists an iced tea in "Boopie" with a capacity of 15 oz. All mine only hold 14 oz.!

	Crystal	Forest Green	Light Blue	Royal Ruby
Bowl, 4", berry	4.00		17.50	
Bowl, 4½", fruit	4.50	7.00	11.00	8.00
Bowl, 5¼", cereal	5.00	12.00	12.50	
Bowl, 7¾", flat soup	6.50		15.00	
Bowl, 8⅜", large berry (Pink-$7.00)	6.50	14.00	16.50	20.00
Bowl, 9", flanged			325.00	
Candlesticks, pr.	16.00	37.50		
Creamer	6.00	12.00	35.00	
*Cup	3.50	7.00	5.00	8.00
Lamp, 3 Styles	40.00			
Pitcher, 64 oz., ice lip	60.00			55.00
Plate, 6¾", bread and butter	2.00	15.00	3.00	
Plate, 9⅜", grill			20.00	
Plate, 9⅜", dinner	6.00	25.00	7.00	22.00
Platter, 12", oval	9.00		16.00	
**Saucer	1.00	4.00	1.50	4.00
***Stem, 3½ oz., cocktail	4.00	10.00		10.00

	Crystal	Forest Green	Light Blue	Royal Ruby
***Stem, 4 oz., juice	4.50	10.00		10.00
Stem, 4½ oz., cocktail	4.00	12.50		12.50
Stem, 5½ oz., juice	5.00	12.50		12.50
***Stem, 6 oz., sherbet	3.00	6.00		7.00
Stem, 6 oz., sherbet	3.50	9.00		9.00
***Stem, 9 oz., goblet	7.00	10.00		12.50
Stem, 9½ oz., goblet	7.00	13.00		13.00
***Stem, 14 oz., iced tea	9.00	14.00		
Sugar	6.00	12.00	20.00	
Tidbit, 2 tier				37.50
Tumbler, 6 oz., juice	3.50			8.00
Tumbler, 8 oz., 3¼", old fashioned		6.00		16.00
Tumbler, 9 oz., water	5.00			9.00
Tumbler, 12 oz., 4½", iced tea	12.00			12.50
Tumbler, 16 oz., 5⅞", lemonade	14.00			16.00

*Pink - $100.00   **Pink - $40.00   ***Boopie

Please refer to Foreword for pricing information

"BUBBLE"

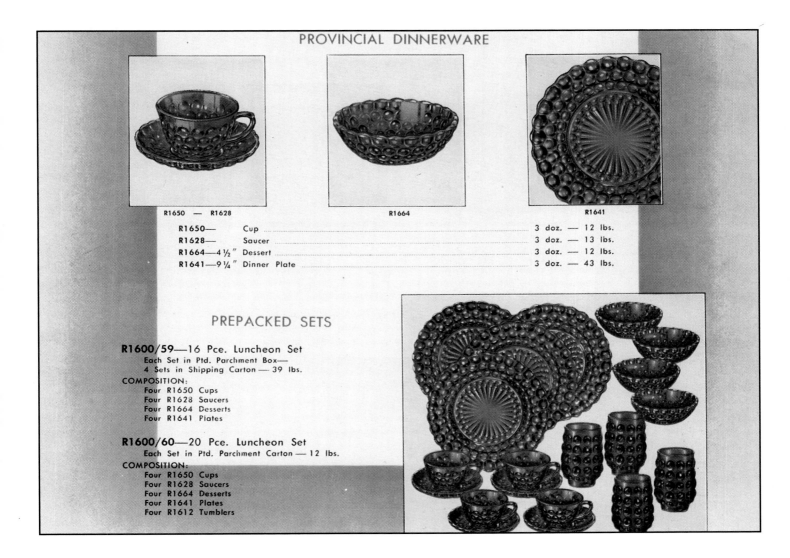

PROVINCIAL DINNERWARE

R1650 — R1628

R1664

R1641

R1650—	Cup	3 doz. — 12 lbs.
R1628—	Saucer	3 doz. — 13 lbs.
R1664—4 ½"	Dessert	3 doz. — 12 lbs.
R1641—9 ¼"	Dinner Plate	3 doz. — 43 lbs.

PREPACKED SETS

R1600/59—16 Pce. Luncheon Set
Each Set in Ptd. Parchment Box—
4 Sets in Shipping Carton — 39 lbs.
COMPOSITION:
    Four R1650 Cups
    Four R1628 Saucers
    Four R1664 Desserts
    Four R1641 Plates

R1600/60—20 Pce. Luncheon Set
Each Set in Ptd. Parchment Carton — 12 lbs.
COMPOSITION:
    Four R1650 Cups
    Four R1628 Saucers
    Four R1664 Desserts
    Four R1641 Plates
    Four R1612 Tumblers

"BUBBLE"

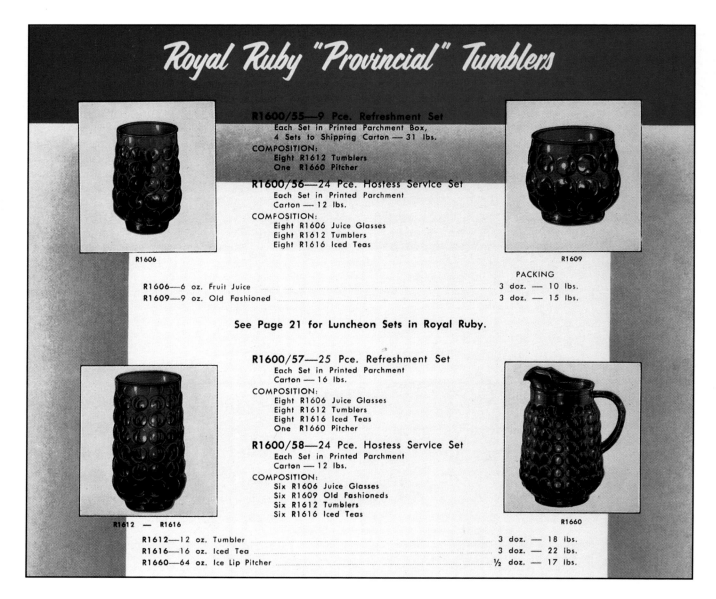

Royal Ruby "Provincial" Tumblers

R1600/55—9 Pce. Refreshment Set
Each Set in Printed Parchment Box,
4 Sets to Shipping Carton — 31 lbs.
COMPOSITION:
    Eight R1612 Tumblers
    One R1660 Pitcher

R1600/56—24 Pce. Hostess Service Set
Each Set in Printed Parchment
Carton — 12 lbs.
COMPOSITION:
    Eight R1606 Juice Glasses
    Eight R1612 Tumblers
    Eight R1616 Iced Teas

R1606

R1609

PACKING

R1606—6 oz. Fruit Juice		3 doz. — 10 lbs.
R1609—9 oz. Old Fashioned		3 doz. — 15 lbs.

See Page 21 for Luncheon Sets in Royal Ruby.

R1600/57—25 Pce. Refreshment Set
Each Set in Printed Parchment
Carton — 16 lbs.
COMPOSITION:
    Eight R1606 Juice Glasses
    Eight R1612 Tumblers
    Eight R1616 Iced Teas
    One R1660 Pitcher

R1600/58—24 Pce. Hostess Service Set
Each Set in Printed Parchment
Carton — 12 lbs.
COMPOSITION:
    Six R1606 Juice Glasses
    Six R1609 Old Fashioneds
    Six R1612 Tumblers
    Six R1616 Iced Teas

R1612 — R1616

R1660

R1612—12 oz. Tumbler		3 doz. — 18 lbs.
R1616—16 oz. Iced Tea		3 doz. — 22 lbs.
R1660—64 oz. Ice Lip Pitcher		½ doz. — 17 lbs.

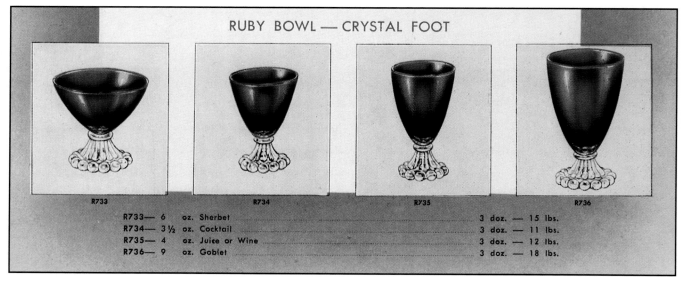

RUBY BOWL — CRYSTAL FOOT

R733   R734   R735   R736

R733— 6 oz. Sherbet			3 doz. — 15 lbs.
R734— 3½ oz. Cocktail			3 doz. — 11 lbs.
R735— 4 oz. Juice or Wine			3 doz. — 12 lbs.
R736— 9 oz. Goblet			3 doz. — 18 lbs.

FOREST GREEN Anchorglass®
Dinnerware

E1600/46—22 PCE. LUNCHEON SET
Each Set in Gift Ctn., 4 Sets to Shipping Ctn.—50 lbs.
COMPOSITION:
Four E1650 Cups   Four E336 Goblets
Four E1628 Saucers   One E1653 Sugar
Four E1665 Cereals   One E1654 Creamer
Four E1641 Dinner Plates

E1600/45—18 PCE. LUNCHEON SET
Each Set in Gift Ctn., 4 Sets
to Shipping Ctn.—42 lbs.
COMPOSITION:
Four E1650 Cups   Four E1641-9¼" Plates
Four E1628 Saucers   One E1653 Sugar
Four E1665 Cereals   One E1654 Creamer

E1600/47—30 PCE. LUNCHEON SET
Each Set in Shipping Ctn.—22 lbs.
COMPOSITION:
Four E1650 Cups   Four E336 Goblets
Four E1628 Saucers   Four E333 Sherbets
Four E1665 Cereals   One E1653 Sugar
Four E1630-6⅜" Plates   One E1654 Creamer
Four E1641-9¼" Plates

FOREST GREEN AND CRYSTAL STEMWARE

E336—9½ OZ. GOBLET
Pkd. 3 doz.—17 lbs.

E335—5½ OZ. F. JUICE
Pkd. 3 doz.—10 lbs.

E334—4½ OZ. COCKTAIL
Pkd. 3 doz.—9 lbs.

E333—6 OZ. SHERBET
Pkd. 3 doz.—16 lbs.

E1650—8 OZ. CUP
Pkd. 6 doz.—22 lbs.

E1628—5¾" SAUCER
Pkd. 6 doz.—24 lbs.

E1665—5¼" CEREAL
Pkd. 6 doz.—35 lbs.

E1630—6⅝" PIE OR SALAD PLATE
Pkd. 6 doz.—38 lbs.

E1641—9¼" DINNER PLATE
Pkd. 3 doz.—38 lbs.

E1653—FOOTED SUGAR
Pkd. 3 doz.—18 lbs.

E1654—FOOTED CREAMER
Pkd. 3 doz.—18 lbs.

BUTTERCUP, ETCHING #340, FOSTORIA GLASS COMPANY, 1941 – 1960

Color: crystal

Buttercup has not yet attained the notoriety of some of Fostoria's other patterns. With a 20 year production there were many brides who chose Buttercup as their wedding crystal. Time is beginning to cause some of these sets to assimilate into the market due to retirement or death. As families downsize or distribute their heirlooms, they are either sold into the collectible market or split up within the family. Collectors are often created from either circumstance of this dispersal; and antique glassware dealers provide one of the few choices left to obtain discontinued glassware.

As I travel, I have noticed that many dealers do not recognize this pattern and bargains can occasionally surface. It is not earth shattering, but I just obtained a set with six cups, eight saucers, and eight salad plates for $30.00. The seller asked me if I knew who made that pretty pattern.

Vases are hard to find in all Fostoria crystal patterns. The smaller vase, pictured on the left of the photo, is the 6", footed #6021. The larger is the 7½", footed #4143. Between these vases is an iced tea tumbler. The small pieces in front are an individual ash tray and a cigarette holder. That cigarette holder might make a better toothpick holder. Stemware, salad, and luncheon plates were in catalog listings as late as 1960. After that, Buttercup disappeared from Fostoria's catalog.

	Crystal		Crystal
Ash tray, #2364, 2⅝", individual	22.00	Plate, #2337, 8½"	17.50
Bottle, #2083, salad dressing	225.00	Plate, #2337, 9½"	40.00
Bowl, #2364, 6", baked apple	18.00	Plate, #2364, 6¾", mayonnaise	7.50
Bowl, #2364, 9", salad	50.00	Plate, #2364, 7¼" x 4½", crescent salad	45.00
Bowl, #2364, 10½", salad	55.00	Plate, #2364, 11¼", cracker	30.00
Bowl, #2364, 11", salad	55.00	Plate, #2364, 11", sandwich	35.00
Bowl, #2364, 12", flared	60.00	Plate, #2364, 14", torte	45.00
Bowl, #2364, 12", lily pond	55.00	Plate, #2364, 16", torte	85.00
Bowl, #2364, 13", fruit	65.00	Relish, #2364, 6½" x 5", 2 part	22.50
Bowl, #2594, 10", 2 hdld.	55.00	Relish, #2364, 10" x 7¼", 3 part	30.00
Candlestick, #2324, 4"	17.50	Saucer, #2350	5.00
Candlestick, #2324, 6"	32.50	Shaker, #2364, 2⅝"	32.50
Candlestick, #2594, 5½"	27.50	Stem, #6030, 3¾", 4 oz., oyster cocktail	18.00
Candlestick, #2594, 8", trindle	45.00	Stem, #6030, 3⅞", 1 oz., cordial	40.00
Candlestick, #6023, 5½", duo	35.00	Stem, #6030, 4⅜", 6 oz., low sherbet	17.50
Candy w/cover, #2364, 3¾" diameter	100.00	Stem, #6030, 5¼", 3½ oz., cocktail	22.50
Celery, #2350, 11"	27.50	Stem, #6030, 5⅝", 6 oz., high sherbet	20.00
Cheese stand, #2364, 5¾" x 2⅞"	20.00	Stem, #6030, 6", 3½ oz., claret-wine	32.50
Cigarette holder, #2364, 2" high	35.00	Stem, #6030, 6⅜", 10 oz., low goblet	22.50
Coaster	15.00	Stem, #6030, 7⅞", 10 oz., water goblet	27.50
Comport, # 2364, 8"	35.00	Sugar, #2350½, 3⅛", ftd	13.00
Comport, #6030, 5"	30.00	Syrup, #2586, sani-cut	250.00
Creamer, #2350½, 3¼", ftd	14.00	Tray, #2364, 11¼", center handled	32.50
Cup, #2350½, ftd.	15.00	Tumbler, #6030, 4⅝", 5 oz., ftd. juice	20.00
Mayonnaise, #2364, 5"	25.00	Tumbler, #6030, 6", 12 oz., ftd. ice tea	27.50
Pickle, #2350, 8"	25.00	Vase, 6", ftd., #4143	90.00
Pitcher, #6011, 8⅞", 53 oz.	265.00	Vase, 6", ftd., #6021	75.00
Plate, #2337, 6"	7.00	Vase, 7½", ftd., #4143	120.00
Plate, #2337, 7½"	12.00	Vase, 10", #2614	135.00

CABOCHON, A.H. HEISEY & COMPANY, 1950 – 1957

Colors: amber, crystal, and Dawn

Cabochon received little notice (outside the world of Heisey collectors) before its introduction in this book. Some collectors find the plainer shapes highly desirable while others think it needs more pizzazz. The name itself means a gem cut in a convex curve with no facets!

Only a small number of Cabochon pieces are found in the desirable amber and Dawn. It is mostly found in crystal. Prices remain reasonable for this pattern manufactured in those last years before the closing of the Heisey plant in 1957. This listing is taken from a 1953 catalog. Most patterns made in the declining years of the factory are harder to find than those made during the glory years from the 1930s to the early 1950s.

Observe the 6¼" Dawn candy dish in the top row. This candy is very seldom seen in this Heisey color. I found a crystal one with Orchid etch that is even more rarely found. Both candy dishes are pictured in *Very Rare Glassware of the Depression Years, Fifth Series*. You will find a few other pieces of Cabochon that are cut or etched, but Orchid and Rose etchings are the desirable designs fascinating a majority of Heisey collectors. Obviously, the original designers of the Cabochon pattern intended the design to stand alone... as a "gem" of glassware!

	Crystal		Crystal
Bon bon, 6¼", hndl.,		Sherbet, 6 oz. #6092 (blown)	4.00
(sides sloped w/squared hndl.) #1951	24.00	Stemware, 1 oz., cordial #6091	22.50
Bottle, oil, w/#101 stopper #1951	30.00	Stemware, 3 oz., oyster cocktail #6091	4.00
Bowl, 4½", dessert #1951	4.00	Stemware, 3 oz., wine #6091	8.00
Bowl, 5", dessert #1951	5.00	Stemware, 4 oz., cocktail #6091	4.00
Bowl, 7", cereal #1951	6.00	Stemware, 5½ oz., sherbet #6091	4.00
Bowl, 13", floral or salad #1951	18.00	Stemware, 10 oz., goblet #6091	8.00
Bowl, 13", gardenia		Sugar, w/cover #1951	14.00
(low w/edge cupped irregularly) #1951	18.00	Tidbit, 7½" (bowl w/sloped outsides) #1951	12.50
Butter dish, ¼ lb. #1951	25.00	Tray, 9", for cream and sugar #1951	45.00
Cake salver, ftd. #1951	65.00	Tumbler, 5 oz. #1951 (pressed)	7.00
Candle holder, 2 lite, ground bottom, pr. #1951	165.00	Tumbler, 5 oz., juice, flat bottomed #6092 (blown)	7.00
Candlette, 1 lite (like bowl), pr. #1951	38.00	Tumbler, 5 oz., juice, ftd. #6091	7.00
Candy, 6¼", w/lid (bowl w/lid) #1951	38.00	Tumbler, 10 oz., beverage #6092 (blown)	8.00
Cheese, 5¾", ftd., compote for cracker plate	17.50	Tumbler, 10 oz., tumbler #6092 (blown)	8.00
Cream #1951	9.00	Tumbler, 12 oz. #1951 (pressed)	12.50
Creamer, cereal, 12 oz. #1951	30.00	Tumbler, 12 oz., ice tea #6092 (blown)	12.50
Cup #1951	6.00	Tumbler, 12 oz., ice tea, ftd. #6091	8.00
Jelly, 6", hndl., (sides and hndl. rounded) #1951	24.00	Tumbler, 14 oz., soda #6092 (blown)	11.00
Mayonnaise, 3 pc. (plate, bowl, ladle) #1951	27.50	Vase, 3½", flared #1951	20.00
Mint, 5¾", ftd., (sides slanted) #1951	22.50		
Pickle tray, 8½" #1951	20.00		
Plate, 8", salad #1951	6.00		
Plate, 13", center hndl. #1951	42.00		
Plate, 14", cracker w/center ring #1951	18.00		
Plate, 14", party (edge cupped irregularly) #1951	18.00		
Plate, 14", sandwich #1951	18.00		
Relish, 9", three part, oblong #1951	22.00		
Relish, 9", three part, square #1951	20.00		
Salt and pepper, square, w/#60 silver			
plated tops, pr. #1951	13.00		
Saucer #1951	1.50		
Sherbet, 6 oz. #1951 (pressed)	4.00		

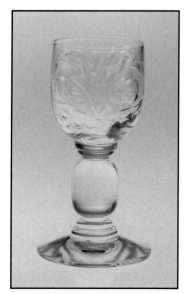

CAMELIA PLATE ETCHING #344, FOSTORIA GLASS COMPANY, 1952 – 1976

Color: crystal

Fostoria's Camelia is often confused by novice dealers and collectors with Heisey's Rose Pattern. Many collectors refer to this pattern as "Camelia Rose." I had a piece brought to me at a glass show over the weekend that had been misidentified as Heisey Rose. The collector was upset because she paid a Heisey Rose price for a cup and saucer that should have been less expensive. She bought it at an antique mall. Have you noticed that almost all antique malls have signs posted — "No Refunds or Returns"?

Camelia was a contemporary of Heisey's Rose, Cambridge's Rose Point, and Tiffin's Cherokee Rose. Fostoria's patterns outlasted all the other companies' rose pattern; but it has never reached the collecting status of those of Heisey or Cambridge.

All pieces in the listing below that have no line number listed are found on #2630 blank, better known as Century. You may find additional pieces in this pattern. Let me know what you discover!

Basket, 10¼" x 6½", wicker hdld.	80.00	Plate, 9½", small dinner	30.00
Bowl, 4½", hdld.	15.00	Plate, 10", hdld., cake	30.00
Bowl, 5", fruit	16.00	Plate, 10¼", dinner	45.00
Bowl, 6", cereal	25.00	Plate, 10½", snack, small center	30.00
Bowl, 6¼", snack, ftd.	20.00	Plate, 14", torte	40.00
Bowl, 7¼", bonbon, 3 ftd.	25.00	Plate, 16", torte	70.00
Bowl, 7⅛", 3 ftd., triangular	18.00	Platter, 12"	47.50
Bowl, 8", flared	30.00	Preserve, w/cover, 6"	65.00
Bowl, 8½", salad	32.00	Relish, 7⅜", 2 part	18.00
Bowl, 9", lily pond	37.50	Relish, 11⅛", 3 part	32.50
Bowl, 9½", hdld., serving bowl	42.50	Salt and pepper, 3⅛", pr.	45.00
Bowl, 9½", oval, serving bowl	45.00	Salver, 12¼", ftd. (like cake stand)	75.00
Bowl, 10", oval, hdld.	45.00	Saucer	4.00
Bowl, 10½", salad	47.50	Stem, #6036, 3¼", 1 oz., cordial	40.00
Bowl, 10¾", ftd., flared	50.00	Stem, #6036, 3¾", 4 oz., oyster cocktail	17.50
Bowl, 11, ftd., rolled edge	55.00	Stem, #6036, 4⅛", 3½ oz., cocktail	22.00
Bowl, 11¼", lily pond	45.00	Stem, #6036, 4⅛", 6 oz., low sherbet	10.00
Bowl, 12", flared	52.50	Stem, #6036, 4¾", 3¼ oz., claret-wine	30.00
Butter, w/cover, ¼ lb.	45.00	Stem, #6036, 4¾", 6 oz., high sherbet	15.00
Candlestick, 4½"	22.50	Stem, #6036, 5⅞", 5½ oz., parfait	25.00
Candlestick, 7", double	37.50	Stem, #6036, 6⅞", 9½ oz., water	25.00
Candlestick, 7¾", triple	50.00	Sugar, 4", ftd.	14.00
Candy, w/cover, 7"	55.00	Sugar, individual	10.00
Comport, 2¾", cheese	20.00	Tid bit, 8⅛", 3 ftd., upturned edge	30.00
Comport, 4⅜"	25.00	Tid bit, 10¼", 2 tier, metal hdld.	45.00
Cracker plate, 10¾"	30.00	Tray, 4¼", for ind. salt/pepper	17.50
Creamer, 4¼"	15.00	Tray, 7⅛", for ind. sugar/creamer	20.00
Creamer, individual	12.00	Tray, 9½", hdld., muffin	32.50
Cup, 6 oz., ftd.	17.00	Tray, 9⅛", hdld., utility	30.00
Ice Bucket	75.00	Tray, 11½", center hdld.	38.00
Mayonnaise, 3 pc.	37.50	Tumbler, #6036, 4⅝", 5 oz., ftd. juice	20.00
Mayonnaise, 4 pc., div. w/2 ladles	42.50	Tumbler, #6306, 6⅛", 12 oz., ftd. ice tea	25.00
Mustard, w/spoon, cover	35.00	Vase, 5", #4121	60.00
Oil, w/stopper, 5 oz.	50.00	Vase, 6", bud	30.00
Pickle, 8¾"	25.00	Vase, 6", ftd., #4143	85.00
Pitcher, 6⅛", 16 oz.	75.00	Vase, 6", ftd., #6021	65.00
Pitcher, 7⅛", 48 oz.	135.00	Vase, 7½", hdld.	85.00
Plate, 6½", bread/butter	7.00	Vase, 8", flip, #2660	85.00
Plate, 7½", crescent salad	45.00	Vase, 8"., ftd., #5092	75.00
Plate, 7½", salad	10.00	Vase, 8½", oval	85.00
Plate, 8", party, w/indent for cup	27.50	Vase, 10", ftd., #2470	110.00
Plate, 8½", luncheon	15.00	Vase, 10½", ftd., #2657	110.00

Please refer to Foreword for pricing information

CAPRI, "SEASHELL," "SWIRL COLONIAL," "COLONIAL," "ALPINE"
HAZEL WARE, DIVISION OF CONTINENTAL CAN, 1960s

Color: Azure blue

"Capri" referred to the blue color of this ware rather than a pattern name per se. Thanks for all the kind words on my efforts to organize the various Capri designs into some form of reference. I will repeat these for those who skipped buying the last book and will be lost trying to understand the terminology. Knowing differences will help when discussing the pattern with dealers or collectors.

Pictured at the top of page 29 is Colony (on the right) and "Colony Swirl" (on the left.) The Colony name comes from actual labels while the "Swirl" is my added name for the same pattern but with a distinct twist in it. Notice that the bases of both patterns are square or rectangular. Until someone finds a piece of the swirled with a pattern name, it will remain "Colony Swirl." That sounds great except I do have a crystal Colony shaped bowl sent me by a reader that has a label "Simplicity." An amber tumbler has also been discovered with a Colony label attached. Perhaps the colored ware was named Colony but the crystal was dubbed Simplicity. "Colony Swirl," at present, seems more scarce than Colony and pricing for "Colony Swirl" is beginning to edge ahead of the Colony.

Pentagonal flat tumblers, hexagonal stems, and octagonal dinnerware items are shown in the bottom photo on page 29. Only Capri labels have been found on these pieces so far. Being a former mathematics teacher, shape names seem the only way to describe these now. Neither the crystal stem nor the avocado green tumbler were found with labels; so their names remain a mystery.

The top of page 30 shows the pattern known as "Seashell." The ash trays all are the same moulds as Moroccan Amethyst; so they are obviously Capri. The tumblers in the back left seem to be the same mould as Moroccan swirl, but they have different blue color than normal Capri. The coaster and candlestick are only Capri possibilities until somebody finds a piece with a label. The square ash tray in the back boasts an IHOP advertisement.

On the bottom of page 30 are more problem children in this pattern. On the right are pieces, I have been calling "Tulip," but a crystal piece with similar characteristics is called "Daisy." The crystal may be made by someone else. It is only similar! On the left is the pattern I have called "Hobnails" to differentiate it from "Dots." Note the small hobs like those seen in some of our Depression era patterns. The creamer and sugars shown here have round bases and seem to fit the handle style of the "Hobnails" cups. The interesting piece here is the swirled creamer similar to the squared "Colony Swirl" pattern. Hopefully, some company catalog information will make an appearance and solve all this speculation! (So far, this has not happened!)

Atop page 31 is the pattern I have dubbed "Dots." Some collectors were calling it "Drip-Drop." The box pictured at the bottom of the page had 24 of these tumblers in three sizes. It says "Skol Swedish style glasses," but the box says "Hazel-Atlas" and not Hazel Ware as you might expect. The tumblers had only Capri labels attached. Prices on the glass ranged from 14 to 19 cents. Since it also says American made, I wonder if they were to be exported. The "Dots" Capri pattern appears to be abundant in my Florida area! Page 32 shows a triangular candy and ash tray that I thought were Capri; and finally, a gift boxed candy was found with the Capri label intact.

Price other colors half or less than the Capri color. There appears to be an abundance of advertising ash trays in this pattern. They might make an interesting collection in themselves! Let me hear what you discover about this appealing pattern!

	Blue		Blue		Blue
Ash tray, 3¼", triangular	6.00	Creamer, round	8.00	Sugar w/lid, round	17.50
Ash tray, 3¼", round	6.00	Cup, octagonal	6.00	Tid bit, 3 tier (round 9⅞" plate,	
Ash tray, 3½", square, embossed		Cup, round, "Hobnails"	5.00	7⅛" plate, 6" saucer)	22.50
flower	15.00	Cup, round, swirled	6.00	Tumbler, 2¾", 4 oz., "Colony Swirl"	7.00
Ash tray, 5", round	7.50	Cup, round, Tulip	7.00	Tumbler, 3", 4 oz., fruit "Dots"	6.00
Ash tray, 6⅞", triangular	12.00	Plate, 5¾", bread and butter,		Tumbler, 3", 5 oz., pentagonal bottom	7.00
Bowl, 4¾", octagonal	7.00	octagonal	5.00	Tumbler, 3¹⁄₁₆", Colony or	
Bowl, 4¾", swirled	8.00	Plate, 7", salad, round, "Colony Swirl"	7.00	"Colony Swirl"	8.00
Bowl, 4⅞", round, "Dots"	7.00	Plate, 7⅛", round, salad, "Colony		Tumbler, 3⅛", 5 oz., pentagonal	8.00
Bowl, 5⅜", salad, round, "Hobnails"	7.00	Swirl"	7.00	Tumbler, 3¼", 8 oz., old fashioned,	
Bowl, 5⅝", "Colony Swirl"	8.50	Plate, 7¼", salad, "Hobnails"	6.50	"Dots"	7.50
Bowl, 5¾", square, deep, Colony	10.00	Plate, 7¼", salad, octagonal	7.50	Tumbler, 3⅝", 3 oz., "Dots"	6.00
Bowl, 6", round, Tulip	12.00	Plate, 8", square	9.00	Tumbler, 4", "Dots"	6.00
Bowl, 6", round, "Dots"	8.00	Plate, 8", square, w/square cup rest	8.00	Tumbler, 4¼", 9 oz., "Colony Swirl"	7.50
Bowl, 6", round, sq. bottom, Colony	8.00	Plate, 8⅞", square	10.00	Tumbler, 4¼", 9 oz., water, pentagonal	
Bowl, 6¹⁄₁₆", round, "Colony Swirl"	8.00	Plate, 8⅞", square, w/round cup rest	9.00	bottom	7.50
Bowl, 7¾", oval, Colony	16.00	Plate, 9½", round, snack w/cup rest,		Tumbler, 5", 12 oz., "Colony Swirl"	9.00
Bowl, 7¾", rectangular, Colony	16.00	Tulip	9.50	Tumbler, 5", 12 oz., tea, pentagonal	
Bowl, 8¾", swirled	18.00	Plate, 9¾", dinner, octagonal	10.00	bottom	9.00
Bowl, 9⅛" x 3" high	25.00	Plate, 9⅞", dinner, round, "Hobnails"	9.00	Tumbler, 5¼", "Dots"	6.50
Bowl, 9½" x 2⅞" high	22.00	Plate, 10", snack, fan shaped w/cup rest	8.50	Tumbler, 5½", 12 oz., tea, swirl	9.00
Bowl, 9½" oval 1½" high	9.00	Saucer, 5½" square	2.00	Tumbler, 6", 10 oz., "Dots"	8.00
Bowl, 10¾", salad, Colony	25.00	Saucer, 6", round, "Hobnails"	1.50	Vase, 8", "Dots"	25.00
Candy jar, w/cover, ftd.	30.00	Saucer, octagonal	2.00	Vase, 8½", ruffled	35.00
Chip and dip, 2 swirled bowls		Stem, 4½", sherbet	7.50		
(8¾" and 4¾" on metal rack)	30.00	Stem, 5½", water	10.00		

Please refer to Foreword for pricing information

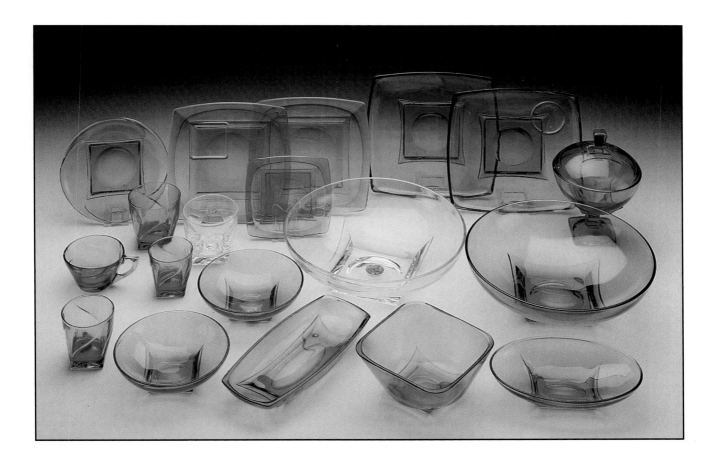

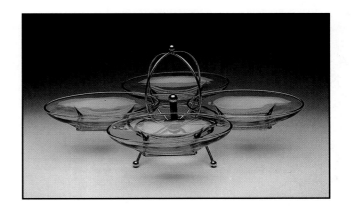

Footed Bowl

Mayonnaise Set

Ash Tray

CASCADE
By CAMBRIDGE

Like a stream of pure light tumbling rhythmically into sun-splashed pools, Cascade brings you one of the most fascinating, brilliant *new* crystal designs to be seen in years. It is hand-made *modern* crystal in a variety of pieces . . . substantial, practical . . . ideal for formal or informal occasions.

You will fall in love with Cascade for yourself and willingly share its beauty in gifts to others. Be sure to see this fine American crystal now . . . at good stores, priced moderately.

THE CAMBRIDGE GLASS COMPANY • CAMBRIDGE, OHIO

CASCADE, 4000 LINE CAMBRIDGE GLASS COMPANY, 1950s

Colors: Crystal, Emerald Green, Mandarin Gold, and Milk White

Cascade is a 1950s pattern made by Cambridge that is just being discovered by collectors. There are two styles of stems on the water goblets, something to notice if you are just beginning to buy this pattern. One is turned upside down from the other. At present, I do not know which is the harder to find. They almost look like they were meant to be different patterns.

Several Cascade items have multiple purposes. The 8" ash tray serves not only in that capacity, but as the punch bowl base when it is turned upside down. Then, too, it rests on top of the 21" plate to make a buffet set. The plate also becomes the punch bowl liner in the punch set. It was a parsimonious use of costly moulds at a time when Cambridge was headed toward insolvency.

	Crystal	Green	Yellow		Crystal	Green	Yellow
Ash tray, 4½"	6.00			Plate, 6½", bread & butter	5.50		
Ash tray, 6"	10.00			Plate, 8½", salad	7.50		
Ash tray, 8"	20.00			Plate, 8", 2 hdld.,			
Bowl, 4½", fruit	7.00			ftd. bonbon	12.50		
Bowl, 6½", relish	13.00			Plate, 11½", 4 ftd.	17.50		
Bowl, 6½", relish, 2 pt.	13.00			Plate, 14", 4 ftd. torte	22.50		
Bowl, 6", 4 ftd. bonbon	11.00			Plate, 21"	50.00		
Bowl, 7",				Punch base (same as			
2 hdld., ftd., bonbon	13.00			8" ash tray)	20.00		
Bowl, 10", 3 pt., celery	20.00			Punch bowl liner, 21"	55.00		
Bowl, 10", 4 ftd., flared	25.00			Punch bowl, 15"	125.00		
Bowl, 10½", 4 ftd., shallow	25.00			Punch cup	7.50		
Bowl, 12", 4 ftd., oval	30.00			Saucer	2.50		
Bowl, 12½", 4 ftd., flared	30.00			Shaker, pr.	18.00		
Bowl, 13", 4 ftd., shallow	30.00			Stem, cocktail	11.00		
Buffet set (21" plate				Stem, sherbet	10.00		
w/8" ash tray)	70.00			Stem, water goblet	14.00		
Candlestick, 5"	15.00	30.00	30.00	Sugar	8.00	20.00	20.00
Candlestick, 6", 2 lite	25.00			Tumbler, 5 oz., flat	10.00		
Candy box, w/cover	35.00	75.00	75.00	Tumbler, 5 oz., ftd.	10.00		
Cigarette box w/cover	22.50			Tumbler, 12 oz., ftd.	13.00		
Comport, 5½"	17.50			Tumbler, 12 oz., flat	12.00		
Creamer	8.50	20.00	20.00	*Vase 9½"	35.00	75.00	75.00
Cup	8.00			Vase, 9½", oval	40.00		
Ice tub, tab hdld.	32.50						
Mayonnaise spoon	7.50			*Milk White $45.00			
Mayonnaise, w/liner	17.50	60.00	60.00				

CASCADE

Reflecting your good taste ...

your choice of

fine handmade Fostoria crystal

to grace your own table

or for a gift to be remembered

Century BY Fostoria   FOSTORIA GLASS COMPANY · MOUNDSVILLE · WEST VIRGINIA

ALL FOSTORIA IS HANDMADE IN AMERICA, AVAILABLE IN OPEN STOCK.

CENTURY LINE #2630, FOSTORIA GLASS COMPANY, 1950 – 1982

Color: Crystal

Century was the blank used for many of Fostoria's etched patterns made after 1950, just as Fairfax was used for various earlier patterns. In order to eliminate duplications in my books, Century will no longer be included in my *Elegant Glassware of the Depression Era*. I used that warning on patterns in my *Collector's Encyclopedia of Depression Glass* when I split it into two time periods and still some collectors wrote wondering why some of the patterns disappeared.

Prices for serving pieces in Century continue to increase. Wines, water goblets, and footed iced teas have stabilized recently as more collectors have turned to etched Century blanks instead of the pattern itself. Nationally, prices are beginning to steady. However, prices for elegant glassware in general are more reasonable in the western states than are the prices for Depression glassware. Dealers at the moment are having a difficult time stocking fundamental patterns in Depression ware, and serving pieces are fetching whatever the market will support. Using that criterion, it's very possible that shortages will occur 20 years hence in the 40s, 50s, and 60s glassware.

Fostoria catalog listings for Century plates conflict with the actual measurements by up to ½ inch. I have tried to include actual measurements for Fostoria patterns in this book. I realize that this has been a profound problem for people ordering through the mail or Internet. (Yes, glassware is now on the net!)

There are two sizes of dinner plates (as happens in most of Fostoria's patterns). The larger plate (usually listed as a service plate) is the harder to find. They were priced higher originally, and many people did without the bigger plates. With use, glass abrasions and scuffs are a proclivity of Century. Since all the pieces are very plain in the center section, scratches show more than with patterns having center designs. The bottom rims of stacked plates is often the culprit since they rub the surface of the underneath plate. Consider using paper plates between the your glass plates — and do not serve guests meats that require cutting.

The ice bucket has button "tabs" for attaching a metal handle. One is pictured in the top photograph. The 8½" oval vase is shaped like the ice bucket but without the tabs. A few damaged ice buckets (sans handles) have been sold as vases. Pay attention to the glass you buy! You can see where the tabs used to be upon close scrutiny.

I recently bought a pair of single candles in pink. Rarely are colors found on the Century blank, so don't pass any colored Century!

	Crystal		Crystal
Ash tray, 2¾"	10.00	Pitcher, 7⅛", 48 oz.	97.50
Basket, 10¼" x 6½", wicker hndl.	70.00	Plate, 6½", bread/butter	6.00
Bowl, 4½", hndl.	12.00	Plate, 7½", salad	8.00
Bowl, 5", fruit	14.00	Plate, 7½", crescent salad	35.00
Bowl, 6", cereal	22.50	Plate, 8", party, w/indent for cup	25.00
Bowl, 6¼", snack, ftd.	14.00	Plate, 8½", luncheon	12.50
Bowl, 7⅛", 3 ftd., triangular	15.00	Plate, 9½", small dinner	25.00
Bowl, 7¼", bonbon, 3 ftd.	20.00	Plate, 10", hndl., cake	22.00
Bowl, 8", flared	25.00	Plate, 10½", dinner	32.00
Bowl, 8½", salad	25.00	Plate, 14", torte	30.00
Bowl, 9", lily pond	30.00	Platter, 12"	47.50
Bowl, 9½", hndl., serving bowl	35.00	Preserve, w/cover, 6"	35.00
Bowl, 9½", oval, serving bowl	32.50	Relish, 7⅜", 2 part	15.00
Bowl, 10", oval, hndl.	32.50	Relish, 11⅛", 3 part	25.00
Bowl, 10½", salad	30.00	Salt and pepper, 2⅜", (individual), pr.	15.00
Bowl, 10¾", ftd., flared	40.00	Salt and pepper, 3⅛", pr.	20.00
Bowl, 11, ftd., rolled edge	40.00	Salver, 12¼", ftd. (like cake stand)	50.00
Bowl, 11¼", lily pond	32.50	Saucer	3.50
Bowl, 12", flared	37.50	Stem, 3½ oz., cocktail, 4⅛"	20.00
Butter, w/cover, ¼ lb.	35.00	Stem, 3½ oz., wine, 4½"	30.00
Candy, w/cover, 7"	37.50	Stem, 4½ oz., oyster cocktail, 3¾"	20.00
Candlestick, 4½"	17.50	Stem, 5½" oz., sherbet, 4½"	12.00
Candlestick, 7", double	30.00	Stem, 10 oz., goblet, 5¾"	22.50
Candlestick, 7¾", triple	40.00	Sugar, 4", ftd.	9.00
Comport, 2¾", cheese	15.00	Sugar, individual	9.00
Comport, 4⅜"	20.00	Tid bit, 8⅛", 3 ftd., upturned edge	18.00
Cracker plate, 10¾"	30.00	Tid bit, 10¼", 2 tier, metal hndl.	25.00
Creamer, 4¼"	9.00	Tray, 4¼", for ind. salt/pepper	14.00
Creamer, individual	9.00	Tray, 7⅛", for ind. sugar/creamer	14.00
Cup, 6 oz., ftd.	13.00	Tray, 9⅛", hndl., utility	25.00
Ice Bucket	65.00	Tray, 9½", hndl., muffin	30.00
Mayonnaise, 3 pc.	30.00	Tray, 11½", center hndl.	30.00
Mayonnaise, 4 pc., div. w/2 ladles	35.00	Tumbler, 5 oz., ftd., juice, 4¾"	22.50
Mustard, w/spoon, cover	27.50	Tumbler, 12 oz., ftd., tea, 5⅞"	27.50
Oil, w/stopper, 5 oz.	45.00	Vase, 6", bud	18.00
Pickle, 8¾"	15.00	Vase, 7½", hndl.	70.00
Pitcher, 6⅛", 16 oz.	50.00	Vase, 8½", oval	67.50

Please refer to Foreword for pricing information

CHINTZ PLATE ETCHING #338, FOSTORIA GLASS COMPANY, 1940 – 1977

Color: Crystal

Fostoria's Chintz was added to this 50s book because it fit the time parameters better than those of the *Elegant Glassware of the Depression Era* in which it was introduced. I repeat, as with the Century pattern, Chintz has now been removed from the Elegant book.

An elusive 9½" oval vegetable bowl is pictured on its side in the top photograph. I found the 17½" plate (in the background of the same photo) at a tent sale outside an antique shop near Pittsburgh. That plate dwarfs the oval vegetable and makes everything else in the picture look very small. That sort of optical illusion always makes selecting pictures for the book difficult. Do you show the rarely seen plate or forget you have it available?

Currently, Chintz stemware is bountiful as is the case for numerous patterns in this era. Evidently, people in the 1950s acquired stemware whether they bought the serving pieces or not. Those serving pieces are evasive as anyone collecting Chintz will tell you. Watch for cream soups, dinner bells, finger bowls, salad dressing bottles, syrups, and any kind of vases. All these pieces are considered to be uncommon.

Contrary to many Fostoria patterns, only one size dinner plate exists in Chintz. You will have to settle for a 9½" plate. Scuffed and worn plates are a nemesis; choose your merchandise carefully. Prices below are for mint condition plates and not ones with so-called "light" damage! If it has light damage, then the price should be less!

The drip cut syrup with metal lid was listed as Sani-cut in sales brochures. Evidently, this was not a significant item then since they are so scarce today. Those oval bowls in the bottom photograph were called sauce dishes by Fostoria. Many collectors refer to them as gravy boats. The oval sauce boat liner came with both, but a brochure listed it as a tray instead of liner. Many pieces of Chintz are found on the #2496 blank (known as Baroque). For novice collectors, a fleur-de-lis in relief is the design for the Baroque blank.

	Crystal		Crystal
Bell, dinner	125.00	Plate, #2496, 9½", dinner	55.00
Bowl, #869, 4½", finger	65.00	Plate, #2496, 10½", hndl., cake	45.00
Bowl, #2496, 4⅝", tri-cornered	22.50	Plate, #2496, 11", cracker	42.00
Bowl, #2496, cream soup	85.00	Plate, #2496, 14", upturned edge	55.00
Bowl, #2496, 5", fruit	30.00	Plate, #2496, 16", torte, plain edge	125.00
Bowl, #2496, 5", hndl.	25.00	Plate, 17½", upturned edge	175.00
Bowl, #2496, 7⅝", bon bon	32.50	Platter, #2496, 12"	100.00
Bowl, #2496, 8½", hndl.	65.00	Relish, #2496, 6", 2 part, square	33.00
Bowl, #2496, 9¼" ftd.	300.00	Relish, #2496, 10" x 7½", 3 part	40.00
Bowl, #2496, 9½", oval vegetable	195.00	Relish, #2419, 5 part	40.00
Bowl, #2496, 9½", vegetable	75.00	Salad dressing bottle, #2083, 6½"	350.00
Bowl, #2484, 10", hndl.	65.00	Salt and pepper, #2496, 2¾", flat, pr.	95.00
Bowl, #2496, 10½", hndl.	70.00	Sauce boat, #2496, oval	65.00
Bowl, #2496, 11½", flared	65.00	Sauce boat, #2496, oval, divided	65.00
Bowl, #6023, ftd.	50.00	Sauce boat liner, #2496, oblong, 8"	30.00
Candlestick, #2496, 3½", double	32.00	Saucer, #2496	5.00
Candlestick, #2496, 4"	20.00	Stem, #6026, 1 oz., cordial, 3⅞"	47.50
Candlestick, #2496, 5½"	35.00	Stem, #6026, 4 oz., cocktail, 5"	24.00
Candlestick, #2496, 6", triple	50.00	Stem, #6026, 4 oz., oyster cocktail, 3⅜"	27.50
Candlestick, #6023, double	45.00	Stem, #6026, 4½ oz., claret-wine, 5⅜"	40.00
Candy, w/cover, #2496, 3 part	140.00	Stem, #6026, 6 oz., low sherbet, 4⅜"	20.00
Celery, #2496, 11"	40.00	Stem, #6026, 6 oz., saucer champagne, 5½"	22.00
Comport, #2496, 3¼", cheese	35.00	Stem, #6026, 9 oz., water goblet, 7⅝"	33.00
Comport, #2496, 4¾"	32.50	Sugar, #2496, 3½", ftd.	16.00
Comport, #2496, 5½"	37.50	Sugar, #2496½, individual	21.00
Creamer, #2496, 3¾", ftd.	17.50	Syrup, #2586, Sani-cut	395.00
Creamer, #2496½, individual	22.50	Tidbit, #2496, 8¼", 3 ftd., upturned edge	26.00
Cup, #2496, ftd.	21.00	Tray, #2496½, 6½", for ind. sugar/creamer	22.00
Ice bucket, #2496	130.00	Tray, #2375, 11", center hndl.	40.00
Jelly, w/cover, #2496, 7½"	85.00	Tumbler, #6026, 5 oz., juice, ftd.	27.50
Mayonnaise, #2496½, 3 piece	60.00	Tumbler, #6026, 9 oz., water or low goblet	27.50
Oil, w/stopper, #2496, 3½ oz.	110.00	Tumbler, #6026, 13 oz., tea, ftd.	32.50
Pickle, #2496, 8"	32.00	Vase, #4108, 5"	95.00
Pitcher, #5000, 48 oz., ftd.	375.00	Vase, #4128, 5"	95.00
Plate, #2496, 6", bread/butter	10.00	Vase, #4143, 6", ftd.	110.00
Plate, #2496, 7½", salad	15.00	Vase, #4143, 7½", ftd.	195.00
Plate, #2496, 8½", luncheon	21.00		

"CHRISTMAS CANDY" NO. 624, INDIANA GLASS COMPANY, 1937 – early 1950s

Colors: Terrace Green (teal) and crystal

"Christmas Candy" is Indiana's #624 line. Prices for Terrace Green (teal) as it was named by the company, have made the largest increase of any pattern in this book. Unfortunately, there is very little Terrace Green found today; but there are numerous collectors! Demand is the engine that drives up prices and a scarcity on top of that creates a dilemma for impatient collectors. Frequently, "Christmas Candy" is found in sets rather than a piece here and there. Any glassware made in the 1950s is often found in sets — having been carefully stored in someone's attic, garage, or basement. Lots of "precious" gifts were never used — or were saved to use later. Nearly all the teal colored pieces I have bought over the years have come from my trips into Indiana. I have also seen several groupings in Florida. "Christmas Candy" may have been regionally distributed. Dunkirk, the home of Indiana Glass, is not far from Indianapolis where I used to attend Depression glass shows each year. Crystal is seen nationally, but not so the teal, as I have been told many times by collectors.

One good thing about buying glassware in Florida, is that "snow birds" (Northerners) yearly bring glass to sell from all over the country. Retirees also bring glassware south with them, and as they move about or leave for a better world, much of that glass comes into the market place!

That round, 9½" vegetable bowl continues to be the only one known! It has created quite a commotion among "Christmas Candy" collectors. There has been such a price offer that by the time you read this, it will have a new home. Yes, it was found in Indiana! I sincerely doubt the company made only one! So, keep your eyes pealed for another.

The bowl atop the crystal tidbit measures 5¾". That bowl is difficult to find and has never been seen in Terrace Green. Crystal Christmas Candy has garnered few collectors, but it is a pattern that can still be found at reasonable prices. Some Terrace Green pieces are no longer reasonably priced as you can see below. (Of course, pricing is relative. Years from now, we may think these were very fair prices for uncommon items!)

I will repeat information found on the only known boxed set. On a 15-piece set was the following: "15 pc. Luncheon set (Terrace Green) To F W Newburger & Co. New Albany Ind Dept M 1346; From Pitman Dretzer Dunkirk Ind 4-3-52." This was valuable dated information because this color had been attributed to a much earlier production in other published material.

	Crystal	Teal
Bowl, 5¾"	4.50	
Bowl, 7⅜", soup	7.00	45.00
Bowl, 9½", vegetable		500.00
Creamer	9.00	30.00
Cup	5.00	30.00
Mayonnaise, w/ladle, liner	22.00	
Plate, 6", bread and butter	3.50	12.50
Plate, 8¼", luncheon	7.00	25.00
Plate, 9⅝", dinner	11.00	45.00
Plate, 11¼", sandwich	16.00	55.00
Saucer	2.00	10.00
Sugar	9.00	30.00
Tidbit, 2-tier	17.50	

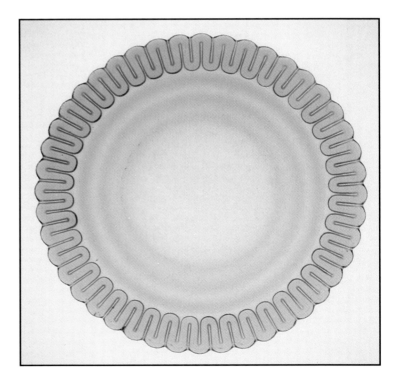

COIN GLASS LINE #1372, FOSTORIA GLASS COMPANY, 1958 – 1982

Colors: amber, blue, crystal, green, Olive, and red

Coin glass is rapidly becoming a hot collectible in today's markets. With that sentence I opened a can of worms in the first edition of this book. Even though I have had hundreds of letters thanking me for finally providing a price guide for Fostoria's Coin Glass, I was sorry that I had included the pattern before the book was ever off the press. I included Coin because it was becoming an increasingly desirable collectible — so desirable, in fact, that Lancaster Colony, who now owns the Fostoria moulds, began remaking it! I do not mean moulding a few pieces, but producing a whole line in many of the original colors! These colors vary somewhat from the originals in amber, blue, and green, but there is almost no way to distinguish the red or crystal made yesterday from that made in the 1950s and 1960s. Most collectors are unaware that Coin is still being produced today. It will be your decision to buy!

I have put an asterisk (*) by all pieces that have been recently made. Recognize that even that could change by the time this book becomes available. Obviously, this has set prices in disarray. Because the newly made pieces are priced so highly, dealers are jacking up the prices on the older pieces. Who can blame them? Why sell an older piece for $50.00 when the newer item sells for $40.00. The older piece is going to be raised to $60.00 or even $75.00. This has happened in other collectibles, oak furniture for an example. The quandary I now have is how to handle it. If you collect Fostoria Coin, never has the following been truer. Know your dealer! Ask him if he can date the piece and keep the dated information with the piece; remember, if the price sounds too good to be true, it probably is!

The blue lamp minus shade (top of page 47) was one of a pair I bought in an antique mall in Ohio a couple of years ago for an outrageously low price of $5.00 per pair. There are still bargains to be found!

The Olive Green is sometimes referred to as avocado, but Olive was the official name. The green that is most desired is often called "emerald" by collectors. This color is represented by the jelly and cruet set shown on bottom of page 47.

If you enjoy this pattern, by all means, collect it. Just be aware that future marketing may be jeopardized by the remaking of older colors. Buy accordingly.

	Amber	Blue	Crystal	Green	Olive	Ruby
Ash tray, 5" #1372/123	17.50	25.00	18.00	30.00	17.50	22.50
Ash tray, 7½", center coin #1372/119	20.00		25.00	35.00		25.00
Ash tray, 7½", round #1372/114	25.00	40.00	25.00	45.00	30.00	20.00
Ash tray, 10" #1372/124	30.00	50.00	25.00	55.00	30.00	
Ash tray, oblong #1372/115	15.00	20.00	10.00	25.00	25.00	
Ash tray/cover, 3" #1372/110	20.00	25.00	25.00	30.00		
Bowl, 8", round #1372/179	30.00	50.00	25.00	70.00	25.00	45.00
Bowl, 8½", ftd. #1372/199	60.00	90.00	50.00	100.00	50.00	70.00
Bowl, 8½", ftd. w/cover #1372/212	100.00	165.00	85.00	185.00		
*Bowl, 9", oval #1372/189	30.00	55.00	30.00	70.00	30.00	50.00
*Bowl, wedding w/cover #1372/162	70.00	90.00	55.00	135.00	55.00	85.00
Candle holder, 4½", pr. #1372/316	30.00	50.00	40.00	50.00	30.00	50.00
Candle holder, 8", pr. #1372/326	60.00		50.00		50.00	110.00
Candy box w/cover, 4⅛" #1372/354	30.00	60.00	30.00	75.00	30.00	60.00
*Candy jar w/cover, 6⁵⁄₁₆" #1372/347	25.00	50.00	25.00	75.00	25.00	50.00
*Cigarette box w/cover, 5¾" x 4½" #1372/374	50.00	75.00	40.00	110.00		
Cigarette holder w/ash tray cover #1372/372	50.00	75.00	45.00	90.00		
Cigarette urn, 3⅜", ftd. #1372/381	25.00	45.00	20.00	50.00	20.00	40.00
Condiment set, 4 pc. (tray, 2 shakers and cruet) #1372/737	210.00	295.00	130.00		205.00	
Condiment tray, 9⅝", #1372/738	60.00	75.00	40.00		75.00	
*Creamer #1372/680	11.00	16.00	10.00	30.00	15.00	16.00
Cruet, 7 oz. w/stopper #1372/531	65.00	110.00	55.00	160.00	80.00	
*Decanter w/stopper, pint, 10³⁄₁₆" #1372/400	120.00	195.00	90.00	350.00	135.00	
*Jelly #1372/448	17.50	25.00	15.00	35.00	15.00	25.00
Lamp chimney, coach or patio #1372/461	50.00	60.00	40.00			
Lamp chimney, hndl., courting #1372/292	45.00	65.00				
Lamp, 9¾", hndl., courting, oil #1372/310	110.00	170.00				
Lamp, 10⅛", hndl., courting, electric #1372/311	110.00	170.00				
Lamp, 13½", coach, electric #1372/321	135.00	195.00	95.00			
Lamp, 13½", coach, oil #1372/320	135.00	195.00	95.00			

Please refer to Foreword for pricing information

	Amber	Blue	Crystal	Green	Olive	Ruby
Lamp, 16⅝", patio, electric #1372/466	160.00	275.00	135.00			
Lamp, 16⅝", patio, oil #1372/459	160.00	275.00	135.00			
Nappy, 4½" #1372/495			22.00			
*Nappy, 5⅜", w/hndl. #1372/499	20.00	30.00	15.00	40.00	18.00	30.00
Pitcher, 32 oz., 6 5/16" #1372/453	55.00	125.00	55.00	165.00	55.00	95.00
Plate, 8", #1372/550			20.00		20.00	40.00
Punch bowl base #1372/602			165.00			
Punch bowl, 14", 1½ gal., #1372/600			165.00			
Punch cup #1372/615			32.00			
*Salver, ftd., 6½" tall #1372/630	110.00	150.00	90.00	250.00	115.00	
Shaker, 3¼", pr. w/chrome top #1372/652	30.00	45.00	25.00	90.00	30.00	45.00
Stem, 4", 5 oz. wine #1372/26			35.00		50.00	70.00
Stem, 5¼", 9 oz., sherbet, #1372/7			25.00		45.00	70.00
Stem, 10½ oz., goblet #1372/2			38.00		50.00	95.00
*Sugar w/cover #1372/673	35.00	45.00	25.00	65.00	35.00	45.00
Tumbler, 3⅝", 9 oz. juice/old fashioned #1372/81			30.00			
Tumbler, 4¼", 9 oz. water, scotch & soda #1372/73			30.00			
Tumbler, 5⅛", 12 oz. ice tea/high ball #1372/64			37.50			
Tumbler, 5⅜", 10 oz. double old fashioned #1372/23			30.00			
Tumbler, 5 3/16", 14 oz. ice tea #1372/58			35.00		40.00	75.00
*Urn, 12¾", ftd., w/cover #1372/829	80.00	125.00	75.00	200.00	80.00	100.00
Vase, 8", bud #1372/799	22.00	40.00	20.00	60.00	25.00	45.00
Vase, 10", ftd. #1372/818			45.00			

Please refer to Foreword for pricing information

CORSAGE PLATE ETCHING #325, FOSTORIA GLASS COMPANY, 1935 – 1960

Color: Crystal

Corsage was introduced before the 40s decade, but nearly all its major production falls within the guidelines of this book. Examine the cone-shaped nosegay of flowers that adorns Corsage. It is occasionally confused with Fostoria's Mayflower pattern that has a cornucopia of flowers as its main design. Turn to page 147 so you can contrast these two Fostoria flower patterns.

Corsage is one of a small number of Fostoria dinnerware lines found on several different blanks. There are three lines illustrated in the picture on the right. The creamer and sugar shown are #2440 or Lafayette blank as are the cup and saucer and a few other serving pieces. The individual creamer and sugar (not pictured) are found on #2496 that is known as Baroque. I can't think of any other pattern that has different blanks for two sizes of sugars. The ice bucket is on the Baroque blank. Oddly enough, the basic plates are from the #2337 line that has plain round plates. The larger cake plate and the 13" torte plate are found on the Lafayette line.

I found all this highly entertaining as I researched this pattern for the book. It's almost as if they were etching remainders for this pattern. You will no doubt have fun unearthing the different blanks on which Corsage is etched. I know I did!

	Crystal		Crystal
Bowl, #869, finger	25.00	Plate, 10", hdld., cake, #2496	35.00
Bowl, 4", #4119, ftd.	22.00	Plate, 11", cracker, #2496	35.00
Bowl, 4⅝", 3 corner, #2496	20.00	Plate, 13", torte, #2440	50.00
Bowl, 7⅜" 3 ftd., bon bon, #2496	20.00	Plate, 16", #2364	85.00
Bowl, 9", hdld., #2536	65.00	Relish, 2 part, #2440	27.50
Bowl, 9½", ftd., #2537	145.00	Relish, 2 part, #2496	22.50
Bowl, 10", hdld., #2484	60.00	Relish, 3 part, #2440	35.00
Bowl, 12", flared, #2496	55.00	Relish, 3 part, #2496	32.50
Bowl, 12½", oval, #2545, "Flame"	45.00	Relish, 4 part, #2419	42.50
Candelabra, 2 light w/prisms, #2527	77.50	Relish, 4 part, #2496	37.50
Candlestick, 5½", #2496	30.00	Relish, 5 part, #2419	57.50
Candlestick, 5½", #2535	35.00	Sauce bowl, 6½", oval, #2440	65.00
Candlestick, 6¾", duo, #2545, "Flame"	45.00	Sauce tray, 8½", oval, #2440	35.00
Candlestick, duo, #2496	40.00	Saucer, #2440	5.00
Candlestick, trindle, #2496	50.00	Stem, #6014, 3¾", 1 oz., cordial	45.00
Candy, w/lid, 3 part, #2496	100.00	Stem, #6014, 3¾", 4 oz., oyster cocktail	17.50
Celery, #2440	32.00	Stem, #6014, 4½", 5½ oz., low sherbet	16.00
Comport, 3¼", cheese	20.00	Stem, #6014, 5¼", 3 oz., wine	30.00
Comport, 5½", #2496	22.50	Stem, #6014, 5⅜", 5½ oz., high sherbet	22.00
Creamer, #2440	17.50	Stem, #6014, 5", 3½ oz., cocktail	22.00
Creamer, ind., #2496	12.50	Stem, #6014, 7⅜", 9 oz., water	27.50
Cup, #2440	18.00	Stem, #6014, 7⅞", 4 oz., claret	35.00
Ice Bucket, #2496	75.00	Sugar, #2440	17.50
Mayonnaise, 2 part, #2440	25.00	Sugar, ind., #2496	12.50
Mayonnaise, 3 pc., #2496½	47.50	Tid bit, 3 footed, #2496	15.00
Pickle, #2440	25.00	Tray, 6½", ind. sug/cr., #2496½	12.50
Pitcher	250.00	Tumbler, #6014, 4¾", 5 oz., ftd. juice	20.00
Plate, 6½", #2337	8.00	Tumbler, #6014, 5½", 9 oz., ftd. water	22.00
Plate, 7½", #2337	10.00	Tumbler, #6014, 6", 12 oz., ftd. ice tea	25.00
Plate, 8½",	12.50	Vase, 8", bud, #5092	55.00
Plate, 9½", #2337	37.50	Vase, 10", ftd., #2470	135.00
Plate, 10½", cake, hdld., #2440	32.50		

"CRINOLINE," RIPPLE, "PETTICOAT," "PIE CRUST," "LASAGNA"
HAZEL ATLAS GLASS COMPANY, early 1950s

Colors: Platonite white and white w/blue or pink trim

"Petticoat" is the name I first heard used for this pattern; then my wife and I heard someone call it "Crinoline" and Cathy thought that more descriptive of the border treatment. The names listed above are ones that I have also seen or heard over the years. All are descriptive and any would work; however, just last week I received a call from an individual visiting Florida from Virginia. She had heard from a dealer that this pattern was being added to my book. She called and told me that she had an original boxed set with the pattern name Ripple on it. Since the layout of this book was already "set in stone," it is alphabetized as "Crinoline" for this one book. Next edition it will be found under its Ripple name if a confirming picture arrives as promised.

We have been buying Ripple for several years and decided to test the waters with pricing at a recent show. Prices below are the actual selling prices that we received. It will take time to ascertain the broader picture, but for now I can say the dinner plate and cereal bowls are harder to find than other pieces. There are at least two sizes of tumblers that go with either color. In fact, a mix of colors works very well! You may find other pieces; I'd appreciate a listing of what you find.

	All colors		All colors
Bowl, berry, 5"	5.00	Plate, dinner	12.50
Bowl, cereal, 5⅝"	8.00	Saucer, 5⅝"	1.00
Creamer	7.50	Sugar	7.50
Cup	4.00	Tid bit, 3 tier	30.00
Plate, salad	5.00	Tumbler, 6", 16 oz.	8.00
Plate, 8⅛", luncheon	8.00	Tumbler, 6¼", 20oz.	10.00

Please refer to Foreword for pricing information

CROCHETED CRYSTAL, IMPERIAL GLASS COMPANY, 1943 – early 1950s

Color: Crystal

Crocheted Crystal was made by Imperial exclusively for Sears, Roebuck and Company. The listing below is from the fall 1943 Sears catalog. In order to show you the stemware in this pattern, I have included an ad showing them (page 53). I have been unable to locate any of these myself. I think the difficulty lies with the fact that no one seems to recognize these as Crocheted Crystal. Besides the stems, the cake stand and narcissus bowl are not easily found.

I first started looking at this pattern because the shapes and styles reminded me of Laced Edge, also made by Imperial. Some of the pieces I have pictured are not in the listing below, although they have all the characteristics of the pattern. I do not have all the Sears catalog listings from this era; so there may be additional pieces not in my list. You will find a number of go-with pieces in this pattern. Not only did Imperial make a multitude of similar designs, but so did other companies. In the lower photograph the center handled plate and ruffled bowl in the back are possible go-with items.

In that same photo is a punch bowl with closed-handled cups, although the catalog ad shows open-handled ones. Cups came both ways and I suspect the earlier cups had the open handles. Consumer complaints of "punch baptisms" may have influenced a design change on this cup! There is no punch liner, but the 14" plate will serve as such. I have not seen a 17" plate, but that might also work. The single candleholder next to the double one is shaped like the Narcissus bowl. Even though the candle is not listed, I have no doubt that this is Crocheted Crystal. The double candleholder may be the most commonly found piece.

An astounding thing I encountered while trying to buy pieces of this pattern was the disparity of prices. No one seemed to know what the pattern was, but they all had proud prices because it was "pretty good glass" or "elegant looking glass." One individual swore that the epergne set was Heisey. She said it was pictured in the Heisey book and she could let it go for a special dealer price of $395.00! I suspect she still owns it!

I have never understood how merchants can come up with a gigantic price when they have no idea what they are pricing! A guess based upon what was paid, I understand; but attempting to tell someone what something is when one has no idea, is a blunder! It's better to put nothing on the label but a price. What's the old saw? Better to be thought a fool, than open your mouth and prove it.

Contrary to what I see on labels of unfamiliar glass, Heisey and Cambridge did not make every smart looking piece of glass in the country!

	Crystal		Crystal
Basket, 6"	27.50	Mayonnaise ladle	5.00
Basket, 9"	37.50	Mayonnaise plate, 7½"	7.50
Basket, 12"	60.00	Plate, 8", salad	7.50
Bowl, 7", Narcissus	35.00	Plate, 9½"	12.50
Bowl, 10½", salad	27.50	Plate, 13", salad bowl liner	22.50
Bowl, 11", console	27.50	Plate, 14"	25.00
Bowl, 12", console	30.00	Plate, 17"	40.00
Buffet set, 14" plate, ftd. sauce bowl, ladle	45.00	Punch bowl, 14"	65.00
Cake stand, 12", ftd.	40.00	Punch cup closed hdld.	5.00
Candleholder, 4½" high, double	17.50	Punch cup, open hdld.	7.00
Candleholder, 6" wide, single	20.00	Relish, 11½", 3 pt.	25.00
Candleholder (Narcissus bowl shape)	30.00	Stem, 4½", 3½ oz., cocktail	12.50
Celery, 10", oval	25.00	Stem, 5½", 4½ oz., wine	17.50
Cheese & cracker, 12" plate, ftd. dish	37.50	Stem, 5", 6 oz., sherbet	10.00
Creamer	17.50	Stem, 7⅛", 9 oz., water goblet	14.00
Epergne, 11", ftd. bowl, center vase	130.00	Sugar	15.00
Hors d'oeuvre dish, 10½", 4 pt., round	30.00	Tumbler, 6", 6 oz., ftd. fruit juice	10.00
Lamp, 11", hurricane	37.50	Tumbler, 7⅛", 12 oz., ftd. iced tea	15.00
Mayonnaise bowl, 5¼"	12.50	Vase, 8"	20.00

Our choice and yours ... Harmony House *Crocheted Crystal*

Your table deserves fine hand-made crystal, and this is it. Harmony House Crocheted Crystal ... unusually elegant, unusually low priced ... exclusive with Sears. You'll want it for yourself, and you'll choose it for impressive gifts. All pieces (except stemware) have graceful "crocheted" openwork edges.

4-piece Salad Set

[A] With this set you'll add sparkle to salads, flatter your dining table. Bowl. 10½-in. diam.; plate, 13-in. diam.; glass serving fork, spoon.
35 E 01732—Shpg. wt., 7 lbs...4-piece set **$2.65**

Charming Epergne Centerpiece

[B] Filled with colorful fruit or flowers, this beautiful epergne will brighten your living room or add a graceful touch to your dining table or buffet. Sparkling, footed crystal glass bowl, 11 inches in diameter, with removable vase. Overall height, 11 inches. Shipping weight, 7 pounds.
35 E 01727 .... Complete centerpiece **$2.89**

Graceful Cake Stand

[C] This beautiful cake stand will even do justice to your prize cakes—and it's equally good for holding smaller tid-bits like cookies, candies, and fruit. Overall diam., 12 in. Height, 4 in.
35 E 1729—Shipping weight, 5 pounds ...Each **$1.49**

Lovely 3-piece Console Set

[D] Glittering crystal and glowing candle-light add charm and glamour to any occasion. Here is a 3-piece console set, consisting of two exquisitely styled crystal glass twin candle-holders, each about 4½ inches high, and a lovely crystal glass bowl, about 11 inches in diameter. Candles not incl.
35 E 01739—Shpg. wt., 6 lbs......3-piece set **$1.45**

Matched Crocheted Stemware

[E] Start your collection of crocheted crystal with this 12-piece set, which includes the most popular, most-used pieces. All have strikingly beautiful shapes and decorated stems. Set of four goblets, four sherbets and four 8-inch salad plates. Makes a romantic gift any bride would treasure.
35 E 01751—Shpg. wt., 10 lbs ...12-piece set **$5.79**

Add more stemware from time to time from open stock

35 E 1750—State pieces.	Height	Shpg. wt., Each	Six for
Goblet......Size 9 oz ....7⅛ in .1 lb..55c..$3.25			
Sherbet.....Size 6 oz .....5 .1 lb..55c..3.25			
Wine ....Size 4½ oz .....5½ in .1 lb..55c..3.25			
Iced Tea ...Size 12 oz ......7⅛ in .1 lb..55c..3.25			
Salad Plate .Size 8-in. diam......2 lbs .38c..2.19			

Narcissus Bowl

[F] Just the thing for growing narcissus or other bulbs; you'll like it, too, for candies, preserves and salted nuts. Deep bowl. 4½-in. high, 7 in. diam.
35 E 1714—Shipping weight, 3 pounds 8 ounces **85c**

14-piece Punch Set

[G] If you're one who plays hostess often, this set will prove practical—really invaluable. It adds a festive touch to any occasion, and is wonderful for holiday entertaining. Cups hook over the edge of the bowl, which can also be used for salads. 4-qt. bowl, 14 in. in diam.; 12 six-ounce cups; glass ladle.
35 E 01719—Shpg. wt., 18 lbs ......14-piece set **$5.75**
35 E 1720—Set of 12 cups only. Shpg. wt., 8 lbs. **$2.89**

3-Piece Mayonnaise Set

[H] Bowl 5¼-in. diam.; plate 7½-in. diam.; ladle.
35 E 1705—Shipping weight, 3 lbs. 8 oz ..Set **89c**

Exquisite Crocheted Plates

[J] Use the 9½-inch size for place plates; 14-inch size plate for cake; 17-inch size for sandwiches.
35 E 01701—9½-in. Shpg. wt., 9 lbs .....Set of six **$2.59**
35 E 01703—14-in. Shpg. wt., 5 lbs ....Each **1.25**
35 E 01704—17-in. Shpg. wt., 8 lbs ....Each **3.45**

3-piece Buffet Set

[K] Ideal for serving snacks that require sauces. 14-in. serving plate, removable bowl for sauce, and ladle.
35 E 01736—Shipping weight, 6 pounds .....Set **$1.65**

Hors d'oeuvre Dish

[L] Useful relish dish with four handy partitions.
35 E 1716—Diam. 10½ in. Shpg. wt., 3 lbs **98c**

Crocheted Crystal can be added to your Easy Terms order ... see inside back cover

"DAISY," NUMBER 620, INDIANA GLASS COMPANY

Colors: crystal, 1933 – 40; fired-on red, late 30s; amber, 1940s; dark green and milk glass, 1960s, 1970s, 1980s.

"Daisy" is one of the small number of patterns that fit the time frame of both *Collector's Encyclopedia of Depression Glass* and *Collectible Glassware of the 40s, 50s, 60s ....* Since more collectors search for amber or green "Daisy," I decided that it best fit this book. Know that the crystal was made in 1930s, but there are few collectors for that today, pretty though it is.

Avocado colored "Daisy" was marketed by Indiana as "Heritage" in the 1960s through 1980s and not under the name "Daisy" or No. 620 as it was called when it was first produced in the late 1930s. I mention this because Federal Glass Company also made a "Heritage" pattern that is rare in green. Federal's green is the brighter, normally found Depression glass color and not the avocado colored green shown here. You can see that rare color on page 121.

Amber "Daisy" has numerous admirers and prices have increased. Besides the indented grill plate, the 12 oz. footed tea, relish dish, 9⅜" berry, and cereal bowls are all scarce, not rare. Perfect (without inner rim roughness) cereal bowls have become the most difficult pieces to find, taking that honor away from the iced tea.

A week after we photographed this shelf set up, I found an amber grill plate with an indent. It amazes me how many times that has happened in the past. It's been four years since we last photographed "Daisy" without turning up that one missing amber piece; and two weeks after this photo session, a stack of those plates was sitting in an antique mall in Kentucky looking for a buyer! They were not cheap enough to buy for resale, but I had to buy one! The pattern shot below shows an indented grill plate in green. Note how large that ring is. It is much larger than the base of a cup, but fits the base of the cream soup perfectly. I never have figured out how the grill plate/cream soup combination came about. If anyone knows why this combo, let me know!

There are a few pieces of fired-on red "Daisy" being found. A reader's letter a few years back said that her family had a red set that was acquired in 1935. That helps date this production. There is a pitcher in a fired-on red being found with the No. 618 tumblers. This pitcher does not belong to either pattern per se, but was sold with both of these Indiana patterns. Thus, it's a legitimate "go-with" pitcher. It has a squared base, if you spot one.

	Crystal	Green	Red, Amber
Bowl, 4½", berry	4.50	6.00	9.00
Bowl, 4½", cream soup	4.50	6.00	12.00
Bowl, 6", cereal	10.00	12.00	32.00
Bowl, 7⅜", deep berry	7.50	9.00	15.00
Bowl, 9⅜", deep berry	13.00	16.00	35.00
Bowl, 10", oval vegetable	9.50	11.00	17.50
Creamer, footed	5.50	5.00	8.00
Cup	4.00	4.00	6.00
Plate, 6", sherbet	2.00	2.00	3.00
Plate, 7⅜", salad	3.50	3.50	7.00
Plate, 8⅜", luncheon	4.00	4.50	6.00
Plate, 10⅜", grill	5.50	7.50	10.00
Plate, 9⅜", dinner	5.50	6.50	9.00
Plate, 10⅜", grill w/indent for cream soup		16.00	25.00
Plate, 11½", cake or sandwich	6.50	7.50	15.00
Platter, 10¾"	7.50	8.50	15.00
Relish dish, 8⅜", 3 part	12.50		35.00
Saucer	1.50	1.50	2.00
Sherbet, footed	5.00	5.50	9.00
Sugar, footed	5.50	5.00	8.00
Tumbler, 9 oz., footed	9.50	9.50	18.00
Tumbler, 12 oz., footed	20.00	22.00	40.00

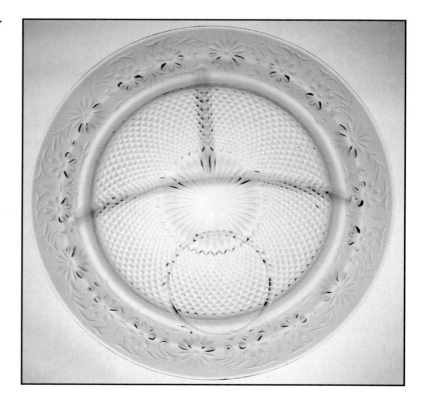

DEWDROP, JEANNETTE GLASS COMPANY, 1953 – 1956

Color: Crystal and iridized

There has been a wave of new collectors looking for Dewdrop recently. Both tumblers are difficult to find, but the iced tea is virtually impossible. I have included a photo of the iced tea tumbler below. I haven't found a smaller tumbler but collectors tell me it is easily located! Unfortunately, many of the shows I attend have few dealers who stock Dewdrop. I think they are making a mistake!

Dewdrop pitchers have caused a stir. There are two styles showing up and I have probably pictured the wrong one previously. The footed one may be a "go-with" type while the flat, iridized one pictured on bottom of page 57 may be the true Dewdrop pitcher. These are also found in crystal, but I was astonished to find one iridized! Notice how the top edge matches the top edge of the creamer while the footed one has a non-scalloped edge. Since I have no catalog listing for this pattern, I will list both styles.

Many collectors in the past bought the Lazy Susan in Dewdrop to obtain the missing ball bearings for their Shell Pink Lazy Susan! The ball bearings are interchangeable in every Jeannette pattern that has Lazy Susans. The boxed Lazy Susan below is an original. The Shell Pink Lazy Susan came in the same decorated floral box, but with pink flowers.

The snack sets were sold in sets of four. I have seen several boxed sets of these in my travels. TV tray sets of various types were something of a phenomenon in the mid 1950s.

Dewdrop will not break your bank account, so buy it now. Besides, nearly all crystal patterns make marvelous table settings.

	Crystal		Crystal
Bowl, 4¾"	5.00	Plate, snack, w/indent for cup	4.00
Bowl, 8½"	12.00	Punch bowl base	10.00
Bowl, 10⅜"	17.50	Punch bowl, 6 qt.	24.00
Butter, w/cover	27.50	Relish, leaf shape w/hndl.	8.00
Candy dish, w/cover, 7", round	22.00	Sugar, w/cover	13.00
Creamer	8.00	Tray, 13", lazy susan	25.00
Cup, punch or snack	4.00	Tumbler, 9 oz., water	15.00
Pitcher, ½ gallon, ftd	25.00	Tumbler, 15 oz., iced tea	17.50
Pitcher, flat	50.00		
Plate, 11½"	16.00		

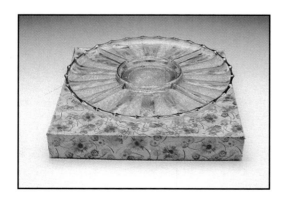

EARLY AMERICAN PRESCUT, ANCHOR HOCKING GLASS CORPORATION, 1960 – 1974

Colors: crystal, some blue and red

Early American Prescut is the pattern most requested to be added to this book. I used catalogs from 1960 to 1974 to assemble this list, but you may see pieces that I do not have listings for at this time. I have seen red ash trays and a blue sugar bowl and lid. You can also find pieces in dark green and amber. I am betting that colored pieces are uncommon and that the punch bowl may have been one of the pieces most promoted. I have seen the punch bowl priced from $5.00 to $69.95. I bought the cheaper one! You can see it pictured here. The average price seems to be about $30.00 on the punch set. The 8½" vase was also made into a lamp!

All Early American Prescut pieces are designated in Hocking's catalogs in the 700 line numbering system. There were other Prescut patterns made at Anchor Hocking, but I'm only listing Early American for this book. Send me a picture to confirm any pieces you have that are not listed below. Thanks!

	Crystal		Crystal
Ash tray, 4" #700/690	3.00	Oil Lamp	20.00
Ash tray, 7¾" #718-G	12.00	Pitcher, 18 oz. #744	8.00
Bowl, 4¼" #726 (plain or ruffled edge)	2.50	Pitcher, 60 oz. #791	12.50
Bowl, 5¼" #775	4.00	Plate, 4⅜"	3.00
Bowl, dessert, 5⅜" #765	2.50	Plate, 10", snack #780	10.00
Bowl, 6¾", three-toed #768	4.50	Plate, 13½", serving #790	12.50
Bowl, 7¼", round #767	6.00	Punch set, 15 pc.	30.00
Bowl, 8¾" #787	9.00	Relish, 8½", oval #778	5.00
Bowl, 9", console #797	10.00	Relish, 10", divided, tab hdld. #770	7.00
Bowl, 9", oval #776	7.00	Server, 12 oz. (Syrup) #707	6.00
Bowl, 9⅜", gondola dish #752	7.50	Shakers, pr., 2¼" individual #700/736	4.00
Bowl, 10¾", salad #788	10.00	Shakers, pr. #700/699	4.00
Bowl, 11¾" #794	12.50	Sugar, w/lid #753	4.00
Butter, w/cover, ¼ lb. #705	6.00	Tray, 6½" x 12", hostess #750	8.00
Cake plate, 13½", ftd. #706	17.50	Tray, 11¾", deviled egg/relish #750	25.00
Candlestick, 7" x 5⅝" double #784	15.00	Tray, cr/sug #700/671	3.00
Candy, w/lid, 5¼" #774	10.00	Tumbler, 3½", flared rim	3.50
Candy, w/cover, 7¼" x 5½" #792	12.00	Tumbler, 4⅜", flared rim	6.00
Chip & dip, 10¾" bowl, 5¼",		Tumbler, 5 oz., 4", juice #730	3.00
brass finish holder #700/733	17.50	Tumbler, 7 oz., 3", old fashioned	6.00
Coaster #700/702	2.00	Tumbler, 10 oz., 4½" tumbler #731	4.00
Creamer #754	3.00	Tumbler, 15 oz., 6", iced tea #732	5.00
Cruet, w/stopper, 7¾" #711	6.00	Vase, basket/block, 6 x 4½" #704/205	15.00
Cup, custard, 4¼" high	2.50	Vase, 8½" #741	10.00
Cup, snack, 6 oz.	2.50	Vase, 10" #742	12.50
Lazy Susan, 9 pc. #700/713	20.00		

EMERALD CREST, FENTON ART GLASS COMPANY, 1949 – 1955

Color: white with green edge

Emerald Crest, introduced in 1949, was listed in Fenton catalogs until January 1955. That means production was finished at least by the end of 1955. This popular line followed the Aqua Crest (blue trimmed) started in 1941, and Silver Crest (crystal trimmed) started in 1943. Prices for Aqua Crest fall between that of Emerald Crest and Silver Crest (priced on pages 222 and 224). I eventually will get the Aqua Crest pictured and listed in this book. The set I intended to use was owned by an individual who divorced and took it to Arizona, a bit far away to photograph it.

Thanks for all the interactions with readers, collectors, and dealers I have had concerning Fenton patterns in this book. I treasure the time and help obtaining price listings for Emerald Crest and Silver Crest.

Most mayonnaise sets are found with crystal spoons, but a green spoon was made. It is rarely found. You can see two green spoons in the mustards. The green stopper for the oil bottle is also difficult to locate. Most of these were also crystal.

Certain pieces of Emerald Crest have two different line numbers. Originally, this line was #680, and all pieces carried that designation. In July 1952, Fenton began issuing a Ware Number for each piece. That is why you see two separate numbers for the different sized plates and vases.

	White w/Green		White w/Green
Basket, 5" #7236	77.50	Mayonnaise set, 3 pc. w/gr. ladle #7203	90.00
Basket, 7" #7237	97.50	Mustard, w/lid and spoon	85.00
Bowl, 5", finger or deep dessert #7221	18.00	Oil bottle, w/green stopper #680, #7269	95.00
Bowl, 5½", soup #680, #7230	37.50	Pitcher, 6" hndl., beaded melon #7116	55.00
Bowl, 8½", flared #680	45.00	Plate, 5½" #680, #7218	15.00
Bowl, 9½" #682	57.50	Plate, 6½" #680, #7219	16.00
Bowl, 10" salad #7220	80.00	Plate, 8½" #680, #7217	32.50
Bowl, dessert, shallow #7222	20.00	Plate, 10" #680, #7210	40.00
Bowl, ftd., tall, square #7330	80.00	Plate, 12" #680, #7212	47.50
Cake plate, 13" high ftd. #680, #7213	85.00	Plate, 12" #682	47.50
Cake plate, low ftd. #5813	67.50	Plate, 16", torte #7216	75.00
Candle holder, flat saucer base, pr. #680	75.00	Saucer #7208	13.00
Comport, 6", ftd., flared #206	37.50	Sherbet, ftd. #7226	22.50
Comport, ftd., double crimped	37.50	Sugar, clear reeded hndls. #7231	36.00
Creamer, clear reeded hndls. #7231	42.50	Tidbit, 2 tier bowls, 5½" & 8½"	65.00
Cup #7208	37.00	Tidbit, 2 tier bowls, 8½" & 10"	85.00
Flower pot w/attached saucer #7299	67.50	Tidbit, 2 tier plates #7297	57.50
Mayonnaise bowl, #7203	32.50	Tidbit, 3 tier plates #7298	77.50
Mayonnaise ladle, crystal #7203	5.00	Vase, 4½", fan #36, #7355	25.00
Mayonnaise ladle, green, #7203	35.00	Vase, 6¼", fan #36, #7357	35.00
Mayonnaise liner, #7203	12.00	Vase, 8", bulbous base #186	65.00
Mayonnaise set, 3 pc. w/crys. ladle #7203	55.00		

EMERALD-GLO, PADEN CITY AND FENTON ART GLASS COMPANY

Color: Emerald green

Originally made by Paden City for Rubel, this pattern was also made by Fenton Art Glass Company in the later years of its production. Labeled pieces have been found which state "Cavalier Emerald-Glo Hand-Made." All "star cut" pieces were made by Paden City, but uncut pieces were made by both companies. Normally, the Fenton manufactured pieces are a darker green color. Fenton pieces are most often found with cast-iron accoutrements as opposed to the brass colored ones pictured here. I now have a box of Fenton pieces that were shipped to me too late for this book, but will be photographed for future books. Fenton made other colors from these moulds; so be on the lookout for white or other colors.

	Emerald Green
Candleholders, pr., ball with metal cups	35.00
Casserole w/metal cover	35.00
Cheese dish w/metal top and handle	55.00
Condiment set (2 jars, metal lids, spoons & tray)	55.00
Condiment set (3 jars, metal lids, spoons & tray)	75.00
Creamer	15.00
Creamer/sugar, individual (metal) w/metal lid, on metal tray	28.00
Creamer/sugar, individual w/metal lid, on metal tray	25.00
Cruet	25.00
Ice bucket, metal holder & tongs	65.00
Marmalade w/metal lid & spoon	25.00
Mayonnaise, divided w/metal underliner & spoons	35.00
Oil bottle	25.00
Relish, 9" divided w/metal handle	25.00
Relish, 9", tab handled w/metal handle	30.00
Relish, heart shaped	17.00
Salad bowl w/metal base, fork and spoon	55.00
Salad bowl, 10"	30.00
Server, five part w/metal covered center	60.00
Sugar	15.00
Sugar w/metal lid & liner	22.00
Syrup w/metal lid & liner	35.00
Tid-bit, 2 tier (bowls, 6" & 8")	45.00

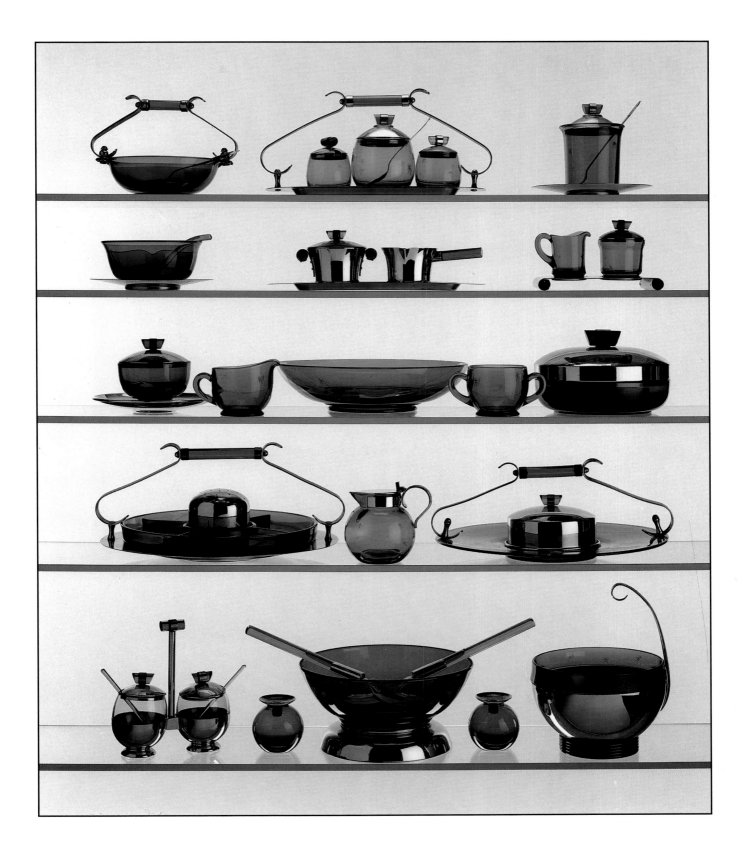

ENGLISH HOBNAIL LINE NO. 555, WESTMORELAND GLASS COMPANY, 1920s – 1983

Colors: amber, crystal, and crystal with various color treatments

English Hobnail has been in my Depression era book since 1972; but crystal and amber English Hobnail were made until Westmoreland closed in 1983. Thus, I am pricing amber and crystal in this book. I realize that crystal, crystal with amber or black feet, and some shades of amber were made before 1940. Yet pricing is fairly consistent for all these colors that essentially fit the time structure of this book. Milk glass was made very late. You can double the price listed for any fruit decorated milk glass. Ruby flashed English Hobnail is difficult to sell at regular crystal prices. There are strong buyers for crystal English Hobnail, but collectors seeking amber are lagging behind.

I bought several old fashioned tumblers. One is pictured on the second row next to the double egg cup. When I put these out for sale, they zipped off the table! I either hit the right customer or they were rarer than I thought. In any case, I have not run into any others. Sometimes rarely found items do not sell because the right collector does not come along or because there are few collectors of that pattern or color. Rarity does not always determine price; but demand does.

The 8" compote on the bottom row was called a sweetmeat by Westmoreland. The ice bucket pictured there can also be a large candy when a lid is present. The two tiered tid-bit could be original, but many of these in numerous patterns were made in the early 1970s by a dealer in St. Louis. Even if old hardware is used there is no way to tell how old these are. Remember that a tid-bit is the cost of two drilled plates plus the cost of the hardware.

	Amber/Crystal		Amber/Crystal		Amber/Crystal
Ash tray, 3"	5.00	Bowl, 11", bell	35.00	Cup, demitasse	18.00
Ash tray, 4½"	7.00	Bowl, 11", rolled edge	22.00	Decanter, 20 oz.	55.00
Ash tray, 4½", sq.	7.50	Bowl, 12", celery	20.00	Egg cup	10.00
Basket, 5", hdld.	20.00	Bowl, 12", flange or console	30.00	Hat, high	18.00
Basket, 6", tall, hdld.	40.00	Bowl, 12", flared	35.00	Hat, low	15.00
Bon bon, 6½", hdld.	12.50	Bowl, 12", oval crimped	40.00	Ice tub, 4"	20.00
Bottle, toilet, 5 oz.	20.00	Bowl, cream soup	15.00	Ice tub, 5½"	40.00
Bowl, 4", rose	15.00	Candelabra, 2-lite	25.00	Icer, sq. base,	
Bowl, 4½", finger	7.50	Candlestick, 3½", rnd. base	10.00	w/patterned insert	45.00
Bowl, 4½", round nappy	7.00	Candlestick, 5½", sq. base	15.00	Lamp, 6½", electric	32.00
Bowl, 4½", sq. ftd., finger	9.00	Candlestick, 9", rnd. base	25.00	Lamp, 9½", electric	45.00
Bowl, 4½", sq. nappy	7.00	Candy dish, 3 ftd.	30.00	Lamp, candlestick	
Bowl, 5", round nappy	9.50	Candy, ½ lb. and cover,		(several types)	30.00
Bowl, 5½", bell nappy	11.50	cone shaped	25.00	Lampshade, 17"	175.00
Bowl, 6", crimped dish	12.50	Chandelier, 17" shade		Marmalade w/cover	22.00
Bowl, 6", rose	17.50	w/200+ prisms	395.00	Mayonnaise, 6"	10.00
Bowl, 6", round nappy	10.00	Cheese w/cover, 6"	35.00	Mustard, sq. ftd., w/lid	20.00
Bowl, 6", sq. nappy	10.00	Cheese w/cover, 8¾"	55.00	Nut, individual, ftd.	6.00
Bowl, 6½", grapefruit	11.00	Cigarette box and cover,		Oil bottle, 2 oz., hdld.	20.00
Bowl, 6½", round nappy	12.00	4½"x2½"	20.00	Oil bottle, 6 oz., hdld.	30.00
Bowl, 6½", sq. nappy	12.50	Cigarette jar w/cover, rnd.	15.00	Oil-vinegar combination, 6 oz.	37.50
Bowl, 7", 6 pt.	20.00	Cigarette lighter		Parfait, rnd. ftd.	15.00
Bowl, 7", oblong spoon	17.50	(milk glass only)	14.00	Pitcher, 23 oz., rounded	50.00
Bowl, 7", preserve	15.00	Coaster, 3"	5.00	Pitcher, 32 oz., straight side	55.00
Bowl, 7", round nappy	15.00	Compote, 5", round, rnd. ftd.	12.00	Pitcher, 38 oz., rounded	65.00
Bowl, 7½", bell nappy	16.00	Compote, 5", sq. ftd., round	12.50	Pitcher, 60 oz., rounded	70.00
Bowl, 8", 6 pt.	25.00	Compote, 5½", ball stem,		Pitcher, 64 oz., straight side	80.00
Bowl, 8", cupped, nappy	25.00	sweetmeat	25.00	Plate, 5½", rnd.	4.50
Bowl, 8", ftd.	30.00	Compote, 5½", bell	15.00	Plate, 6", sq.	5.00
Bowl, 8", hexagonal ftd.,		Compote, 5½", sq. ftd., bell	15.00	Plate, 6", sq. finger bowl liner	5.00
2-hdld.	40.00	Compote, 6", honey, rnd. ftd.	16.00	Plate, 6½", depressed center, rnd.	6.00
Bowl, 8", pickle	15.00	Compote, 6", sq. ftd., honey	16.00	Plate, 6½", round.	6.00
Bowl, 8", round nappy	25.00	Compote, 8", ball stem,		Plate, 6½, rnd. finger bowl liner	6.50
Bowl, 9", bell nappy	30.00	sweetmeat	35.00	Plate, 8", rnd.	7.50
Bowl, 9", celery	17.50	Creamer, hexagonal, ftd.	9.00	Plate, 8", rnd., 3 ftd.	15.00
Bowl, 9½", round crimped	30.00	Creamer, low, flat	7.50	Plate, 8½", plain edge	8.00
Bowl, 10", flared	32.50	Creamer, sq. ftd.	8.50	Plate, 8½", rnd.	8.00
Bowl, 10", oval crimped	35.00	Cup	6.00	Plate, 8¾", sq.	8.00

Please refer to Foreword for pricing information

ENGLISH HOBNAIL (cont.)

	Amber/Crystal
Plate, 10½", grill, rnd	15.00
Plate, 10", rnd.	15.00
Plate, 10", sq.	15.00
Plate, 12", sq.	22.00
Plate, 15", sq.	35.00
Plate, 14", rnd., torte	30.00
Plate, 20½", rnd., torte	55.00
Plate, cream soup liner, rnd.	5.00
Puff box, w/ cover, 6", rnd.	20.00
Punch bowl	195.00
Punch bowl stand	65.00
Punch cup	6.50
Punch set (bowl, stand, 12 cups, ladle)	335.00
Relish, 8", 3 part	15.00
Saucer, demitasse, rnd.	10.00
Saucer, demitasse, sq.	10.00
Saucer, rnd.	2.00
Saucer, sq.	2.00
Shaker, pr., rnd. ftd.	20.00
Shaker, pr., sq. ftd.	20.00
Stem, 1 oz., rnd. ftd., cordial	15.00
Stem, 1 oz., rnd., ball, cordial	18.00
Stem, 1 oz., sq. ftd., cordial	15.00
Stem, 2 oz., rnd. ftd., wine	10.00
Stem, 2 oz., sq. ftd., wine	10.00
Stem, 2¼ oz., rnd. ball, wine	9.00
Stem, 3 oz., rnd. cocktail	8.00
Stem, 3 oz., sq. ftd., cocktail	8.00
Stem, 3½ oz., rnd. ball, cocktail	7.00

	Amber/Crystal
Stem, 5 oz., rnd. claret	12.50
Stem, 5 oz., sq. ftd., oyster cocktail	9.00
Stem, 8 oz., rnd. water goblet	10.00
Stem, 8 oz., sq. ftd., water goblet	10.00
Stem, sherbet, low, one ball, rnd ftd.	6.00
Stem, sherbet, rnd. low foot	7.00
Stem, sherbet, sq. ftd., low	7.00
Stem. champagne, two ball, rnd ftd.	8.00
Stem. sherbet, high, two ball, rnd ftd.	9.00
Stem. sherbet, rnd. high foot	9.00
Stem. sherbet, sq. ftd., high	9.00
Sugar, hexagonal, ftd.	8.50
Sugar, low, flat	7.50
Sugar, sq. ftd.	8.50
Tid-bit, 2 tier	22.50
Tumbler, 1½ oz., whiskey	11.00
Tumbler, 3 oz., whiskey	10.00
Tumbler, 5 oz., ginger ale	8.00
Tumbler, 5 oz., old fashioned cocktail	10.00
Tumbler, 5 oz., rnd. ftd., ginger ale	8.00
Tumbler, 5 oz., sq. ftd., ginger ale	8.00
Tumbler, 7 oz., rnd. ftd. juice	9.00

	Amber/Crystal
Tumbler, 7 oz., sq. ftd., juice	9.00
Tumbler, 8 oz., rnd., ball, water	10.00
Tumbler, 8 oz., water	10.00
Tumbler, 9 oz., rnd., ball, water	10.00
Tumbler, 9 oz., rnd., ftd. water	10.00
Tumbler, 9 oz., sq. ftd., water	10.00
Tumbler, 10 oz., ice tea	12.00
Tumbler, 11 oz., rnd., ball, ice tea	10.00
Tumbler, 11 oz., sq. ftd., ice tea	12.00
Tumbler, 12 oz., ice tea	12.50
Tumbler, 12½ oz., rnd. ftd. iced tea	10.00
Urn, 11", w/cover	30.00
Vase, 6½", ivy bowl, sq., ftd., crimp top	27.50
Vase, 6½", sq., ftd., flower holder	20.00
Vase, 7½", flip	25.00
Vase, 7½", flip jar w/cover	60.00
Vase, 8", sq. ftd.	35.00
Vase, 8½", flared top	37.50
Vase, 10" (straw jar)	65.00

Please refer to Foreword for pricing information

66

Westmoreland's Handmade "English Hobnail" Crystal
Catalog No. 555

WESTMORELAND GLASS COMPANY
GRAPEVILLE, PENNSYLVANIA

Handmade Glassware of Quality
Since 1889

ENGLISH HOBNAIL

Westmoreland's Handmade "English Hobnail" Crystal — Line No. 555

WESTMORELAND'S "English Hobnail" Crystal Pattern is handmade in one hundred and thirty-seven open stock items. It is fashioned in three Line Numbers: Line 555 with round foot; Line No. 555/2 has square plates and all stemware items are made with square foot. Line No. 555/3 stemware is barrel-shape, with ball stem and round foot. All three versions are identical in pattern, except for difference in foot as illustrated on the following pages. The various items of all three Lines intermix charmingly, and provide a wide choice for complete luncheon or dinner service.

555/12½ oz. Ice Tea, ftd.

555/9 oz. Tumbler, ftd.

555/7 oz. Tumbler, ftd.

555 Parfait

555 Sherbet High foot.

555 Sherbet Low foot.

555/3 oz. Cocktail

555/8 oz. Goblet

555/5 oz. Claret

555/2 oz. Wine

555 Cordial

555 Old Fashioned Cocktail

1½ oz. Whiskey. Also 3 oz.

555/5 oz. Ginger Ale

555/8 oz. Tumbler

555/10 oz. Ice Tea

555/12 oz. Ice Tea

555/2 oz. Oil

555/6 oz. Oil

555/6 oz. Oil-Vinegar Comb.

555/20 oz. Decanter

555/1 qt. Jug Also in ½ Gal.

555/38 oz. Jug. Also 23 oz., 60 oz.

555 Sugar & Cream Set, footed.

555 Sugar & Cream Set, Low.

555 Salt and Pepper

555/5½ Bell Compote

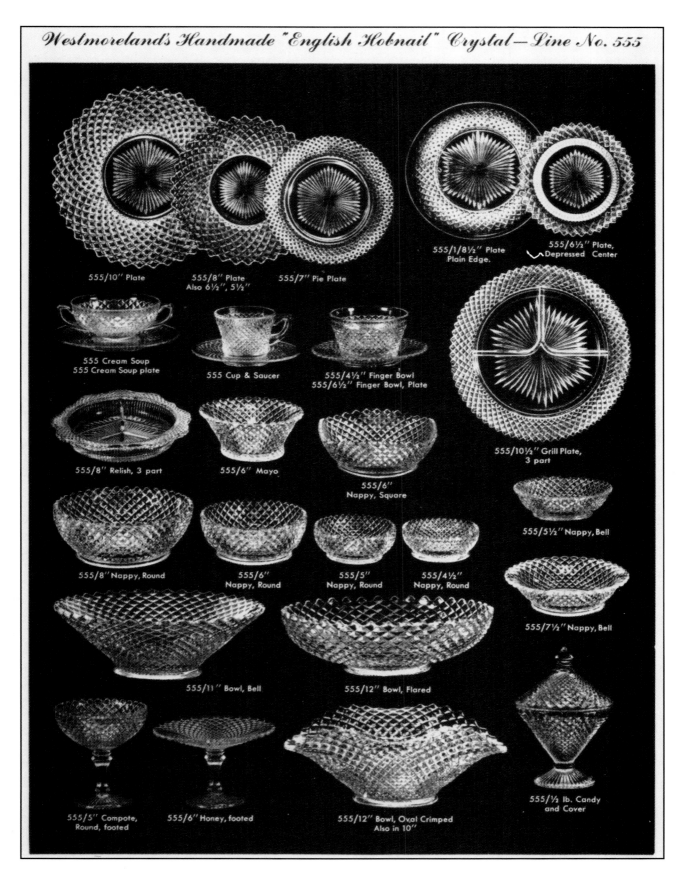

Westmoreland's Handmade "English Hobnail" Crystal—Line No. 555

555/10" Plate

555/8" Plate
Also 6½", 5½"

555/7" Pie Plate

555/1/8½" Plate
Plain Edge.

555/6½" Plate,
Depressed Center

555 Cream Soup
555 Cream Soup plate

555 Cup & Saucer

555/4½" Finger Bowl
555/6½" Finger Bowl, Plate

555/10½" Grill Plate,
3 part

555/8" Relish, 3 part

555/6" Mayo

555/6"
Nappy, Square

555/5½" Nappy, Bell

555/8" Nappy, Round

555/6"
Nappy, Round

555/5"
Nappy, Round

555/4½"
Nappy, Round

555/7½" Nappy, Bell

555/11" Bowl, Bell

555/12" Bowl, Flared

555/5" Compote,
Round, footed

555/6" Honey, footed

555/12" Bowl, Oval Crimped
Also in 10"

555/½ lb. Candy
and Cover

ENGLISH HOBNAIL

Westmoreland's Handmade "English Hobnail" Crystal — Line No. 555

555/4½ x 2½" Cigarette Box & Cover

High Hat

Low Hat

555/4½" Ash Tray.

555 Ind. Nut, ftd.

3" Ash Tray

555 3" Coaster

555/6½" Grapefruit

555/6½" Bon Bon, H'ld.

555/8" Pickle

555/6" Crimped Dish

555/6" Rose Bowl

4" Rose Bowl

555/8"/6 Pt. Bowl. Also in 7"

555/2-Lite Candelabra

555/6" Basket, Tall Handled.

555/6" Three-Footed Covered Dish

555 Marmalade and Cover

555/3½" Candlestick

555/9½" Bowl, Round, Crimped

555/12" Celery, Also 9"

555/14" Torte Plate, Also in 20½"

555/15 Piece Punch Set

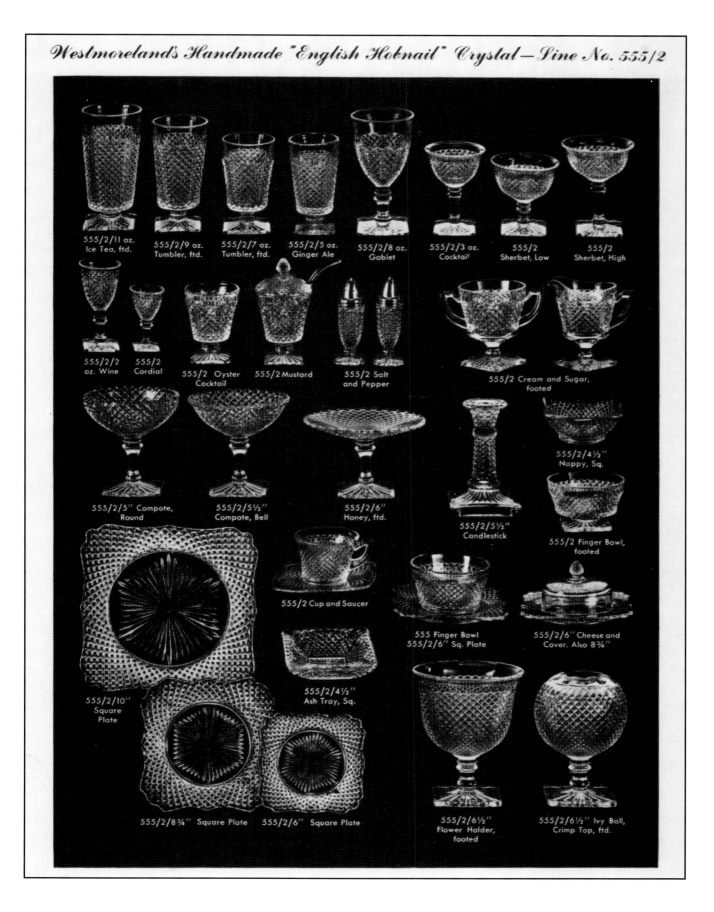

Westmoreland's Handmade "English Hobnail" Crystal — Line No. 555/2

555/2/11 oz. Ice Tea, ftd.

555/2/9 oz. Tumbler, ftd.

555/2/7 oz. Tumbler, ftd.

555/2/5 oz. Ginger Ale

555/2/8 oz. Goblet

555/2/3 oz. Cocktail

555/2 Sherbet, Low

555/2 Sherbet, High

555/2/2 oz. Wine

555/2 Cordial

555/2 Oyster Cocktail

555/2 Mustard

555/2 Salt and Pepper

555/2 Cream and Sugar, footed

555/2/5" Compote, Round

555/2/5½" Compote, Bell

555/2/6" Honey, ftd.

555/2/5½" Candlestick

555/2/4½" Nappy, Sq.

555/2 Finger Bowl, footed

555/2/10" Square Plate

555/2 Cup and Saucer

555/2/4½" Ash Tray, Sq.

555 Finger Bowl
555/2/6" Sq. Plate

555/2/6" Cheese and Cover. Also 8¾"

555/2/8¾" Square Plate

555/2/6" Square Plate

555/2/6½" Flower Holder, footed

555/2/6½" Ivy Ball, Crimp Top, ftd.

FIRE-KING DINNERWARE "ALICE"
ANCHOR HOCKING GLASS CORPORATION, early 1940s

Colors: Jade-ite, white w/trims of blue or red

"Alice" is available in plain white or white trimmed in red or blue, as well as, Jade-ite. Some of the red-trimmed pieces fade to pink; and there are two shades of blue-trimmed pieces being found. I bought some red-trimmed "Alice" in Zanesville, Ohio, but I notice they did not get to the photography session. When you buy as much glass for use in books as I do, you might expect a few mistakes to occur. Actually, we are finally getting more organized and by the next century, we might even know where most pieces are! My father-in-law told one of our northern visitors that he had built us more shelves for glass than there were in the Sanford, Florida, glass show. The visitor took in a glimpse of the show and said, "No way!" He really has — but we have moved several times leaving marvelous shelving behind!

During my travels I am always buying glass for photography. That glassware is eventually all packed by book category: Depression, 50s, Elegant, or Kitchen. When a photo session approaches, all of this glass is unpacked (usually by Cathy and her mom) and sorted into separate patterns. These pieces are then added to the proper boxes. Sometimes a piece or two out of the muddle does not end up where it belongs! We tried a new approach and took the new pieces unsorted this year. Same result, but it takes more room at the photography studio!

Dinner plates are the pieces to own in this diminutive "Alice" pattern. Evidently, few people bought the plates to go with those cups and saucers that were packed in oatmeal boxes. That was the reason that Hocking's Forest Green Sandwich has six easily found small pieces with all the larger pieces difficult to find. They, too, were packed in "Crystal Wedding Oats." The larger pieces were not premiums; the retailing operation obviously failed (in these cases) at stimulating balanced sales of the rest of the pattern. Today, the larger items are in minute supply!

	Jade-ite	White/Blue trim	White/Red trim
Cup	3.50	12.00	20.00
Plate, 9½"	22.50	25.00	30.00
Saucer	2.00	4.00	6.00

Please refer to Foreword for pricing information

FIRE-KING DINNERWARE CHARM, ANCHOR HOCKING GLASS CORPORATION, 1950 – 1954

Colors: Azur-ite, Jade-ite, Forest Green, and Royal Ruby

Charm refers to the square dishes made by Anchor Hocking from 1950 through 1954. The Jade-ite and Azur-ite were advertised alongside Forest Green and Royal Ruby; however, the color names of Forest Green and Royal Ruby prevailed on those instead of Charm. Because I have had numerous requests to put Forest Green and Royal Ruby under Charm, I have acquiesced. They are now found here.

The ash tray pictured on top of page 74 sneaked into the photograph; please disregard that as a piece of Charm! It is priced under Forest Green where it belongs. There are only a few pieces of Royal Ruby. You will only find five pieces in that color. Sorry, but there are no creamer, sugar, or dinner plates.

Jade-ite continues to evade collectors, but there seems to be an adequate supply of Azur-ite except for soups and dinner plates. This squared shape is the most troublesome Jade-ite to find. At present, the platter and dinner plates are very elusive. Prices have risen considerably in the last couple of years. I mentioned that I sold a platter to an individual who had been searching for one for three years in the last book; however, I failed to keep one to photograph! I find Azur-ite dinner plates in my area, and they are, frankly, hard to sell there. It is a fact that some patterns remained in one geographical area, and are relatively scarce elsewhere.

The 8⅜" plate is listed in a 1950 catalog as a dinner plate, but in later years as a luncheon plate. Apparently, promotion writers at Hocking felt that 8⅜" was a seriously small dinner plate and changed the dimension size after that first year.

	Azur-ite	Forest Green	Jade-ite	Royal Ruby
Bowl, 4¾", dessert	5.00	5.50	10.00	6.00
Bowl, 6", soup	15.00	18.00	22.00	
Bowl, 7⅜", salad	17.50	14.00	24.00	15.00
Creamer	8.00	7.50	18.00	
Cup	4.00	5.00	9.00	6.00
Plate, 6⅝", salad	5.00	5.00	7.00	
Plate, 8⅜", luncheon	5.00	7.00	9.00	9.00
Plate, 9¼", dinner	18.00	30.00	30.00	
Platter, 11" x 8"	18.00	22.00	30.00	
Saucer, 5⅜"	1.50	1.50	2.50	2.50
Sugar	8.00	7.50	18.00	

FIRE-KING DINNERWARE FLEURETTE and HONEYSUCKLE
ANCHOR HOCKING GLASS CORPORATION, 1958 – 1960

Color: white w/decal

Fleurette first appeared in Anchor Hocking's 1959 – 1960 catalog printed in April 1958, with Honeysuckle showing up the following year. Both patterns seem to have given way to Primrose by the 1960 – 1961 catalog. Both Fleurette and Honeysuckle are in shorter supply than Primrose.

I chose catalog reprints for Fleurette on pages 76 – 78 and Honeysuckle on page 75 instead of actual photographs. These catalog sheets are more educational than the pieces I had gathered. There were three sizes of tumblers listed for Honeysuckle, but I have never seen ones in Fleurette. The only worn decals in all the Fire-King patterns seem to occur on Fleurette. Maybe that problem was corrected for later patterns.

Note on page 77 the various sized sets of Fleurette that were available: 16 pc., 19 pc., 35 pc., and 53 pc. On page 78, you can see wholesale prices of these sets when they were first issued.

All Fire-King sugar lids are interchangeable. They are plain white without a pattern. Be sure to check these out. Sometimes you may find an American sweetheart lid that has been misplaced. It happened at a farmer's market in Plant City, Florida, not long ago!

	Fleurette	Honeysuckle		Fleurette	Honeysuckle
Bowl, 4⅝", dessert	2.00	2.25	Platter, 9" x 12"	13.00	14.00
Bowl, 6⅝", soup plate	6.00	9.00	Saucer, 5¾"	.50	.50
Bowl, 8¼", vegetable	10.00	12.00	Sugar	3.00	3.50
Creamer	4.00	4.50	Sugar cover	3.00	3.00
Cup, 5 oz., snack	2.00		Tumbler, 5 oz., juice		7.00
Cup, 8 oz.	3.50	4.00	Tumbler, 9 oz., water		8.00
Plate, 6¼", bread and butter	1.50		Tumbler, 12 oz., iced tea		10.00
Plate, 7⅜", salad	2.50	3.00	Tray, 11"x 6", snack	2.50	
Plate, 9⅛", dinner	3.50	5.00			

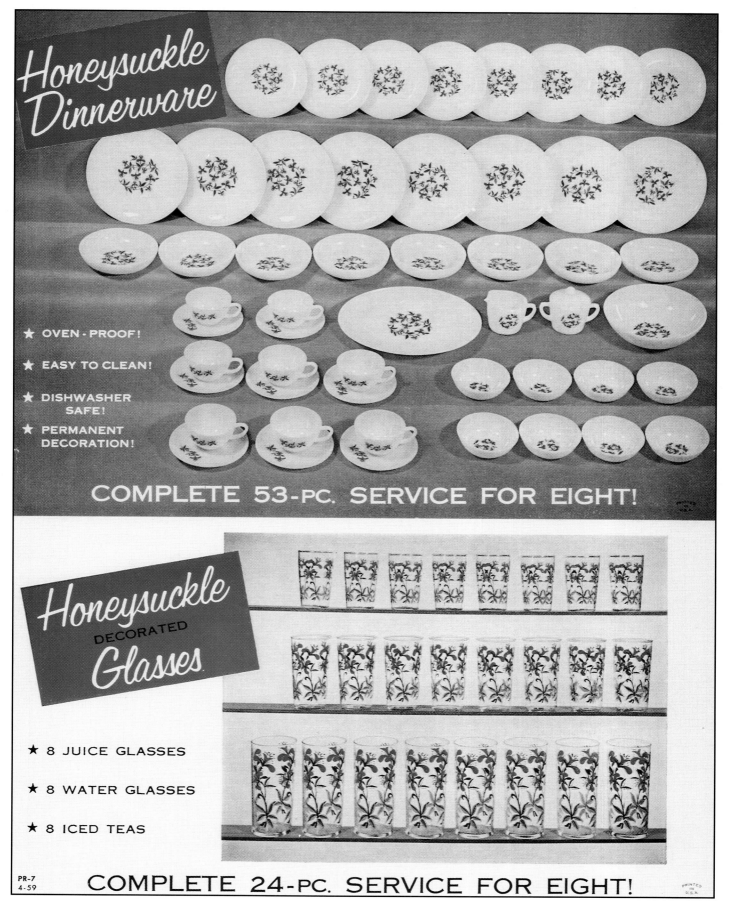

Honeysuckle Dinnerware

★ OVEN - PROOF!

★ EASY TO CLEAN!

★ DISHWASHER SAFE!

★ PERMANENT DECORATION!

COMPLETE 53-PC. SERVICE FOR EIGHT!

Honeysuckle DECORATED Glasses

★ 8 JUICE GLASSES

★ 8 WATER GLASSES

★ 8 ICED TEAS

PR-7
4-59

COMPLETE 24-PC. SERVICE FOR EIGHT!

FLEURETTE® DINNERWARE

W4679/58 — W4629/58

W4674/58

W4637/58 — W4638/58 — W4641/58

PACKING

W4679/58—8 oz.	Cup	6 doz. — 25 lbs.
W4629/58—5 ¾"	Saucer	6 doz. — 27 lbs.
W4674/58—4 ⅝"	Dessert	6 doz. — 21 lbs.
W4637/58—6 ¼"	Bread & Butter Plate	3 doz. — 16 lbs.
W4638/58—7 ⅜"	Salad Plate	3 doz. — 23 lbs.
W4641/58—9 ⅛"	Dinner Plate	3 doz. — 39 lbs.

W4667/58

Fleurette
Prepacked Sets
are shown on
Page 3.

W4647/58

W4667/58— 6 ⅝"	Soup Plate	3 doz. — 27 lbs.
W4647/58—12 x 9"	Platter	1 doz. — 20 lbs.

W4678/58

See Prepacked
Serva-Snack Set
on Page 3.

W4653/58 — W4654/58

W4678/58—8 ¼"	Vegetable Bowl	1 doz. — 15 lbs.
W4653/58—	Sugar & Cover	2 doz. — 16 lbs.
W4654/58—	Creamer	2 doz. — 12 lbs.

HEAT-PROOF

FLEURETTE® PREPACKED SETS

W4600/4—16 Pce. Starter Set
Each Set in Gift Display Carton,
4 Sets to Shipping Carton — 37 lbs.
COMPOSITION:
Four W4679/58 Cups
Four W4629/58 Saucers
Four W4674/58 Desserts
Four W4641/58 Dinner Plates

W4600/2—35 Pce. Dinner Set
Each Set in Shipping Carton — 21 lbs.
COMPOSITION:
Six W4679/58 Cups   One W4678/58 Vegetable Bowl
Six W4629/58 Saucers   One W4647/58 Platter
Six W4674/58 Desserts   One W4653/58 Sugar & Cover
Six W4638/58 Salad Plates   One W4654/58 Creamer
Six W4641/58 Dinner Plates

W4600/1—19 Pce. Luncheon Set (Not Illustrated)
Each Set in Gift Carton, 4 Sets to Shipping Carton — 41 lbs.
COMPOSITION:
Four W4679/58 Cups   Four W4641/58 Dinner Plates
Four W4629/58 Saucers   One W4653/58 Sugar & Cover
Four W4674/58 Desserts   One W4654/58 Creamer

W4600/3—53 Pce. Dinner Set (Not Illustrated)
Each Set in Shipping Carton — 32 lbs.
COMPOSITION:
Eight W4679/58 Cups   Eight W4641/58 Dinner Plates
Eight W4629/58 Saucers   One W4678/58 Vegetable Bowl
Eight W4674/58 Desserts   One W4647/58 Platter
Eight W4638/58 Salad Plates   One W4653/58 Sugar & Cover
Eight W4667/58 Soup Plates   One W4654/58 Creamer

SERVA-SNACK SET

W4600/9—8 Pce. Snack Set
Each Set in Die-Cut Display Carton,
6 Sets to Shipping Carton — 48 lbs.
COMPOSITION:
Four 5 oz. Cups
Four 11 x 6" Rectangular Trays

(See Crystal Serva-Snack Sets on Page 10.)

PROMOTE PREPACKED SETS

HEAT-PROOF

W4674/58

W4678/58

HEAT-PROOF

W4647/58

W4667/58

W4653/58

W4679/58 — W4629/58

W4654/58

OPEN STOCK

			Per Doz. Net Pkd.	Doz. Ctn.	Wt. Ctn.
W4679/58—	8 oz.	Cup	$ .90	6	25#
W4629/58—	5¾″	Saucer	.90	6	28#
W4674/58—	4⅝″	Dessert	.90	6	21#
W4637/58—	6¼″	B & B Plate	1.20	3	16#
W4638/58—	7⅜″	Salad Plate	1.50	3	23#
W4667/58—	6⅝″	Soup Plate	1.60	3	24#
W4641/58—	9⅛″	Dinner Plate	1.80	3	39#
W4678/58—	8¼″	Vegetable Bowl	2.40	1	14#
W4647/58—	12 x 9″	Platter	3.60	1	20#
W4653/58—		Sugar & Cover	1.50	2	11#
W4654/58—		Creamer	1.25	2	12#

Anchorglass®

SETS

W4600/4—16 PCE. STARTER SET .... $1.55 Set 4 Sets 39#
(Each Set in Gift Display Ctn.)
COMPOSITION: Four each Cups, Saucers,
Desserts and Dinner Plates

W4600/1—19 PCE. LUNCHEON SET ...... 1.75 Set 4 Sets 40#
(Each Set in Gift Carton)
COMPOSITION: Four each Cups, Saucers,
Desserts and Dinner Plates.
One Sugar & Cover and one Creamer

W4600/2—35 PCE. DINNER SET .... 3.95 Set 1 Set 21#
(Each Set in Shipping Carton)
COMPOSITION: Six each Cups, Saucers,
Desserts, Salad Plates and Dinner Plates.
One each Vegetable Bowl, Platter,
Sugar & Cover and Creamer.

W4600/3—53 PCE. DINNER SET .... 6.00 Set 1 Set 32#
(Each Set in Shipping Carton)
COMPOSITION: Eight each Cups, Saucers,
Desserts, Salad Plates, Soup Plates and
Dinner Plates. One each Vegetable Bowl,
Platter, Sugar & Cover and Creamer.

W4637/58   W4638/58   W4641/58

FIRE-KING DINNERWARE "GAME BIRD"
ANCHOR HOCKING GLASS CORPORATION, 1959 – 1962

Color: white w/decal decoration

Anchor Hocking called these both "Wild Bird" and "Game Bird," but the "Game Bird" seemed more apropos when I was first writing *Collectible Glassware from the 40s, 50s, 60s....* I have had fun trying to find one of each of these birds. I now have one of everything except I've only flushed one pheasant ash tray. Others were pictured in catalogs, but so far they've flown from me.

The Ringed-Neck Pheasant seems to be the only game in town if you are looking for serving pieces. No one has notified me of any other bird decoration on the sugar, creamer, 8¼" vegetable, or platter. It is possible to collect an entire set of Pheasant decorated dinnerware, but no other bird can be collected in a full set as far as I can determine.

You will find the following birds on this pattern: Canada Goose, Ringed-Necked Pheasant, Ruffled Grouse, and Mallard Duck. I have catalog sheets of mugs, cereals, and ash trays listed for 1960 – 1961, but as you can see below, there are many more pieces available than those.

Our excursion to Tulsa, Oklahoma, convinced me that a bird hunting trip to southwestern Missouri and Oklahoma would be the way to go if you are looking for this pattern. Either through promotional sales or give-aways, this area is cover for "Game Birds." I will say that I only saw mugs and tumblers on my last trip.

Prices on this little pattern have increased due to the number of collectors searching for these feathered friends. Serving pieces are becoming more than a problem for the many collectors looking for them. Mugs and tumblers can be found with some work, and many of these are being used. Mugs are microwaveable and great for tea or ... hot chocolate!

	White w/decals		White w/decals
Ash tray, 5¼"	9.00	Plate, 9⅛", dinner	6.50
Bowl, 4⅝", dessert	4.25	Platter, 12" x 9"	20.00
Bowl, 5", soup or cereal	8.00	Sugar	10.00
Bowl, 8¼", vegetable	20.00	Sugar cover	3.00
Creamer	10.00	Tumbler, 5oz., juice	15.00
Mug, 8 oz.	8.00	Tumbler, 11 oz., iced tea	9.00
Plate, 7⅜", salad	4.00		

ANCHORGLASS

Anchorwhite heat-resistant Mugs and Bowls

With authentic game bird decorations

Colorful game bird decorations lend a touch of rustic charm to these practical Anchorwhite mugs and bowls. The mugs are as ideal for in-home use as they are for outdoors. Versatile, too, they're perfect for coffee as well as for cocoa, hot chocolate and milk. The cereal-soup bowls, with their matching decorations, will brighten up any table setting. Both mugs and bowls are heat-resistant and safe to use with hot liquids and foods.

No.	Size	Item	Doz. Ctn.	Lbs. Ctn.
W1212/5931	8 oz.	Ruffed Grouse Mug	4	27
W1212/5932	8 oz.	Ring-Necked Pheasant Mug	4	27
W1212/5933	8 oz.	Canada Goose Mug	4	27
W1212/5934	8 oz.	Mallard Duck Mug	4	27
W291/5931	5"	Ruffed Grouse Bowl	4	27
W291/5932	5"	Ring-Necked Pheasant Bowl	4	27
W291/5933	5"	Canada Goose Bowl	4	27
W291/5934	5"	Mallard Duck Bowl	4	27

ANCHOR HOCKING GLASS CORPORATION
Lancaster, Ohio, U.S.A.

FIRE-KING DINNERWARE JADE-ITE RESTAURANT WARE
ANCHOR HOCKING GLASS CORPORATION, 1950 – 1956

Jade-ite collectors are flocking to the Restaurant Ware line. Several pieces are in increasingly short supply. The smaller platter (9½") comes in two different widths. I ran into a stack in Missouri that were 7⅞" wide. The ones I normally see are 6" wide. I only bought one because they were badly scratched. I do not know which is the more common. Let me know about yours!

I have added the 9¼" flanged rim soup and the ball jug to the listings here for lack of some other place to list them. I guess both could be considered Restaurant Ware, but neither are shown in the catalogs I have. The 5-compartment plate and the oval partitioned plates (already discontinued before 1953) are not seen as regularly as most collectors would wish. Still, not all collectors want these pieces.

Anchor Hocking's Restaurant Ware line is adaptable to microwave use. As far as I know, any of these pieces can be used this way. Remember to put the dish in the microwave for just a little time to see if it gets hot as you would test any other dish.

You can see a catalog sheet on page 82 to show you the differences in the three sizes of cups and the mug. This mug appears to come in both thick and thin styles. Most collectors collect only one style; the thick one seems to be the least desired.

White Restaurant Ware is being found in small quantities and will fetch Jade-ite prices!

	Jade-ite		Jade-ite
Bowl, 4¾", fruit G294	7.50	Plate, 5½", bread/butter G315	3.50
Bowl, 9¼", flat soup	55.00	Plate, 6¾", pie or salad G297	5.00
Bowl, 8 oz., flanged rim, cereal G305	13.00	Plate, 8⅞", oval partitioned G211	30.00
Bowl, 10 oz., deep G309	13.00	Plate, 8", luncheon G316	15.00
Bowl, 15 oz., deep G300	12.50	Plate, 9⅝", 3-compartment G292, 2 styles	10.00
Cup, demitasse	20.00	Plate, 9⅝", 5-compartment G311	15.00
Cup, 6 oz., straight G215	6.00	Plate, 9", dinner G306	10.00
Cup, 7 oz., extra heavy G299	8.00	Platter, 9½", oval G307	20.00
Cup, 7 oz., narrow rim G319	6.00	Platter, 11½", oval G308	18.00
Mug, coffee, 7 oz. G212	7.00	Saucer, 6" G295	2.00
Pitcher, ball jug, 3 styles	150.00	Saucer, demitasse	20.00

JADE-ITE *Fire-King** RESTAURANT WARE

Reg. U. S. Pat. Off. **INEXPENSIVE ● HEAT-RESISTANT ● RUGGED ● STAIN-RESISTANT ● SANITARY ● COLORFUL**

A COMPLETE SERVICE FOR MASS FEEDING ESTABLISHMENTS

Cat. No.	Description	Actual Size or Capacity	Std. Pkg.	Weight
G215	Cup (Straight)	6 oz.	4 doz.	35#
G299	Cup (Extra Heavy)	7 oz.	4 doz.	36#
G319	Cup (Narrow Rim)	7 oz.	4 doz.	32#
G295	Saucer	6″	4 doz.	31#
G212	Coffee Mug (Extra Heavy)	7 oz.	4 doz.	48#
G294	Fruit	4¾″	6 doz.	30#
G305	Grapefruit——Cereal	8 oz.	4 doz.	37#
G309	Bowl	10 oz.	4 doz.	30#
G300	Bowl	15 oz.	4 doz.	43#
G315	B & B Plate	5½″	4 doz.	30#
G297	Pie or Salad Plate	6¾″	4 doz.	35#
G316	Luncheon Plate	8″	2 doz.	26#
G306	Dinner Plate	9″	2 doz.	31#
G292	3-Compartment Plate	9⅝″	2 doz.	38#
G211	Oval Partitioned Plate	8⅞″	2 doz.	23#
G307	Oval Platter	9½″	2 doz.	24#
G308	Oval Platter	11½″	1 doz.	20#
G311	5-Compartment Plate	9⅝″	2 doz.	37#

*REG. U. S. PAT. OFF.

PRINTED IN U.S.A.

ANCHOR HOCKING GLASS CORP.
LANCASTER, OHIO, U. S. A.

FIRE-KING DINNERWARE "JANE RAY"
ANCHOR HOCKING GLASS CORPORATION, 1945 – 1963

Colors: Ivory, Jade-ite, Peach Lustre, crystal, white, and white trimmed in gold

"Jane Ray" is a name that collectors have given this pattern. This ribbed Fire-King pattern is the most commonly found Jade-ite. "Jane Ray" is one of the most collected Anchor Hocking patterns from this 1950s era. It was listed in catalogs for almost 20 years. As with "Bubble" pattern, there was a profusion of "Jane Ray" manufactured. A Jade-ite set is still possible to attain in this dinnerware, though many collectors are using the Restaurant Ware line to supplement their sets.

A 1947 chain store catalog of glassware by Anchor Hocking lists this as "Jade-ite Heat Proof Tableware," which is the only true name known. That record also lists the vegetable bowl as 8⅛" instead of 8¼" as indexed in later catalogs. I have never seen this smaller version, but there may be some.

"Jane Ray" is synonymous with Jade-ite to most collectors. I had it listed exclusively in Jade-ite in my first book. Notice that there are other colors! It is highly likely that a smaller set can be found in Ivory. I have seen a few pieces other than the plate, cup, saucer, and dessert bowls shown below. I have recently had several specific requests for Ivory at shows!

There are two new listings in Jade-ite and one in crystal. There are 9¼" flat soups and a 6¼" bread and butter plate as well as demitasse cup and saucers in crystal. The flat soup is pictured in *Very Rare Glassware of the Depression Years*, fourth edition. A local Florida dealer called me about the 6¼" plates. I checked all my Anchor Hocking catalogs and found no mention of this size plate. If you have some in your collection, let me know. Crystal demitasse sets are not commonly found, but over a dozen have been seen in the last year. Amazingly, I have not seen any other crystal pieces. That is true for Peach Lustre and white also.

"Jane Ray" demitasse sets were the most difficult pieces to find until flat soups were unearthed. Remember that the demitasse saucers are harder to find than the cups. These may be the presently scarce Iris demitasse sets of tomorrow!

Availability, as with blue "Bubble" and green Block, puts this pattern in front of many new collectors. Prices are climbing due to an ever-increasing demand and the quandary of locating some pieces. If you like this pattern, start collecting now and buy the harder-to-find pieces when you discover them! You will not be sorry!

	Ivory/White	Jade-ite		Ivory/White	Jade-ite
Bowl, 4⅞", dessert	8.00	4.50	Plate, 6¼"	5.00	20.00
Bowl, 5⅞", oatmeal	7.50	8.00	Plate, 7¾", salad	7.00	7.00
Bowl, 7⅝", soup plate	12.00	15.00	Plate, 9⅛", dinner	12.00	9.00
Bowl, 8¼", vegetable	15.00	15.00	Platter, 9" x 12"	14.00	16.00
Bowl, 9", flat soup	35.00	75.00	Saucer	2.50	1.50
Cup	7.50	3.00	**Saucer, demitasse	25.00	35.00
*Cup, demitasse	15.00	20.00	Sugar	5.00	4.00
Creamer	7.50	4.50	Sugar cover	4.00	8.00

*Peach Lustre $15.00

**Peach Lustre $22.50

FIRE-KING DINNERWARE PEACH LUSTRE/GRAY LAUREL
ANCHOR HOCKING GLASS CORPORATION, 1952 – 1963

"The New Sensation" is how Peach Lustre color/pattern was described in a 1952 catalog. This laurel leaf design was also made as Gray Laurel in 1953. A 1953 catalog is the only time that Gray Laurel is mentioned in Anchor Hocking records. Gray has turned out to be scarce when compared to the quantity of Peach Lustre ("laurel leaf" design) found. Of course Peach Lustre was listed continuously until the 1963 catalog. Page 85 is taken from a 1954 catalog. From its introduction until its demise in 1963, the name Peach Luster was used for the color as well as the pattern.

The 11" serving plate was discontinued as of 8-25-60. It is the most difficult piece to find particularly with good color. That is the major detraction to both patterns — the colors wear through and show white streaks. Dishwashers are deadly on both colors!

Three sizes of tumblers were made to go with Gray Laurel. These tumblers are "complementary decorated" with gray and maroon bands. There is a 5 ounce juice, a 9 ounce water, and a 13 ounce iced tea. To date, I have not spotted any of these. It would be great to get one pictured! Do you have any?

Crystal stemware like shown under "Bubble" and "Boopie" was also engraved with a "Laurel" cutting to go with these patterns.

A few pieces of Ivory Laurel are being seen, so watch for them!

	Gray Laurel	Peach Lustre		Gray Laurel	Peach Lustre
Bowl, 4⅞", dessert	4.00	3.00	Plate, 7⅜", salad	4.00	3.00
Bowl, 7⅝", soup plate	8.00	7.50	Plate, 9⅛", dinner	7.50	4.00
Bowl, 8¼", vegetable	12.00	9.50	Plate, 11", serving	16.00	14.00
Creamer, ftd.	5.00	3.50	Saucer, 5¾"	.75	.75
Cup, 8 oz.	4.00	3.50	Sugar, ftd.	5.00	3.50

Please refer to Foreword for pricing information

Peach Lustre Dinnerware
HEAT-RESISTANT

L4379 — L4329

L4374

L4338 — L4341

PACKING

L4379—8 oz. Cup	6 doz. —	25 lbs.
L4329—5 ¾″ Saucer	6 doz. —	27 lbs.
L4374—4 ⅞″ Dessert	6 doz. —	25 lbs.
L4338—7 ¾″ Salad Plate	3 doz. —	28 lbs.
L4341—9 ⅛″ Dinner Plate	3 doz. —	37 lbs.

L4367

L4378

L4353 — L4354

L4367—7 ⅝″ Soup Plate	3 doz. —	29 lbs.
L4378—8 ¼″ Vegetable Bowl	1 doz. —	14 lbs.
L4353— Sugar	2 doz. —	11 lbs.
L4354— Creamer	2 doz. —	10 lbs.

PREPACKED SET

L4300/33—18 Pce. Luncheon Set

Each Set in Gift Carton, 4 Sets to Shipping Carton — 41 lbs.

COMPOSITION:
Four L4379 Cups
Four L4329 Saucers
Four L4374 Desserts
Four L4341 Dinner Plates
One L4353 Sugar
One L4354 Creamer

PROMOTE SETS

L4300/33

FIRE-KING DINNERWARE & OVENWARE, MEADOW GREEN
ANCHOR HOCKING GLASS CORPORATION, 1968 – 1976

Meadow Green has not yet been as embraced by collectors as Primrose. It may be that it is newer or the green colored decals are not as acceptable as the pink and red. Cups, sugars, and creamers are solid green like those in blue Mosiac.

In any case this pattern is still inexpensively priced and can be used in ovens and microwaves. Be sure to test for hot spots before leaving it in the microwave for very long. Casseroles came with (non-decaled) white lids as well as crystal. A premium of a couple of dollars is asked for white lids. Add that to the price listed below since prices are for items with clear lids. I find the crystal lids more practical; you can see in the dish without raising the lid. Perhaps that fact is why there is a shortage of white lids today!

	White w/decal		White w/decal
Bowl, 4⅝", dessert	2.50	Creamer	3.00
Bowl, 5", cereal	3.00	Cup	2.50
Bowl, 6⅝", soup	4.50	Custard, 6 oz.	1.50
Bowl, 8¼", vegetable	7.00	Loaf pan, 5" x 9"	6.50
Cake dish, 8", square	6.00	Mug, 9 oz.	3.00
Cake dish, 9" round	6.50	Plate, 7⅜", salad	2.50
Casserole, 12 oz., hdld.	3.50	Plate, 10", dinner	4.00
Casserole, 1 qt. w/cover	7.00	Platter, 12" x 9"	8.00
Casserole, 1½ qt. w/cover	8.00	Saucer	.50
Casserole, 1½ qt., oval w/cover	8.00	Sugar w/lid	5.00
Casserole, 2 qt., w/cover	9.00	Utility dish, 1½ qt.	6.00
Casserole, 3 qt., w/cover	10.00	Utility dish, 2 qt.	7.00

FIRE-KING DINNERWARE & OVENWARE PRIMROSE
ANCHOR HOCKING GLASS CORPORATION, 1960 – 1962

Primrose was the pattern that Anchor Hocking used to bridge the gap between dinnerware and ovenware usage. Primrose was produced with pieces intended for either task. Although many of Anchor Hocking's lines were issued as dinnerware, they are marked ovenware on the bottom to let customers know that they were "heat-proof" and could be "pre-warmed" in the oven. None of these were designed for use on the range top, but some can be used in the microwave with the usual precautions of any other ware not designed specifically for the microwave.

Primrose seems to be the pattern that Hocking tried to thrust on the public more than they did Fleurette and Honeysuckle; but Primrose may not have been as successful as many earlier Fire-King patterns. It was only listed in the 1960 – 1961 and 1961 – 1962 catalogs. From the availability I see in the ovenware line, it might be scarce — or, as with the blue Fire-King ovenware, many homemakers may still be using it instead of parting with it to buy newer wares!

Tumblers, along with most of the lidded ovenware items, are the most difficult pieces to find in this pattern. The white tumblers are the only Fire-King ones known besides those of the "Game Bird." Crystal Primrose tumblers were packed in boxed sets and came in three sizes, but how the rarely found 11 oz. white tumblers were distributed remains a mystery. Many a Primrose set has been collected without finding tumblers of any kind!

All casserole covers are clear crystal Fire-King. All pieces of ovenware were guaranteed against oven breakage for two years. Dealers would exchange a new item for the broken pieces. The one quart casserole, baking pan, and oval casserole were all sold with a brass finished candle warmer and candle. I have received numerous letters saying that those brass holders are still working as they were intended!

The deep loaf pan was sold as a baking pan by adding a crystal glass cover. All the crystal glass lids are harder to find than their respective pans. Lids always did have a tendency to be dropped or broken. Have you ever heard, "Not me!" or "I didn't do it!" at your house?

White w/decal		White w/decal		White w/decal	
Bowl, 4⅝", dessert	2.25	Casserole, 2 qt., knob cover	14.00	Plate, 7⅜", salad	2.50
Bowl, 6⅝", soup plate	7.50	Creamer	4.00	Plate, 9⅛", dinner	5.00
Bowl, 8¼", vegetable	10.00	Cup, 5 oz., snack	2.50	Platter, 9" x 12"	13.50
Cake pan, 8", round	9.00	Cup, 8 oz.	3.00	Saucer, 5¾"	1.00
Cake pan, 8", square	9.00	Custard, 6 oz., low or dessert	3.00	Sugar	3.50
Casserole, pt., knob cover	7.50	Pan, 5" x 9", baking, w/cover	15.00	Sugar cover	3.00
Casserole, ½ qt., oval,		Pan, 5" x 9", deep loaf	13.00	Tray, 11" x 6", rectangular, snack	4.00
au gratin cover	15.00	Pan, 6½" x 10½", utility baking	10.00	*Tumbler, 5 oz., juice (crystal)	6.00
Casserole, 1 qt., knob cover	12.00	Pan, 8" x 12½", utility baking	13.00	*Tumbler, 9 oz., water (crystal)	6.50
Casserole, 1½ qt., knob cover	12.00	Plate, 6¼", bread and butter	3.00	*Tumbler, 11 oz., (white)	20.00
				*Tumbler, 13 oz., iced tea (crystal)	7.00

* Triple price for white

87

ANCHORGLASS

NEW!

Primrose

Anchorwhite heat-resistant ovenware

The delicate red, tan and grey tones of stylized flowers enhance this new gleaming white ovenware. It's glamorous...on the table...in the kitchen. It's perfect for special occasions or everyday use ...just right for oven-to-table service, storing and reheating. Build more colorful displays with this eye-catching, traffic-stopping, Primrose Ovenware. It will sell on sight! Available in 8 and 11 piece sets in gift cartons...also in open stock.

ANCHOR HOCKING GLASS CORPORATION
Lancaster, Ohio, U. S. A.

W424/62

W410/62

W411/62

W450/62

W409/62

W452/62

New
Primrose
Anchorglass
Ovenware

Number	Size	Item	Doz. Ctn.	Lbs. Ctn.
W424/62	6 Oz.	Dessert	4	15
W405/62	1 Pt.	Casserole, Cover	1	16
W406/62	1 Qt.	Casserole, Cover	½	14
W407/62	1½ Qt.	Casserole, Cover	½	19
W467/62	1½ Qt.	Oval Casserole, Au Gratin Cover	½	19
W408/62	2 Qt.	Casserole, Cover	½	21
W450/62	8"	Round Cake Pan	½	12
W452/62	8"	Square Cake Pan	½	17
W409/62	5" x 9"	Deep Loaf Pan	½	11
W410/62	6½" x 10½"	Utility Baking Pan	½	15
W411/62	8" x 12½"	Utility Baking Pan	½	23
W469/62	5" x 9"	Baking Pan and Cover	½	21
W400/245*		8 Pc. Set	4 Sets	34
W400/246**		11 Pc. Set	4 Sets	53

*Composition: One each 1 qt. Casserole, Cover, 10½" Utility Baking Pan, 8" Round Cake Pan; four 6 oz. Desserts, Gift Ctn.

**Composition: One each 1½ qt. Casserole, Cover, 5" x 9" Deep Loaf Pan, 8" x 12½" Utility Baking Pan, 8" Square Cake Pan; six 6 oz. Desserts, Gift Ctn.

FIRE-KING OVEN GLASS, ANCHOR HOCKING GLASS CORPORATION, 1942 – 1950s

Colors: Sapphire blue, crystal; some Ivory and Jade-ite

Fire-King Sapphire blue oven glass is readily recognized. When the word Fire-King is mentioned, it is this blue that most people think of and not any of the other multitude of Fire-King patterns. Nearly every family still has a piece or two in use! It was the ovenware that was recognized for its durability. Fire-King had a two year guarantee. All you had to do was take the broken pieces to your local dealer and your piece was replaced at no charge.

Fire-King is grand for standard ovens, but it tends to develop heat cracks from sudden temperature changes if used in the microwave. We learned that the hard way — experience!

Collectors favor the casseroles with pie plate covers above those with knobbed covers. Maybe it has to do with availability. Knobbed lids abound and they are easier to lift when hot than the pie plate style — but there are fewer bottoms for these!

The 8 ounce nurser (bottle) is not as available as the 4 ounce. In the late 1970s, cases of the smaller nurser were found in a warehouse. That supply has kept the market fairly well saturated over the years. The skillet and nipple cover on page 92 are shown compliments of Anchor-Hocking's photographer. The skillets are still hiding. Infrequently, nipple covers have surfaced. These blue covers are embossed "BINKY'S NIP CAP U.S.A." (and not Fire-King). The boxed display set on page 92 was found in a Rhode Island consignment shop for $2.00. A couple of Okies rounded that up for their collection!

A dry cup measure was brought into a Michigan show last year for me to authenticate. It was the real thing! That dry cup measure has ounce measurements up the side and no spout for pouring. Without these measurements on the side, it is the normally found mug! Those mugs come in two styles — thick and thin. Speaking of different styles, the 6 ounce custard cup can be found in three different styles.

The reason that juice saver pie plate is so high in price comes from the fact that most were heavily used. Many are deeply marred. To obtain the price below, this pie plate has to be mint! Jade-ite ones are rarely seen; I recently had a report of one in Ivory!

The prices with asterisks under the Ivory listing are for Jade-ite items with the Fire-King embossing. All the Ivory is plain with no design. You will find plain Ivory and Jade-ite mugs, but they hold eight ounces, not seven. The Jade-ite mug with the embossed Fire-King pattern is rare!

All listings below are from Anchor Hocking's catalog "L."

There are two styles of table servers being found; and you can find a casserole lid on a Bersted Mfg. Co. popcorn popper. One of these can be seen on page 92. Only the lid is Fire-King, but that is enough to excite most collectors!

	Ivory	Sapphire		Ivory	Sapphire
Baker, 1 pt., 4½" x 5"		5.50	Loaf pan, 9⅛" x 5⅛", deep	13.50	18.00
Baker, 1 pt., round	4.00	5.00	Mug, coffee, 7 oz., 2 styles	*45.00	25.00
Baker, 1 qt., round	6.00	7.00	Nipple cover		235.00
Baker, 1½ qt., round	6.00	15.00	Nurser, 4 oz.		20.00
Baker, 2 qt., round	8.50	16.00	Nurser, 8 oz.		30.00
Baker, 6 oz., individual	3.00	5.00	Percolator top, 2⅛"		5.00
Bowl, 4⅜", individual pie plate		15.00	Pie plate, 8⅜", 1½" deep		7.50
Bowl, 5⅜", cereal or deep dish pie plate	6.50	16.00	Pie plate, 9⅝", 1½" deep		9.50
Bowl, measuring, 16 oz.		25.00	Pie plate, 9", 1½" deep	7.00	8.50
Cake pan (deep), 8¾" (½ roaster)		25.00	Pie plate, 10⅜", juice saver	*100.00	110.00
Cake pan, 9"	13.00		Refrigerator jar & cover, 4½" x 5"	**10.00	12.00
Casserole, 1 pt., knob handle cover	8.50	12.00	Refrigerator jar & cover, 5⅛" x 9⅛"	**30.00	32.50
Casserole, 1 qt., knob handle cover	10.00	12.50	Roaster, 8¾"		55.00
Casserole, 1 qt., pie plate cover		18.00	Roaster, 10⅜"		75.00
Casserole, 1½ qt., knob handle cover	12.00	13.00	Table server, tab handles (hot plate)	13.00	20.00
Casserole, 1½ qt., pie plate cover		18.00	Utility bowl, 6⅞", 1 qt.		16.00
Casserole, 2 qt., knob handle cover	13.50	22.00	Utility bowl, 8⅜", 1½ qt.		20.00
Casserole, 2 qt., pie plate cover		25.00	Utility bowl, 10⅛"		22.00
Casserole, individual, 10 oz.		13.00	Utility pan, 8⅛" x 12½", 2 qt.		40.00
Cup, 8 oz. measuring, 1 spout		22.00	Utility pan, 10½" x 2" deep	15.00	25.00
Cup, 8 oz., dry measure, no spout		250.00			
Cup, 8 oz., measuring, 3 spout		25.00	*Jade-ite w/embossed design		
Custard cup or baker, 5 oz.	3.00	3.25	**Jade-ite		
Custard cup or baker, 6 oz.	3.25	4.00			

Please refer to Foreword for pricing information

FIRE - KING OVEN GLASS

Housewives prefer to cook in glass for they are then able to actually see their foods cooking, eliminating the possibility of improperly cooked foods. Glass is also more easily cleaned than metal utensils, saving time and labor.

A three-fold purpose—bake, serve, and store in the same dish. Fire-King oven glass is not only suitable for oven cooking but makes ideal serving dishes for the table and in addition is safe and practical for refrigerator use.

Not only does Fire-King possess unusual cooking qualities but it is attractive, a complement to any table, and above all—the lowest priced oven glass on the market.

FIRE-KING OVEN WARE, TURQUOISE BLUE
ANCHOR HOCKING GLASS CORPORATION, 1957 – 1958

Color: Turquoise Blue

Turquoise Blue was advertised as dinnerware, but all pieces are marked ovenware except the egg plate. Most dinnerware made by Anchor Hocking is marked ovenware. This let the customer know that the glassware could be pre-warmed in the oven before serving. Turquoise Blue has become very popular with collectors.

We used Turquoise Blue as our dinnerware for five years. Conclusions concerning buying and using it come to mind as I write. The 10" serving plates are rarely found in quantity. It is an ideal size for a dinner plate if you raise hungry children! The traditional 9" dinner with its upturned edges did not hold enough for my sons. Soup and cereal bowls are more scarce than their price indicates. My teenagers always used the 8" vegetable bowl for cereal and thankfully, those were commonly found. The 6⅛" plate may be as hard to find as the 10" one. Since most collectors only buy one 10" plate and six, eight, or twelve of the smaller ones, there are not as many to go around! Numerous collectors have told me they have never seen either one!

The batter bowl was never shown in catalogs. Few of these have been found and big prices are being asked. I do not believe Anchor Hocking only made eight of these as one dealer tried to tell his customer.

The 5¾" ash tray was discontinued before the 1957–58 catalog was out of print. It should be scarcer than the others. Especially promoted were the three-part relish, egg plate, and the snack sets with 22K gold decorations. Do not put these gold-edged pieces in the microwave because the gold creates sparks. All other pieces worked well in our microwave. The 10" plate will heat a complete dinner!

Cups, saucers, 9" dinner plates, creamer, and sugar are easily found. Mugs and small berry bowls are the next easiest pieces to gather. Although the 9" plate with cup indent is not as plentiful as the dinner plate, it does not command the price of the dinner since not every buyer wants to own snack sets…yet! The 1 quart round mixing bowl and the 3 quart tear-shaped mixing bowls are the most difficult sizes to find in these bowl sets. However, the 1 quart tear-shaped bowl is always the first to sell at shows. Many people want these to use as small serving dishes. I can vouch for their being great for egg scrambling.

	Blue		Blue
Ash tray, 3½"	7.00	Plate, 6⅛"	15.00
Ash tray, 4⅝"	10.00	Plate, 7"	11.00
Ash tray, 5¾"	15.00	Plate, 9"	7.00
Batter bowl, w/spout	250.00	Plate, 9", w/cup indent	6.00
Bowl, 4½", berry	6.00	Plate, 10"	28.00
Bowl, 5", cereal	15.00	Relish, 3 part, 11⅛"	12.00
Bowl, 6⅝", soup/salad	15.00	Saucer	1.00
Bowl, 8", vegetable	15.00	Sugar	6.00
Bowl, tear, mixing, 1 pt.	15.00		
Bowl, tear, mixing, 1 qt.	18.00		
Bowl, tear, mixing, 2 qt.	25.00		
Bowl, tear, mixing, 3 qt.	30.00		
Bowl, round, mixing, 1 qt.	12.50		
Bowl, round, mixing, 2 qt.	14.00		
Bowl, round, mixing, 3 qt.	16.00		
Creamer	6.00		
Cup	4.00		
Egg plate, 9¾"	15.00		
Mug, 8 oz.	10.00		

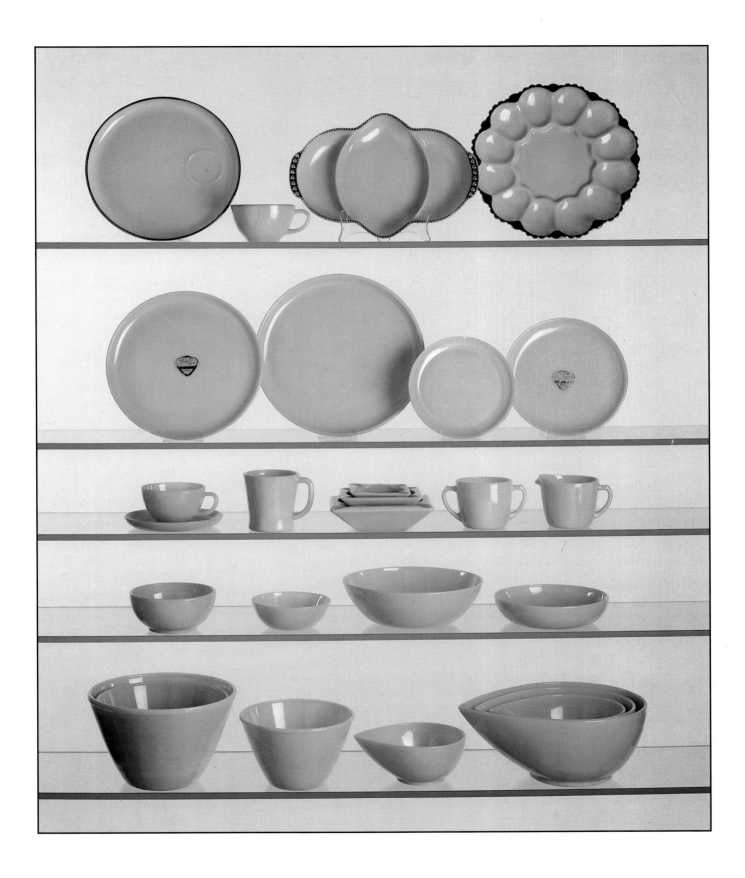

TURQUOISE-BLUE TABLEWARE — HEAT-PROOF

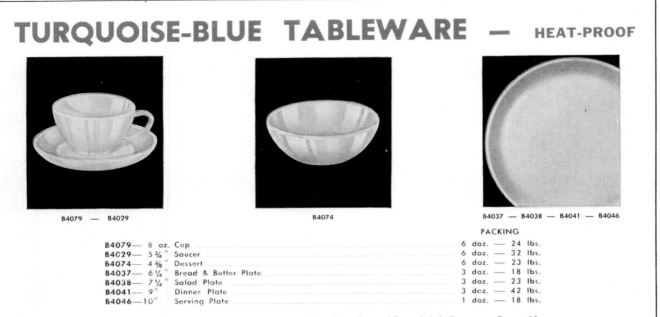

B4079 — B4029

B4074

B4037 — B4038 — B4041 — B4046

PACKING

B4079—	8 oz.	Cup	6 doz.	24 lbs.
B4029—	5¾"	Saucer	6 doz.	32 lbs.
B4074—	4⅝"	Dessert	6 doz.	23 lbs.
B4037—	6¼"	Bread & Butter Plate	3 doz.	18 lbs.
B4038—	7¼"	Salad Plate	3 doz.	23 lbs.
B4041—	9"	Dinner Plate	3 doz.	42 lbs.
B4046—	10"	Serving Plate	1 doz.	18 lbs.

See Mixing Bowls on Page 27, Mug and Bowl on Page 23 and Ash Trays on Page 41.

B4067

B4078

B4053 — B4054

B4067—	6⅝"	Soup Plate	3 doz.	26 lbs.
B4078—	8¼"	Vegetable Bowl	1 doz.	17 lbs.
B4053—		Sugar	2 doz.	11 lbs.
B4054—		Creamer	2 doz.	11 lbs.

B4000/18

PREPACKED SETS

B4000/18—12 Pce. Starter Set
Each Set in Display Style Carton, 6 Sets to Shipper — 48 lbs.
COMPOSITION: Four Each B4079 Cups, B4029 Saucers and
B4041 Dinner Plates

B4000/19—18 Pce. Luncheon Set
Each Set in Gift Carton, 4 Sets to Shipper — 40 lbs.
COMPOSITION: Four Each B4079 Cups, B4029 Saucers, B4074 Desserts,
and B4041 Dinner Plates; One Each B4053 Sugar and B4054
Creamer

B4000/21—34 Pce. Dinner Set
Each Set in Shipping Carton — 20 lbs.
COMPOSITION: Six Each B4079 Cups, B4029 Saucers, B4074 Desserts,
B4038 Salad Plates and B4041 Dinner Plates; One Each B4078
Vegetable Bowl, B4046 Serving Plate, B4053 Sugar and B4054
Creamer

B4000/22—52 Pce. Dinner Set
Each Set in Shipping Carton — 32 lbs.
COMPOSITION: Eight Each B4079 Cups, B4029 Saucers, B4074 Desserts,
B4038 Salad Plates, B4067 Soup Plates and B4041 Dinner Plates;
One Each B4078 Vegetable Bowl, B4046 Serving Plate, B4053 Sugar
and B4054 Creamer

FIRE-KING OVEN WARE, "SWIRL"
ANCHOR HOCKING GLASS CORPORATION, 1950s

Colors: Azur-ite, Ivory, Ivory trimmed in gold or red, white or white trimmed in gold, and Pink

I looked at assorted "swirled" patterns that Anchor Hocking produced since 1950, and spent an entire day trying to find a way to organize patterns into a sensible order. Heretofore, colors determined name and not pattern which has created a quandary for collectors of Anchor Hocking's glassware. There were two dissimilar swirled patterns and even a modification in sugar styles. The obvious answer was Swirls of the 1950s and Swirls of the 1960s.

The first "Swirl," introduced in 1950, was Azur-ite which is the light blue shown on top of page 99; that was followed by Sunrise (red trimmed, shown on top of page 100). In 1953 Ivory "Swirl" was introduced; later in the 1950s, Anchorwhite took over for the Ivory. Golden Anniversary was introduced in 1955 by adding 22K gold trim to Ivory "Swirl." In the latter 1950s a gold border was added to Anchorwhite, but labels on this say 22K. The Ivory is a beige tint as opposed to the flatter white of Anchorwhite. They are sometimes confused when shopping by flashlight at early morning flea markets. Both patterns were heavily marketed, so they are available! Watch out for worn gold edges, since most collectors avoid those pieces for collections. If you are buying these to use, pieces with worn gold edges may be a bargain!

Pink (bottom page 99) was introduced in 1956. I bought a stack of 22 Pink soup bowls a few weeks before we had our photography session. At the studio, I realized that one soup bowl was all I needed for the picture, but not one of those bowls had been kind enough to pack itself for the trip. I did keep one for next time! These are not frequently found!

Note the Pink footed sugar and creamer at the bottom of page 99. These do not have the typical white bottoms normally found on Pink. They are from a pattern called Rosite. Other pieces found in Rosite includes berry and soup bowls and a footed sherbet. Tumblers were made to go with only the Pink as far as I can determine. The tumbler pictured is from an original boxed set. You might find a pitcher to match these tumblers, but I have not been so lucky!

At Houston in February, I traded for an Azur-ite 9¼" flanged soup which was the first I'd seen. One of my Fire-King addicts suggested I mention the Azur-ite mixing bowl in the photo. It's rare. She wants it badly! Some pieces of Azur-ite have been found with gold decorations.

	Anchorwhite Ivory White	Golden Anniversary	Pink	Azur-ite Sunrise
Bowl, 4⅞", fruit or dessert	2.50	2.75	6.00	4.00
Bowl, 7¼", vegetable			18.00	12.50
Bowl, 7⅝", soup plate	2.75	3.00	15.00	10.00
Bowl, 8¼", vegetable	5.00	5.00		16.00
Bowl, 9¼", flanged soup				50.00
Creamer, flat	3.50		8.00	7.00
Creamer, ftd.	2.75	3.25		
Cup, 8 oz.	2.75	3.00	5.50	5.50
Plate, 7⅜", salad	2.50	2.50		6.00
Plate, 9⅛", dinner	3.00	4.00	8.00	7.50
Plate, 11", serving				17.50
Platter, 12" x 9"	6.00	6.50	20.00	17.50
Saucer, 5¾"	.50	.50	1.25	1.00
Sugar lid, for flat sugar	2.50		7.00	5.00
Sugar lid, for ftd. sugar	2.50			
Sugar, flat, tab handles	3.50		7.00	6.00
Sugar, ftd., open handles	3.00	3.50		
Tumbler, 5 oz., juice			5.00	
Tumbler, 9 oz., water			7.00	
Tumbler, 12 oz., iced tea			8.00	

GOLDEN ANNIVERSARY DINNERWARE

W4100/57

W4100/57—18 Pce. Luncheon Set
Each Set in Gift Carton, 4 Sets to Shipping Carton — 41 lbs.
COMPOSITION:

Four W4179/50 Cups	Four W4141/50 Dinner Plates
Four W4129/50 Saucers	One W4153/50 Sugar
Four W4174/50 Desserts	One W4154/50 Creamer

W4100/58—34 Pce. Dinner Set (Not illustrated)
Each Set in Shipping Carton — 23 lbs.
COMPOSITION:

Six W4179/50 Cups	One W4178/50 Vegetable Bowl
Six W4129/50 Saucers	One W4147/50 Platter
Six W4174/50 Desserts	One W4153/50 Sugar
Six W4138/50 Salad Plates	One W4154/50 Creamer
Six W4141/50 Dinner Plates	

W4100/59—52 Pce. Dinner Set (Not illustrated)
Each Set in Shipping Carton — 35 lbs.
COMPOSITION:

Eight W4179/50 Cups	Eight W4141/50 Dinner Plates
Eight W4129/50 Saucers	One W4178/50 Vegetable Bowl
Eight W4174/50 Desserts	One W4147/50 Platter
Eight W4138/50 Salad Plates	One W4153/50 Sugar
Eight W4167/50 Soup Plates	One W4154/50 Creamer

OPEN STOCK

W4179/50 — W4129/50

W4174/50

W4138/50 — W4141/50

W4167/50

			PACKING
W4179/50—		Cup	6 doz. — 26 lbs.
W4129/50—		Saucer	6 doz. — 28 lbs.
W4174/50—4 ⅞″	Dessert		6 doz. — 24 lbs.
W4138/50—7 ¾″	Salad Plate		3 doz. — 26 lbs.
W4141/50—9 ⅛″	Dinner Plate		3 doz. — 40 lbs.
W4167/50—7 ⅝″	Soup Plate		3 doz. — 29 lbs.

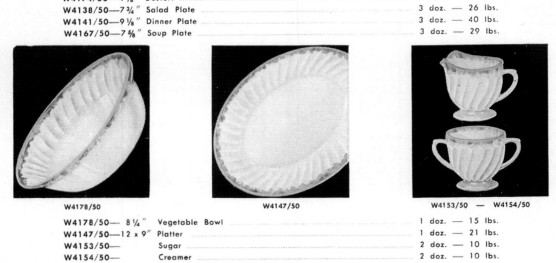

W4178/50   W4147/50   W4153/50 — W4154/50

W4178/50— 8 ¼″	Vegetable Bowl		1 doz. — 15 lbs.
W4147/50—12 x 9″	Platter		1 doz. — 21 lbs.
W4153/50—	Sugar		2 doz. — 10 lbs.
W4154/50—	Creamer		2 doz. — 10 lbs.

HEAT-PROOF   **ANCHORWHITE — 22 K. GOLD TRIMMED**

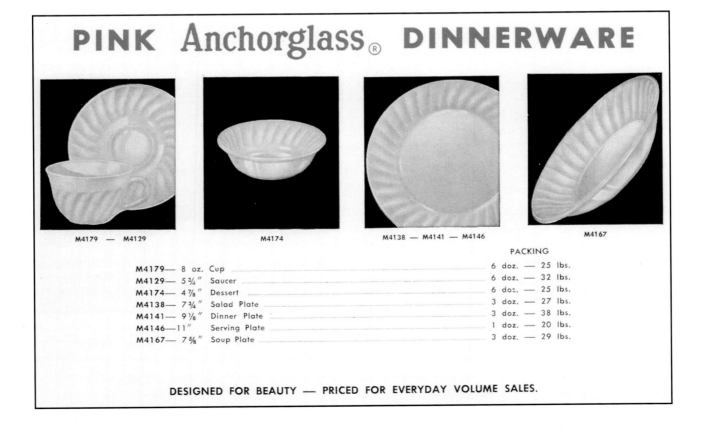

PINK Anchorglass® DINNERWARE

M4179 — M4129

M4174

M4138 — M4141 — M4146

M4167

		PACKING
M4179— 8 oz. Cup		6 doz. — 25 lbs.
M4129— 5¾″ Saucer		6 doz. — 32 lbs.
M4174— 4⅞″ Dessert		6 doz. — 25 lbs.
M4138— 7¾″ Salad Plate		3 doz. — 27 lbs.
M4141— 9⅛″ Dinner Plate		3 doz. — 38 lbs.
M4146—11″ Serving Plate		1 doz. — 20 lbs.
M4167— 7⅝″ Soup Plate		3 doz. — 29 lbs.

DESIGNED FOR BEAUTY — PRICED FOR EVERYDAY VOLUME SALES.

FIRE-KING OVEN WARE, "SWIRL"

ANCHOR HOCKING GLASS CORPORATION, 1960s – 1975

Colors: White, white trimmed in gold, Jade-ite, and iridized Lustre

Anchorwhite "Swirl" continued to be made into the early 1960s. In 1963, Hocking changed the "Swirl" design by making the edge more predominately scalloped. This new design with the 22K gold edge was called Golden Shell and it was manufactured into the late 1970s. Pages 102 and 103 show catalog pages of this new design. Note the taller, footed creamer and sugar in this line. The Golden Shell is on white just as was the earlier 22K.

You can see the major differences in the 22K and Golden Shell by studying the catalog picture of Golden Anniversary (page 98) and Golden Shell (page 102). 22K used the same 4100 line blanks as those of Golden Anniversary. Although similar, Golden Shell and 22K do not blend as well as other analogous patterns since the serving pieces are decidedly more scalloped on the Golden Shell.

Using this new "Swirl" design, Anchor Hocking introduced a Jade-ite set in 1964. The catalog called it an "English Regency style." You can see an example of this pattern on the top of page 106. This pattern's name was only Jade-ite. It was shown in catalogs through 1972.

In 1966, Lustre Shell was introduced and was in catalogs until the late 1970s. This Lustre Shell was the same color used for Peach Lustre, introduced in 1952. Peach Lustre was dropped in 1963. This Lustre finish also deteriorates easily; so look for pieces that were used sparingly. Some Lustre only comes on the outside of plates.

The soup bowl in Lustre Shell was enlarged from 6⅜" to 7⅝". Lustre was Anchor Hocking's name for the color and shell was the design. Now why didn't they add shell to the Jade-ite and solve our pattern name problems today? "Jade-ite Shell" should be the name!

A demitasse cup and saucer were introduced to the Lustre Shell line in 1972. As with other Fire-King patterns, demitasse saucers are harder to find than cups.

On page 104 and 105 are two photographs of "Swirl" with hand-painted scenes. No one has contacted me about having any information on the J. Kinney who painted this ware. However, I have had several calls about other pieces found with a J. Kinney signature and several wanted to buy these pictured. All signed pieces have been Pyrex or Anchor Hocking.

	Golden Shell	Jade-ite "Shell"	Lustre Shell
Bowl, 4¾", dessert	1.75	4.00	3.00
Bowl, 6⅜", cereal	2.50	7.00	4.50
Bowl, 7⅝", soup plate	5.00	12.00	5.00
Bowl, 6⅜", soup	4.00	5.00	
Bowl, 8½", vegetable	5.50	11.00	9.00
Creamer, ftd.	3.50	7.50	5.50
Cup, 8 oz.	3.25	5.00	4.00
Cup, 3¼ oz., demitasse			8.50
Saucer, 4¾", demitasse			6.50
Plate, 7¼", salad	2.50	5.00	3.50
Plate, 10", dinner	4.00	7.00	7.00
Plate, 11", serving			11.00
Platter, 9½" x 13"	9.00	20.00	
Saucer, 5¾"	.50	1.00	.50
Sugar, ftd.	2.75	8.00	6.00
Sugar cover	4.00	8.00	4.00

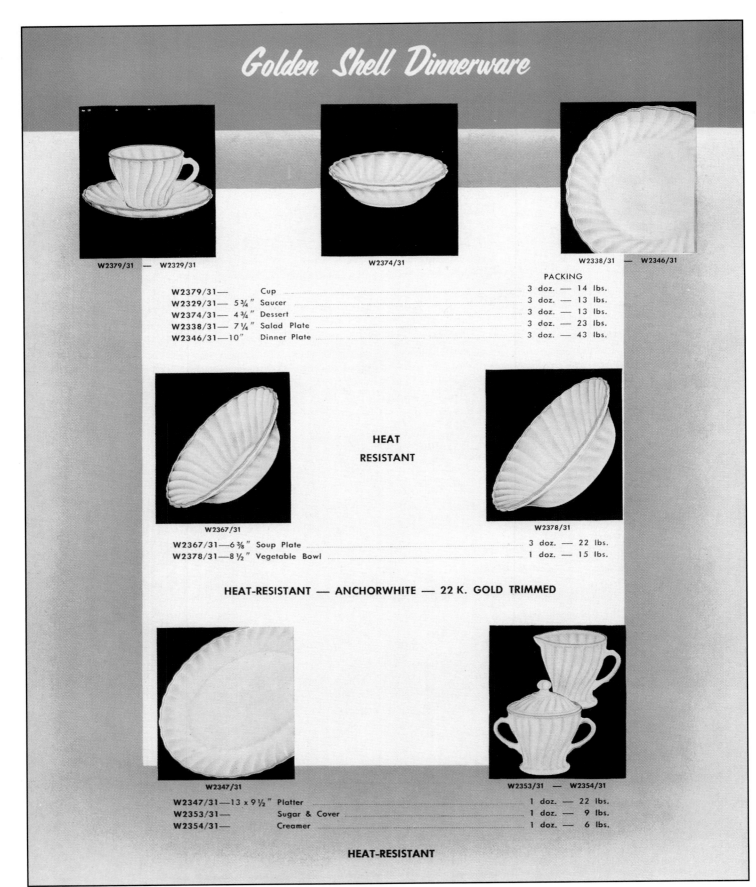

Golden Shell Dinnerware

W2379/31 — W2329/31   W2374/31   W2338/31 — W2346/31

		PACKING
W2379/31—	Cup	3 doz. — 14 lbs.
W2329/31—5¾"	Saucer	3 doz. — 13 lbs.
W2374/31—4¾"	Dessert	3 doz. — 13 lbs.
W2338/31—7¼"	Salad Plate	3 doz. — 23 lbs.
W2346/31—10"	Dinner Plate	3 doz. — 43 lbs.

HEAT RESISTANT

W2367/31   W2378/31

W2367/31—6⅜"	Soup Plate	3 doz. — 22 lbs.
W2378/31—8½"	Vegetable Bowl	1 doz. — 15 lbs.

HEAT-RESISTANT — ANCHORWHITE — 22 K. GOLD TRIMMED

W2347/31   W2353/31 — W2354/31

W2347/31—13 x 9½"	Platter	1 doz. — 22 lbs.
W2353/31—	Sugar & Cover	1 doz. — 9 lbs.
W2354/31—	Creamer	1 doz. — 6 lbs.

HEAT-RESISTANT

Golden Shell Dinnerware Sets

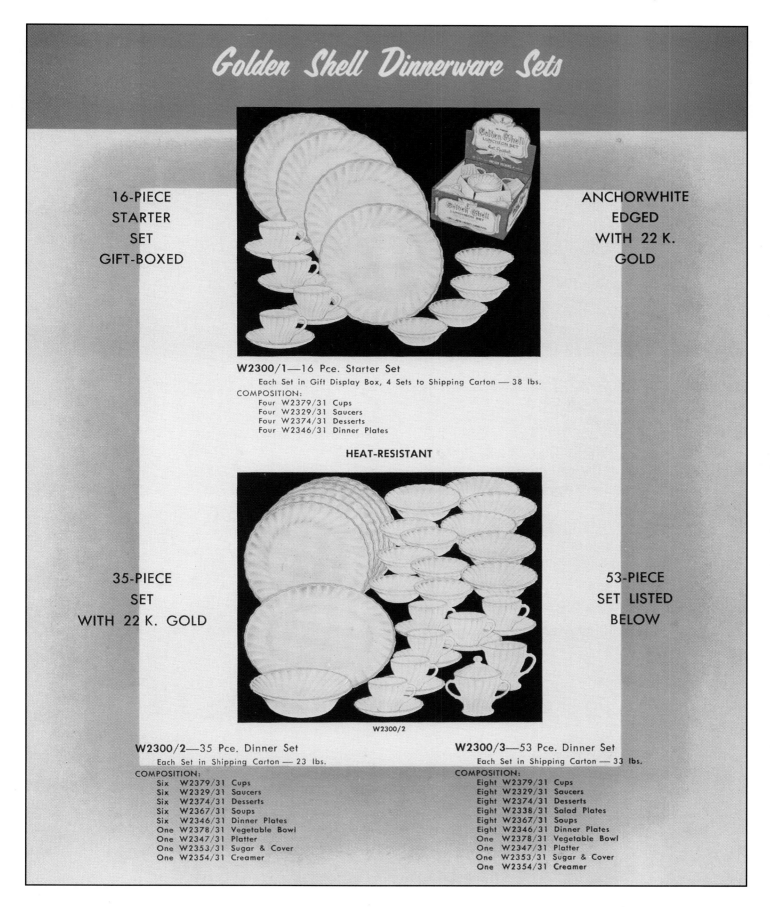

16-PIECE STARTER SET GIFT-BOXED

ANCHORWHITE EDGED WITH 22 K. GOLD

W2300/1—16 Pce. Starter Set

Each Set in Gift Display Box, 4 Sets to Shipping Carton — 38 lbs.

COMPOSITION:
Four W2379/31 Cups
Four W2329/31 Saucers
Four W2374/31 Desserts
Four W2346/31 Dinner Plates

HEAT-RESISTANT

35-PIECE SET WITH 22 K. GOLD

53-PIECE SET LISTED BELOW

W2300/2

W2300/2—35 Pce. Dinner Set

Each Set in Shipping Carton — 23 lbs.

COMPOSITION:
Six W2379/31 Cups
Six W2329/31 Saucers
Six W2374/31 Desserts
Six W2367/31 Soups
Six W2346/31 Dinner Plates
One W2378/31 Vegetable Bowl
One W2347/31 Platter
One W2353/31 Sugar & Cover
One W2354/31 Creamer

W2300/3—53 Pce. Dinner Set

Each Set in Shipping Carton — 33 lbs.

COMPOSITION:
Eight W2379/31 Cups
Eight W2329/31 Saucers
Eight W2374/31 Desserts
Eight W2338/31 Salad Plates
Eight W2367/31 Soups
Eight W2346/31 Dinner Plates
One W2378/31 Vegetable Bowl
One W2347/31 Platter
One W2353/31 Sugar & Cover
One W2354/31 Creamer

FIRE-KING OVEN WARE, "SWIRL"

FIRE-KING OVEN WARE, WHEAT & BLUE MOSAIC
ANCHOR HOCKING GLASS CORPORATION, 1962 – late 1960s

Blue Mosaic was surely distributed in Florida since I see it here more than any place I frequent. For those who wrote me about the sugar and creamer not being shown, I should point out that they are solid blue as is the cup shown. The sugar is a cup with no handles and a white lid and the creamer is a cup with a spout. I ended up with two pairs of these to photograph, but both pairs were pulled from the Blue Mosaic box instead of only one. Use your imagination until the next book, please! The snack tray in this pattern is oval and not rectangular as are most of Fire-King patterns. The same cup design was used for both the saucer and the snack tray! No mosaic cups, sugars, or creamers were made insofar as I can ascertain. This briefly-made Anchor Hocking pattern was illustrated only in a 1967 catalog.

Production of wheat began in 1962, and was one of Anchor Hocking's most prolific lines. Like Sapphire blue Fire-King of the 1940s, everyone has seen the Wheat pattern of the 1960s! Oven ware lids create dilemmas today. Casserole sizes of yesteryear do not accept most modern day lids!

Both the oval and round 1½ quart casseroles and the 10½" baking pan were used with candle warmers. These candle warmers were brass finished with walnut handles and candle. Many of these were never used! They are being found with the original candles intact! Replacement candles can be found at most kitchenware stores should you need one.

	Wheat	Blue Mosaic		Wheat	Blue Mosaic
Bowl, 4⅝", dessert	2.50	4.00	Cup, 8 oz.	3.00	
Bowl, 6⅝", soup plate	7.00	10.00	Custard, 6 oz., low or dessert	2.50	
Bowl, 8¼", vegetable	8.00	15.00	Pan, 5" x 9", baking, w/cover	15.00	
Cake pan, 8", round	9.00		Pan, 5" x 9", deep loaf	8.00	
Cake pan, 8", square	9.00		Pan, 6½" x 10½" x 1½",		
Casserole, 1 pt., knob cover	5.00		utility baking	11.00	
Casserole, 1 qt., knob cover	7.50		Pan, 8" x 12½" x 2",		
Casserole, 1½ qt., knob cover	9.50		utility baking	13.00	
Casserole, 1½ qt., oval,			Plate, 7⅜", salad	2.50	4.00
au gratin cover	14.00		Plate, 10", dinner	4.00	6.00
Casserole, 2 qt., knob cover	15.00		Platter, 9" x 12"	11.00	17.50
Casserole, 2 qt., round,			Saucer, 5¾"	1.00	1.50
au gratin cover	15.00		Sugar	3.50	6.00
Creamer	4.00	6.00	Sugar cover	3.00	4.00
Cup, 5 oz., snack	3.00		Tray, 11" x 6", rectangular, snack	3.50	
Cup, 7½ oz.		4.50	Tray, 10" x 7½", oval, snack		3.50

FIRE-KING OVEN WARE, WHEAT

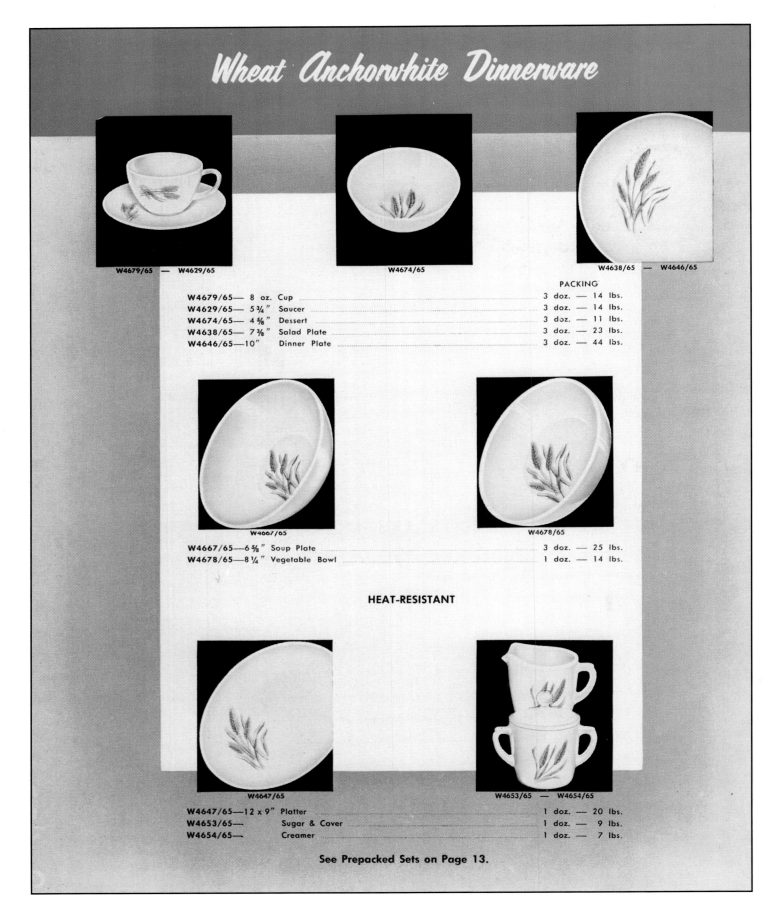

Wheat Anchorwhite Dinnerware

W4679/65 — W4629/65

W4674/65

W4638/65 — W4646/65

PACKING

W4679/65— 8 oz.	Cup	3 doz. — 14 lbs.
W4629/65— 5¾"	Saucer	3 doz. — 14 lbs.
W4674/65— 4⅝"	Dessert	3 doz. — 11 lbs.
W4638/65— 7⅜"	Salad Plate	3 doz. — 23 lbs.
W4646/65—10"	Dinner Plate	3 doz. — 44 lbs.

W4667/65

W4678/65

W4667/65—6⅝"	Soup Plate	3 doz. — 25 lbs.
W4678/65—8¼"	Vegetable Bowl	1 doz. — 14 lbs.

HEAT-RESISTANT

W4647/65

W4653/65 — W4654/65

W4647/65—12 x 9"	Platter	1 doz. — 20 lbs.
W4653/65—	Sugar & Cover	1 doz. — 9 lbs.
W4654/65—	Creamer	1 doz. — 7 lbs.

See Prepacked Sets on Page 13.

Wheat Dinnerware Sets

W4600/46—16 Pce. Starter Set
Each Set in Gift Display Carton, 4 Sets to Shipping Carton — 38 lbs.
COMPOSITION:
- Four W4679/65 Cups
- Four W4629/65 Saucers
- Four W4674/65 Desserts
- Four W4646/65 Dinner Plates

W4600/47—35 Pce. Dinner Set
Each Set in Shipping Carton — 23 lbs.
COMPOSITION:

Six W4679/65 Cups	One W4678/65 Vegetable Bowl
Six W4629/65 Saucers	One W4647/65 Platter
Six W4674/65 Desserts	One W4653/65 Sugar & Cover
Six W4667/65 Soup Plates	One W4654/65 Creamer
Six W4646/65 Dinner Plates	

W4600/48—53 Pce. Dinner Set
Each Set in Shipping Carton — 34 lbs.
COMPOSITION:

Eight W4679/65 Cups	Eight W4646/65 Dinner Plates
Eight W4629/65 Saucers	One W4678/65 Vegetable Bowl
Eight W4674/65 Desserts	One W4647/65 Platter
Eight W4638/65 Salad Plates	One W4653/65 Sugar & Cover
Eight W4667/65 Soup Plates	One W4654/65 Creamer

Wheat Anchorwhite Ovenware

W424/65

W405/65 — W406/65

W407/65 — W408/65

PACKING

W424/65—6	oz. Dessert or Low Custard	4 doz. — 14 lbs.
W405/65—1	Pt. Casserole—Knob Cover	1 doz. — 16 lbs.
W406/65—1	Qt. Casserole—Knob Cover	½ doz. — 14 lbs.
W407/65—1½	Qt. Casserole—Knob Cover	½ doz. — 19 lbs.
W408/65—2	Qt. Casserole—Knob Cover	½ doz. — 22 lbs.

All Covers are Clear Crystal Fire-King.

W467/65

W450/65

W452/65

W467/65—1½	Qt. Casserole—Au Gratin Cover	½ doz. — 18 lbs.
W450/65—8″	Round Cake Pan	½ doz. — 12 lbs.
W452/65—8″	Square Cake Pan	½ doz. — 17 lbs.

GUARANTEED 2 YEARS AGAINST OVEN BREAKAGE.

To be replaced Free by dealer in exchange for broken pieces.

W409/65

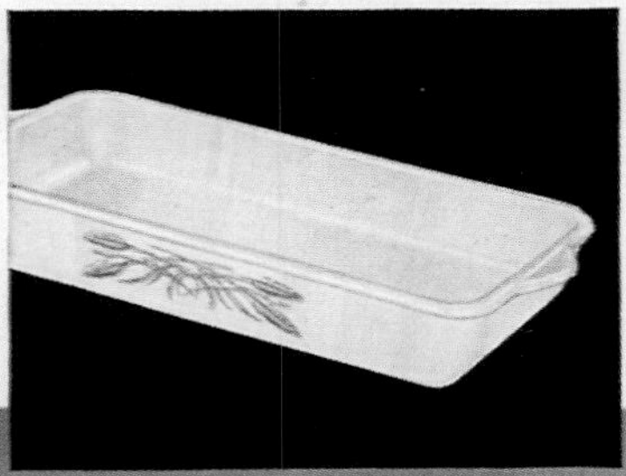

W410/65 — W411/65

W409/65—5 x 9″	Deep Loaf Pan	½ doz. — 12 lbs.
W410/65—6½ x 10½″	Utility Baking Pan	½ doz. — 15 lbs.
W411/65—8 x 12½″	Utility Baking Pan	½ doz. — 22 lbs.

"Fire-King" — The World's Finest Baking Ware. Also available in Crystal, Anchorwhite and Copper-Tint.

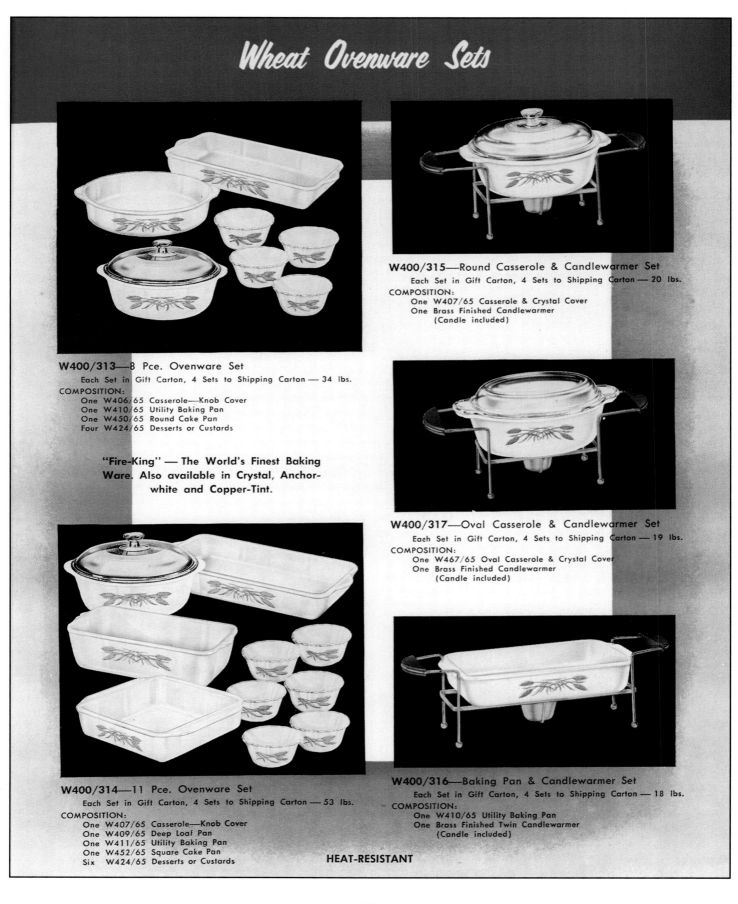

Wheat Ovenware Sets

W400/313—8 Pce. Ovenware Set
Each Set in Gift Carton, 4 Sets to Shipping Carton — 34 lbs.
COMPOSITION:
One W406/65 Casserole—Knob Cover
One W410/65 Utility Baking Pan
One W450/65 Round Cake Pan
Four W424/65 Desserts or Custards

**"Fire-King" — The World's Finest Baking
Ware. Also available in Crystal, Anchorwhite and Copper-Tint.**

W400/314—11 Pce. Ovenware Set
Each Set in Gift Carton, 4 Sets to Shipping Carton — 53 lbs.
COMPOSITION:
One W407/65 Casserole—Knob Cover
One W409/65 Deep Loaf Pan
One W411/65 Utility Baking Pan
One W452/65 Square Cake Pan
Six W424/65 Desserts or Custards

W400/315—Round Casserole & Candlewarmer Set
Each Set in Gift Carton, 4 Sets to Shipping Carton — 20 lbs.
COMPOSITION:
One W407/65 Casserole & Crystal Cover
One Brass Finished Candlewarmer
(Candle included)

W400/317—Oval Casserole & Candlewarmer Set
Each Set in Gift Carton, 4 Sets to Shipping Carton — 19 lbs.
COMPOSITION:
One W467/65 Oval Casserole & Crystal Cover
One Brass Finished Candlewarmer
(Candle included)

W400/316—Baking Pan & Candlewarmer Set
Each Set in Gift Carton, 4 Sets to Shipping Carton — 18 lbs.
COMPOSITION:
One W410/65 Utility Baking Pan
One Brass Finished Twin Candlewarmer
(Candle included)

HEAT-RESISTANT

FLORAGOLD, "LOUISA," JEANNETTE GLASS COMPANY, 1950s

Colors: Iridescent, some Shell Pink, ice blue, and crystal

Floragold is a pattern that was previously in *The Collector's Encyclopedia of Depression Glass*. Floragold was made long after the Depression era and rightly belongs here. Floragold is often confused with an old carnival glass pattern called "Louisa." Some antique dealers, who do not sell much glassware, will price this early 1950s glassware quite high believing it to be carnival glass. Collectors of carnival glass often accept glassware made through the 1920s and occasionally a piece or two from the 1930s; but I have not met one who considers this pattern carnival glass. The rose bowl in carnival "Louisa" is frequently offered for sale as Floragold which turns the confusion around the other way.

Make sure the vase or the 15 ounce tumblers have a strong iridized color before you spend your money for them. For such a large investment, you do not need a weakly sprayed color. This color was made by applying an iridized spray over crystal and reheating. Heating it too hotly burned out the color! That rarely found vase was made by taking a 15 ounce tumbler and fluting the top. These large, 15 ounce tumblers can be found in crystal selling in the $12.00 to 15.00 range; add the iridized spray and you have to add another zero to that price. Evidently, many of these tumblers were never sprayed. I seem to find more crystal tumblers than iridized ones. Occasionally, you will see a crystal vase.

Perfect shaker tops are hard to find. Only white or brown plastic tops are originals. They were made of plastic, and many were broken by tightening them too much. Tops are worth $15.00, which makes the tops themselves more than half the price of the shakers!

Cups were sold without saucers in two similar ways, creating an abundance of cups in Floragold. The large bowl and the pitcher were both sold with 12 cups as "egg nog" sets for the Christmas market. Every set sold added another dozen cups to production; so, today, saucers are scarce! That 5¼" saucer has no cup ring and is the same as the sherbet plate.

Ice blue, crystal, red-yellow, Shell Pink and iridized large comports were made in the late 1950s and into the early 1970s. See Shell Pink for a look at the shape of this piece. All colored comports are selling in the $10.00 to $12.00 range. (That 9" iridized comport I saw for sale at a flea market for $175.00 had been reduced to $100.00 last year and is now on a half price table marked rare carnival.)

For those who have never seen the 5½" butter dish, it is pictured in the *Very Rare Glassware of the Depression Years*, fourth edition. There are two different 5¼" comports in Floragold. Both of these are pictured in the first edition of *Very Rare Glassware of the Depression Years*. One has a ruffled top, and the other has a plain top. You can see the ruffled style below. Currently, none of these are for sale at any price.

	Iridescent
Ash tray/coaster, 4"	5.50
Bowl, 4½", square	5.50
Bowl, 5½", round cereal	37.50
Bowl, 5½", ruffled fruit	8.00
Bowl, 8½", square	14.00
Bowl, 9½", deep salad	42.50
Bowl, 9½", ruffled	8.00
Bowl, 12", ruffled large fruit	7.00
Butter dish and cover, ¼ lb. oblong	25.00
Butter dish and cover, round, 6¼" sq. base	45.00
Butter dish bottom	14.00
Butter dish top	28.50
Butter dish and cover, round, 5½" sq. base	750.00
Candlesticks, double branch, pr.	50.00
Candy dish, 1 handle	12.00
Candy or Cheese dish and cover, 6¾"	52.50
*Candy, 5¼" long, 4 feet	7.50
Comport, 5¼", plain top	600.00
Comport, 5¼", ruffled top	700.00
Creamer	9.00
Cup	6.00
Pitcher, 64 oz.	37.50
Plate or tray, 13½"	22.00
Plate or tray, 13½", with indent	60.00
Plate, 5¼", sherbet	12.00
Plate, 8½", dinner	40.00
Platter, 11¼"	22.00
**Salt and pepper, plastic tops	50.00
Saucer, 5¼" (no ring)	12.00
Sherbet, low, footed	16.00
Sugar	6.50
Sugar lid	10.00

	Iridescent
Tid-bit, wooden post	35.00
Tumbler, 10 oz., footed	20.00
Tumbler, 11 oz., footed	20.00
Tumbler, 15 oz., footed	110.00
Vase or celery	400.00

* Shell pink $20.00
**Tops $15.00 each included in price

FOREST GREEN, ANCHOR HOCKING GLASS COMPANY CORPORATION, 1950 – 1967

Color: Forest Green

Forest Green was the color name of glassware made by Anchor Hocking. In the past it was not a collectible pattern name! Even Hocking's "Bubble" was called Forest Green as you can see by the catalog sheet on page 21. Forest Green was used for the square Charm blank (1950), but the glassware became better known by its color. I have removed all of the Charm pieces from the listing below and you will now find them listed only under Charm.

The photo at the bottom of page 20 shows stemware that was sold along with "Bubble." These have been called "Boopie" by collectors. The prices of the Forest Green "Boopie" have recently leveled off while "Bubble" stemware (shown on page 21) has risen in price. I suspect it has more to do with the bountifulness of "Boopie" than any other explanation. Both lines are priced below.

The Forest Green oval vegetable is scalloped along the edges and has a swirled effect on the sides. This bowl is in the foreground atop page 115. These were a premium item for a flour company in the South; so look for them there.

You will find many odd dark green pieces on the market that are labeled Forest Green. To be truly Forest Green, it must have been made by Anchor Hocking! That name was patented by them!

Decorated tumblers such as "A Bicycle for Two" will bring a dollar or two more than regular tumblers. Yet undecorated tumblers sell faster to collectors!

The paperweight below was one of five I encountered a few years back. They were evidently from this era and may have been promotional items from Anchor Hocking!

Forest Green was widely distributed as premium items. Hocking must have provided their products at an extremely attractive price since so many tumblers and vases are found today. Notice the 9 ounce tumblers in the bottom picture with metal caps which covered dairy products, most frequently, cottage cheese. In the Kentucky area, they were Sealtest brand dairy products. A reader reported finding an unopened box of twenty-four 7 ounce tumblers marked, "Clover Honey Delight, Packed by National Honey Packers Mt. Sterling Illinois." Tea bags were another commodity often found in Anchor Hocking tumblers.

Massive quantities of 4" ball ivy vases testify to successful sales of Citronella candles packed in those vases. The bottom photograph shows a boxed set of "Moskeeto-Lites." This pair of candles originally sold for $1.19. After using the candles, you had two free vases. I considered using these on my dock in Florida!

	Green		Green		Green
Ash tray, 3½", square	5.00	Stem, 6 oz., sherbet	9.00	Tumbler, 10 oz., ftd., 4½"	6.50
Ash tray, 4⅝", square	6.00	*Stem, 6 oz., sherbet	6.00	Tumbler, 11 oz.	7.00
Ash tray, 5¾", square	9.00	*Stem, 9 oz., goblet	10.00	Tumbler, 13 oz., iced tea	7.50
Ash tray, 5¾", hexagonal	8.00	Stem, 9½ oz., goblet	13.00	Tumbler, 14 oz., 5"	7.50
Batter bowl w/spout	25.00	*Stem, 14 oz., iced tea	14.00	Tumbler, 15 oz., long boy	10.00
Bowl, 4¾", dessert	5.50	Tumbler, 5 oz., 3½"	4.00	Tumbler, 15 oz., tall iced tea	12.00
Bowl, 5¼" deep	8.50	Tumbler, 7 oz.	4.00	Tumbler, 32 oz., giant iced tea	17.00
Bowl, 6", mixing	9.00	Tumbler, 9 oz, table	5.00	Vase, 4" ivy ball	4.00
Bowl, 8½", oval vegetable	21.00	Tumbler, 9 oz., fancy	6.00	Vase, 6⅜"	5.00
Pitcher, 22 oz.	22.50	Tumbler, 9½ oz., tall	6.50	Vase, 9"	8.00
Pitcher, 36 oz.	25.00				
Pitcher, 86 oz., round	30.00			* "Boopie"	
Plate, 6¾", salad	5.00				
Punch bowl	22.50				
Punch bowl stand	22.50				
Punch cup (round)	2.25				
Saucer, 5⅜"	1.50				
Sherbet, flat	7.50				
*Stem, 3½ oz., cocktail	10.00				
*Stem, 4 oz., juice	10.00				
Stem, 4½ oz., cocktail	12.50				
Stem, 5½ oz., juice	12.50				

Please refer to Foreword for pricing information

GOLDEN GLORY, FEDERAL GLASS COMPANY, 1959 – 66; 1978 – 79

Color: White with 22K gold decorations

Golden Glory is beginning to blossom in collecting circles. Be aware that the 22K gold decorations wear easily and detergent will bleach them. This makes for obstacles in finding mint condition pieces, unless you can run across some that were rarely used or still boxed. Dishes were bought to be used, and using them caused wear marks and deterioration that collectors should remember to take into account.

I received a picture of a boxed set purportedly showing additional pieces that I did not have listed. Was I ever excited about that information! Unfortunately, the picture was not of Golden Glory, but some other pattern made by Federal.

Initially, there were only a dozen pieces cataloged. When reissued in 1978, three additional pieces were included. These were the larger 10" dinner plate, the smaller 6⅝" soup and the 11¼" round platter. However, the reissue did not include the oval platter, larger soup, sugar, creamer, and tumblers. This should make those items harder to find; but, according to an enthusiastic collector, the hardest-to-find pieces are the 8¼" vegetable bowl, tumblers, and the 7¾" salad plate. I have had no luck in locating a platter, so they may not be prevalent either!

Bowl, 4⅞", dessert	4.50	Plate, 10", dinner	6.50
Bowl, 6⅜", soup	8.00	Platter, 11¼", round	14.00
Bowl, 8½", vegetable	12.00	Platter, 12", oval	11.00
Bowl, 8", rimmed soup	9.00	Saucer	.50
Creamer	4.00	Sugar	3.00
Cup	3.00	Sugar lid	3.00
Plate, 7⅔", salad	3.00	Tumbler, 9 oz., ftd.	10.00
Plate, 9⅛", dinner	5.00	Tumbler, 10 oz., 5"	10.00

HARP, JEANNETTE GLASS COMPANY, 1954 – 1957

Colors: crystal, crystal with gold trim, and cake stands in Shell Pink, pink, iridescent white, red, and ice blue

Harp cup and saucer prices have skyrocketed! With so many new collectors starting on smaller sized patterns, the demand for basic pieces has more than doubled the prices in the last few years. There is simply not enough of this smaller pattern to provide everyone a set who wishes one. Many collectors use Harp for their bridge parties. With the cake stand, cups, saucers, and the 7" plates, it's ideal for small parties. Originally, cake sets comprised of the cake stand and eight 7" plates must have sold well. Cake plates abound and there is an adequate supply of the 7" plates for now; but if you run into the cup and saucers, do not hesitate — buy!

Numerous pieces found with gold trim bother some collectors. An art gum eraser will take care of the problem with a little elbow grease! This was 22K gold and it did not anneal well to most glass; so, it has a tendency to wear if used at all.

The vase does stand 7½" and not 6" as once listed! A telephone report of a completely different style vase proved to be true; however I still do not have its measurements. Stay tuned!

I thought Harp cake stand varieties were completely cataloged and the collector of Harp cake stands should have reached the end of the line. I have missed him the last few years at the Michigan show. However, another Harp cake stand has been reported in a fired-on red color! There are thirteen types with eight colors and we're still counting! You can see two styles of ice blue below. A ruffled, gold-trimmed crystal and an iridescent one are also pictured. Note the color variations on the blue. The Shell Pink Harp cake stand can be seen under that pattern.

The thirteen documented varieties of Harp cake stands are as follows:

1, 2. Crystal with smooth or ruffled rim	10. Pink transparent
3, 4. Either of above with gold trim	11. Platinum decorated with smooth rim
5. Iridescent with smooth rim	12. Red
6, 7. White or Shell Pink (opaque) with beads on rim and foot	13. Fired-on red
8, 9. Ice blue with beads on foot and smooth or ruffled rim	

The Harp cake stand is reminiscent of late 1800s and early 1900s glassware. Most patterns after that time had cake plates instead of a stand.

	Crystal		Crystal
Ash tray/coaster	5.00	Plate, 7"	12.50
Coaster	4.50	Saucer	10.00
Cup	27.50	**Tray, 2-handled, rectangular	35.00
*Cake stand, 9"	22.50	Vase, 7½"	22.50

    * Ice blue, white, pink or Shell Pink - $45.00
    ** Shell Pink $60.00

HEATHER ETCHING #343, FOSTORIA GLASS COMPANY, 1949 – 1976

Colors: crystal

Heather is a Fostoria pattern that was introduced in *Elegant Glassware of the Depression Era* because of reader's requests. Heather is now found only in this book. Heather is another 50s pattern that is being split among family; second and third generation family members are pursuing it as replacements or to fill in partial sets.

Everything listed in Heather that does not have a line number is etched on Century blank #2630. The pattern shot below is of the #2470, 10" footed vase. I have tried to give as accurate a listing for this pattern as possible from old catalogs, but I am sure there are additional pieces. Any help from readers will be appreciated.

Heather, like any pattern etched on #2630 blank has problems with scratches and scuffs on the surfaces of any flat piece. All plates, and in particular dinner plates, have been, and still are, subject to that abuse. Protect them by what you serve on them and by how you store them between use! These dishes were meant to be used and most were! No one knew that someday they would become collectible!

Basket, 10¼" x 6½", wicker hdld.	85.00	Plate, 7½", salad	10.00	Tray, 9⅛", hdld., utility	33.00
Bowl, 4½", hdld.	15.00	Plate, 8½", luncheon	15.00	Tray, 11½", center hdld.	37.50
Bowl, 5", fruit	16.00	Plate, 8", party, w/indent for cup	30.00	Tumbler, #6037, 4⅞", 5 oz., ftd.,	
Bowl, 6", cereal	25.00	Plate, 9½", small dinner	35.00	juice	20.00
Bowl, 6¼", snack, ftd.	20.00	Plate, 10", hdld., cake	30.00	Tumbler, #6037, 6⅛", 12 oz.,	
Bowl, 7⅛", 3 ftd., triangular	20.00	Plate, 10½", dinner,		ftd., tea	25.00
Bowl, 7¼", bonbon, 3 ftd.	25.00	large center	45.00	Vase, 5", #4121	50.00
Bowl, 8", flared	32.50	Plate, 10½", snack tray,		Vase, 6", bud	30.00
Bowl, 9", lily pond	37.50	small center	30.00	Vase, 6", ftd. bud, #6021	55.00
Bowl, 9½", hdld., serving bowl	42.50	Plate, 14", torte	45.00	Vase, 6", ftd., #4143	55.00
Bowl, 9½", oval, serving bowl	45.00	Plate, 16", torte	70.00	Vase, 7½", hdld.	75.00
Bowl, 10", oval, hdld.	45.00	Platter, 12"	85.00	Vase, 8", flip, #2660	95.00
Bowl, 10½", salad	47.50	Preserve, w/cover, 6"	65.00	Vase, 8", ftd., bud, #5092	85.00
Bowl, 10¾", ftd., flared	50.00	Relish, 7⅜", 2 part	20.00	Vase, 8½", oval	85.00
Bowl, 11, ftd., rolled edge	55.00	Relish, 11⅛", 3 part	32.50	Vase, 10", ftd., #2470	115.00
Bowl, 11¼", lily pond	45.00	Salt and pepper, 3⅛", pr.	47.50		
Bowl, 12", flared	52.00	Salver, 12¼", ftd. (like cake stand)	65.00		
Butter, w/cover, ¼ lb.	75.00	Saucer	4.50		
Candlestick, 4½"	22.00	Stem, #6037, 4", 1 oz., cordial	42.00		
Candlestick, 7", double	37.50	Stem, #6037, 4", 4½ oz., oyster			
Candlestick, 7¾", triple	50.00	cocktail	18.00		
Candy, w/cover, 7"	55.00	Stem, #6037, 4¾", 7 oz.,			
Comport, 2¾", cheese	20.00	low sherbet	14.00		
Comport, 4⅜"	30.00	Stem, #6037, 5", 4 oz., cocktail	20.00		
Cracker plate, 10¾"	30.00	Stem, #6037, 6⅛", 6 oz., parfait	25.00		
Creamer, 4¼"	15.00	Stem, #6037, 6⅜", 9 oz.,			
Creamer, individual	15.00	low goblet	30.00		
Cup, 6 oz., ftd.	17.00	Stem, #6037, 6", 4 oz.,			
Ice Bucket	75.00	claret-wine	32.50		
Mayonnaise, 3 pc.	37.50	Stem, #6037, 6", 7 oz., saucer			
Mayonnaise, 4 pc., div. w/2 ladles	42.50	champagne	18.00		
Mustard, w/spoon, cover	35.00	Stem, #6037, 7⅞", 9 oz., goblet	26.00		
Oil, w/stopper, 5 oz.	50.00	Sugar, 4", ftd.	14.00		
Pickle, 8¾"	25.00	Sugar, individual	15.00		
Pitcher, 6⅛", 16 oz.	75.00	Tid bit, 8⅛", 3 ftd., upturned edge	30.00		
Pitcher, 7⅛", 48 oz.	135.00	Tid bit, 10¼", 2 tier, metal hdld.	45.00		
Plate, 6", bread/butter	7.00	Tray, 7⅛", for ind. sug/cr.	17.50		
Plate, 7½", crescent salad	45.00	Tray, 9½", hdld., muffin	33.00		

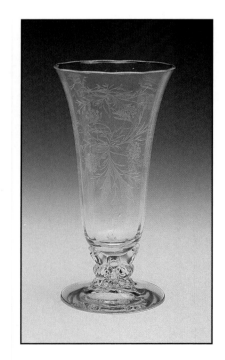

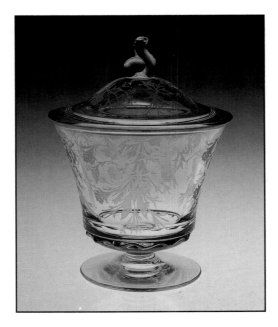

HERITAGE FEDERAL GLASS COMPANY, 1940 – 1955

Colors: crystal, some pink, blue, green, and cobalt

Heritage is one of the smaller patterns that catches the eyes of discerning collectors. Due to current collectors' demand, prices for crystal creamers, sugars, and 8½" berry bowls continue to increase. These are the most troublesome pieces to find. The sugar, turns up with more frequency than the creamer. Actually, most creamers are harder to find than their counterparts. I have seen few 8½" berry bowls for sale in the last several years. You will see dozens of 10½" bowls for every 8½" one.

Reproduction berry bowls are so crudely made that they are causing little trouble for collectors. Reproductions of Heritage bowls were marketed by McCrory's, and other similar stores in the late 1980s and early 1990s. These were made in amber, crystal, and green. Many are marked "MC" in the center. I say "many" because not all reports from readers have mentioned this mark. In any case, the smaller berry bowls sold three for $1.00 and the larger for $1.59 each. The pattern on these pieces is not very good and should not fool even beginning collectors. Compare the fully designed hobs in the photograph to the sparsely designed hobs on the reproductions. The green reproduction is much darker and closer to the 1970s avocado green. Notice the Depression green of the original bowl in the photo. Federal never made Heritage in amber.

Authentic pink, blue, and green berry bowls remain scarce. These are unquestionably rare! It is a shame that only berry bowl sets were made in these colors.

Heritage was advertised as late as 1954 in certain women's magazines.

Crystal Heritage sets can be assembled more easily than sets of many other patterns since there are so few pieces. There are only 10 separate objects to find. The only limitation you have is whether to search for four, six, eight, or twelve place settings. Thankfully, you only have to find one creamer and one 8½" berry bowl no matter how many place settings you collect. Some collectors are buying several of the larger fruit bowls and ignoring the harder to find berry bowl.

Refer to Daisy (page 54) for an explanation of Indiana's green Heritage pattern.

	Crystal	Pink	Blue Green		Crystal	Pink	Blue Green
Bowl, 5", berry	8.00	45.00	60.00	Plate, 8", luncheon	9.00		
Bowl, 8½", large berry	40.00	125.00	195.00	Plate, 9¼", dinner	12.00		
Bowl, 10½", fruit	15.00			Plate, 12", sandwich	14.00		
Cup	7.00			Saucer	4.00		
Creamer, footed	27.50			Sugar, open, footed	25.00		

HOBNAIL FENTON ART GLASS COMPANY

Color: white

We were able to capture Fenton's Hobnail for this book because opportunity knocked and this large collection was made available to us. A dealer friend insisted (joke!) that his spouse collect this pattern — and did she collect it! With all this unloaded in the photography studio, there was hardly room for anything else!

Measurements were done as we photographed and not all these agree with catalog listings. I have used actual measurements when we had the piece in our photograph. Hope you enjoy this wonderful collection! Listings from catalogs were furnished by Carrie Domitz. Catalog numbers are listed for each piece. See what you can find!

	White		White		White
Apothecary jar, 11", w/cover #3689	200.00	Basket, 5¾", 1¾" base #3336	22.00	Bonbon, 5" x 2" #3630	15.00
Ash tray, 3¼" x 4½", rectangular #3693	8.00	Basket, 6½" x 4½", oval, 2-hdld. #838	57.50	Bonbon, 5" x 2¾", star #3921	12.00
Ash tray, 3½", round #3972	10.00	Basket, 6½" x 7½", double crimped #3736	27.50	Bonbon, 6" x 1⅝", double crimped #3926	9.00
Ash tray, 4", ball #3648	35.00	Basket, 7" x 7", deep #3637	85.00	Bonbon, 7" x 2½", two-hdld. #3937	15.00.
Ash tray, 4", octagon #3876	12.50	Basket, 7½" x 7", #3837	27.50	Bonbon, 8" x 2¼" #3716	18.00
Ash tray, 5", round #3973	12.00	Basket, 8" x 7¾", 3" base #3032	30.00	Bonbon, 8" x 5½" #3706	20.00
Ash tray, 5", square #3679	17.50	Basket, 8", 2¼" diameter base #3335	30.00	Boot, 4" #3992	14.00
Ash tray, 5¼", octagon #3877	15.00	Basket, 8½", double crimped #3638	45.00	Bottle, vanity, 5⅜" w/stopper #3865	45.00
Ash tray, 6½", octagon #3878	20.00	Basket, 10" #3830	55.00	Bowl, 4", berry, square #3928	15.00
Ash tray, 6½", pipe w/center flower #3773	115.00	Basket, 10½" x 11½", deep #3734	50.00	Bowl, 4", candle orifice #3873	22.50
Ash tray, 6½", round #3776	15.00	Basket, 13" x 7", oval, #3839	60.00	Bowl, 5", cereal, 2" high #3719	75.00
Basket, 4" x 6", 4-ftd., oval #3634	45.00	Bell, 5½" #3645	15.00	Bowl, 5½" x 6¾", candy, ribbon top #3730	85.00
Basket, 4½" #3834	22.50	Bell, 6" #3667	25.00	Bowl, 5½", rose #3022	15.00
Basket, 5½" x 5½", double crimped #3735	25.00	Bell, 6¾" #3067	18.00	Bowl, 6" x 6", octagonal, peanut #3627	18.50
		Bonbon, 5" x 2½", two-hdld. #3935	20.00	Bowl, 6½", candle orifice #3872	17.50

Please refer to Foreword for pricing information

HOBNAIL (cont.)

Item	Price
Bowl, 7", double crimped #3927	12.50
Bowl, 7½", candle, ftd., 5" high #3971	50.00
Bowl, 8", 3-toed #3635	22.00
Bowl, 8", candle, double crimped #3771	27.50
Bowl, 8", double crimped #3639	30.00
Bowl, 8", oval #3625	25.00
Bowl, 8½", console, rippled top #3724	65.00
Bowl, 9", cupped #3735	125.00
Bowl, 9", double crimped, 5" high #3924	22.50
Bowl, 9", oval, ftd. #3621	55.00
Bowl, 9", scalloped/flared #3626	55.00
Bowl, 9", square #3929	65.00
Bowl, 9½", chip n' dip candle #3924	25.00
Bowl, 10", ftd., double crimped #3731	38.50
Bowl, 10¼", shallow #3622	55.00
Bowl, 10½" #3623	85.00
Bowl, 10½", double crimped #3624	30.00
Bowl, 10½", ftd., crimped #3723	35.00
Bowl, 11", 3 holes for hanging, #3705	125.00
Bowl, 12" x 5", banana #3620	40.00
Bowl, 12" x 7", banana #3720	45.00
Bowl, 12", double crimped #3938	25.00
Butter and cheese, 4¼", w/8" plate, cover #3677	150.00
Butter, ¼ lb., oval, 7¾" x 3¾", #3777	35.00
Butter, ¼ lb., rectangular, 7½" x 2⅛" #3977	20.00
Cake plate, 12⅞" x 5", pie crust crimped edge #3913	50.00
Candleholder, 2" x5", pr. #3670	28.00
Candleholder, 2¾" x4¼", ftd., pr. #3673	40.00
Candleholder, 3", flat, ruffled edge, pr. #3974	30.00
Candleholder, 3½", cornucopia, pr. #3971	70.00
Candleholder, 3½", hdld., pr. #3870	50.00
Candleholder, 3½", rounded, flared top, pr. #3974	30.00
Candleholder, 3½", single, ruffled edge, pr. #3770	135.00
Candleholder, 5½", 2-light, pr. #3672	125.00
Candleholder, 6½", cornucopia, pr. #3874	57.50
Candleholder, 6", pr. #3674	28.00
Candleholder, 7" #3745	35.00
Candleholder, 8", crescent, pr. #3678	200.00
Candleholder, 10", pr. #3774	65.00
Candy box, 5¼", shoe w/cover #3700	35.00
Candy box, 6", w/cover #3600	32.00
Candy box, 6", w/cover, 6" diameter #3984	50.00
Candy box, 6¾", w/cover #3886	35.00
Candy box, 8⅛", w/cover, ftd. #3784	42.50
Candy dish, 6½" x 4¾" #3668	42.50
Candy dish, 6½" x 6½" #3668	42.50
Candy dish, 6½", heart #3033	22.50
Candy jar, 5¼", w/cover #3883	32.00
Candy jar, 6½", w/cover, 4½" wide #3688	45.00
Candy jar, 7½", w/cover #3688	45.00
Candy jar, 8½", ftd., w/pointed knob cover #3885	38.50
Candy jar, 8½", ftd., w/rounded knob cover #3887	35.00
Celery, 12" #3739	100.00
Chip -n'- dip, 12¼" x 3¼" bowl w/division #3922	250.00
Comport #3703	45.00
Cigarette box, 4¼", sq. #3685	35.00
Cigarette lighter 2¼", cube #3692	18.00
Comport, 3¾", double crimped #3727	17.50
Comport, 5½", double crimped #3920	86.00
Comport, 5¼", double crimped #3728	16.00
Comport, 6" x 5½", octagonal stem #3628	18.00
Cookie jar, 11", w/lid #3680	100.00
Creamer, 2⅛", plain handle and edge #3900	9.00
Creamer, 3½", plain handle #3901	10.00
Creamer, 3½", scalloped edge #3708	17.50
Creamer, 3", beaded handle and edge #3665	20.00
Creamer, 3", beaded handle and ruffled edge #3702	20.00
Creamer, 3", star shaped edge #3906	12.50
Creamer, 4" #3606	10.00
Creamer, 4¾", scalloped edge #3902	22.50
Cruet, 7¾" #3863	50.00
Cup, child's #489	60.00
Decanter, 12", hdld., w/stopper #3761	225.00
Egg cup, 4" #3647	125.00
Epergne candle, 2" high x 5" wide, petite #3671	40.00
Epergne candle, 6" wide, for 7" candleholder #3746	70.00
Epergne set, 6½", 2 pc. 7" horn #3704	75.00
Epergne set, 6½", 4 pc., 6" tri-horns #3801	50.00
Epergne set, 9½", 4-pc. 8" tri-horns #3701	50.00
Epergne set, 9", 5 pc. (#3920 comport, frog, 5" tri-horns) #3800	350.00
Fairy light, 4½", 2-pc. #3608	14.00
Fairy light, 8½", 3-pc. #3804	85.00
Goblet, 3⅞", 3 oz., wine #3843	15.00
Goblet, 4½", 4 oz., wine #3843	14.00
Goblet, 5⅝", 8 oz., water #3845	12.50
Hat, 2⅝", burred #3991	15.00
Hat, 2⅝", plain #3991	25.00
Jam & jelly set, 2 4¾" jars, lid, ladle/ double crimped chrome hdld. tray #3915	45.00
Jam set, 4 pc., 4¾" jar, lid, label, and 6" crimped saucer #3903	50.00
Jar, 5", jam w/spoon and lid #3601	35.00
Jar, 7¼", honey, round, ftd., w/cover #3886	65.00
Jardiniere, 4½", scalloped #3994	12.00
Jardiniere, 5½", scalloped #3898	35.00
Jardiniere, 6", scalloped, 6" diameter #3898	25.00
Jelly, 5½" x 4½" #3725	30.00
Kettle, 2½", 3-toed, 3" diameter #3990	14.00
Lamp, 8", hurricane, hdld. base scalloped top #3998	65.00
Lamp, 9", courting, electric, crimped top #3713	150.00
Lamp, 9", courting, oil, crimped top #3713	150.00
Lamp, 11", hurricane, crimped top #3713	115.00
Lamp, 19", student, crimped top #3707	195.00
Lamp, 21", student, double crimped top #3807	175.00
Lamp, 22", Gone with the Wind #3808	200.00
Lamp, 22½", student, w/prisms #1174	225.00
Lamp, 26", double crimped, pillar #3907	200.00
Lavabo, 3 pc. (urn w/lid and basin) #3867	75.00
Margarine tub, 5¼" #3802	22.00
Mayonnaise set, 3 pc., bowl, 6" ruffled saucer, ladle #3803	30.00
Mustard jar, 3½", w/spoon and lid #3605	35.00
Mustard jar, 3½", w/spoon and lid #3889	22.00
Mustard, 3⅝", kettle #3979	20.00
Napkin ring, 2" diameter #3904	35.00
Nut dish, 2½" x 4¾" $3650	58.00
Nut dish, 2½" x 5" $3729	45.00
Nut dish, 2¾" x 4", ftd. #3631	35.00
Nut dish, 5" x 3¼", oval, #3732	20.00
Nut dish, 5" x 5½", ftd. #3629	17.00
Nut dish, 7" x 3½", oval, #3633	14.00
Oil, 4¾", w/stopper #3869	15.00
Oil, 8", w/stopper #3767	55.00
Pickle, 8" x 4", oval #3640	15.00
Pitcher, 5¼", squat, 4" diameter top #3965	37.50
Pitcher, 7" #3365	32.00
Pitcher, 7¾", 80 oz., no ice lip (fat neck) #3967	125.00
Pitcher, 8", 54 oz., no ice lip (fat neck) #3764	65.00

HOBNAIL (cont.)

Pitcher, 9½",w/ice lip, 70 oz. #3664   55.00
Pitcher, 11" #3360   60.00
Planter, 4½", square, scalloped top
  #3699   14.00
Planter, 8½" long, scalloped top
  #3690   20.00
Planter, 8", crescent, 4-ftd., #3798   30.00
Planter, 9½" long, scalloped top
  #3690   27.50
Planter, 9" wall, #3836   57.50
Planter, 10" long, rectangular box
  #3799   27.50
Planter, 10", crescent, 4-ftd., #3698   47.50
Plate, 8½", round, pie crust crimped
  edge #3912   25.00
Plate, 8¼", round, pie crust crimped
  edge #3816   25.00
Plate, 13½", crimped edge #3714   50.00
Plate, 16", torte #3817   95.00
Powder box, 6½", round w/lid
  #3880   48.00
Puff box, 4½", round #3885   75.00
Punch base, 3¾" x 8½" #3778   100.00
Punch bowl, 10½"" x 5¼", plain
  edge #3827   260.00
Punch bowl, 11¼"" x 6½", octagon
  #3820   450.00
Punch bowl, 15" x 7½", crimped
  edge #3722   360.00
Punch cup, 2½" x 3", octagonal
  #3840   20.00
Punch cup, 2¼" x 2¾" #3847   15.00
Punch ladle #9520   55.00
Punch ladle (crystal) #9527   30.00
Relish, 5¼" x 7½", 3-part #3607   35.00
Relish, 7½", 3-sections #3822   16.00
Relish, 7½", non divided #3822   50.00
Relish, 7½", scalloped, 3-sections
  #3822   16.00
Relish, 8½", heart shaped #3733   25.00
Relish, 12⅜", 3-sections #3740   35.00
Salt & pepper, 3", flat, pr. #3806   20.00
Salt & pepper, 3¾" pr. #3609   24.00
Salt & pepper, 4¼" pr. #3602   40.00
Salt dip, 2⅜" x 2¼" x ⅜", shell shape
  #9496   40.00
Server, 10", two tier, 12" bowl &
  3-section top #3709   47.50
Shaker, 4¾", cinnamon sugar
  #3797   125.00
Sherbet, 4" #3825   15.00

Slipper, 5", kitten head and paws
  #3995   10.00
Spoon holder, 7¼" long #3612   105.00
Stein, 6¾". 14 oz., #3646   100.00
Sugar, 2⅛", plain handle and edge
  #3900   9.00
Sugar, 3", beaded handle and edge
  #3665   20.00
Sugar, 3", beaded handle and ruffled
  edge #3702   20.00
Sugar, 3", star shaped edge #3906   12.50
Sugar, 3½", plain handle #3901   10.00
Sugar, 3½", scalloped edge #3708   17.50
Sugar, 4¾", scalloped edge #3902   22.50
Sugar, 5¾" w/lid #3606   12.50
Syrup pitcher, 5¼", 12 oz. #3660   32.50
Syrup pitcher, 5¾", 12 oz. #3762   27.50
Tidbit, two tier, 13½" and 8½"
  #3794   55.00
Toothpick, 2¾" #3895   38.50
Toothpick, 3" #3795   12.00
Tray, 7½" x 3¾", oil/mustard #3715   12.50
Tray, 7¾", chrome handle #3879   25.00
Tray, 12½" x 7", vanity #3775   95.00
Tray, 13½" sandwich w/metal
  handle #3791   55.00
Tumbler, 3½", 5 oz., flat #3945   10.00
Tumbler, 4¾", 9 oz. Flat #3949   15.00
Tumbler, 5", 12 oz., ice tea #3942   18.50
Tumbler, 5", 12 oz., ice tea, barrel
  shape #3947   37.50
Tumbler, 5¾", ice tea, ftd. #3842   38.50
Tumbler, 6", 16 oz., flat #3946   50.00
Urn, 11", covered #3986   175.00
Vanity boxtle, 7⅛", 3 pc. #3986   225.00
Vase, 2¼", violet, ribbon crimped
  #3754   35.00
Vase, 3", crimped #3855   12.50
Vase, 3¾", double crimped #3850   10.00
Vase, 4", 3¾" diameter #3952   10.00
Vase, 4", 4¾" diameter #3775   50.00
Vase, 4", fan, pie crust edge #3953   12.50
Vase, 4½", double crimped #3854   15.00
Vase, 5", 3-toed #3654   12.50
Vase, 5", double crimped #3850   17.50
Vase, 5", scalloped #3655   17.50
Vase, 5½", double crimped #3656   37.50
Vase, 5½", ivy ball, ruffled, ped. ft.
  #3726   20.00
Vase, 5¾", ivy, ribbed, ped. ft.
  #3757   20.00

Vase, 6", double crimped #3856   20.00
Vase, 6", double crimped #3954   25.00
Vase, 6", ftd., swung, handkerchief
  #3651   40.00
Vase, 6", hand #3355   30.00
Vase, 6¼", 3" diameter base, fan
  #3957   22.00
Vase, 6¼", 5" diameter, double
  crimped #3954   25.00
Vase, 6½", ftd., swung, handkerchief
  #3651   50.00
Vase, 6½", swung, handkerchief
  #3750   22.50
Vase, 7½", handkerchief #3657   22.50
Vase, 8", 4" diameter base, fan
  #3959   40.00
Vase, 8", bud, ftd., swung #3756   18.00
Vase, 8", double crimped, 3½"
  diameter #3859   145.00
Vase, 8", double crimped, 6½"
  diameter #3958   28.00
Vase, 8", double crimped, 6¼"
  diameter #3858   50.00
Vase, 8½" fan #3852   175.00
Vase, 8½", Jack in the Pulpit
  #3356   28.00
Vase, 9" #3659   55.00
Vase, 9", swung #3755   100.00
Vase, 10", swung, ftd., bud #3950   15.00
Vase, 10", swung, handkerchief
  #3855   40.00
Vase, 11", double crimped #3752   40.00
Vase, 12", 3-toed #3658   200.00
Vase, 12", swung, ftd., 2½"
  diameter #3758   25.00
Vase, 12", swung, ftd., 3¼"
  diameter #3753   27.50
*Vase, 14", swung, handkerchief
  #3755   50.00
*Vase, 14", swung, pitcher, 3¼"
  diameter #3750   45.00
Vase, 18", ftd., 3¼" diameter #3753   47.50
Vase, 24", swung #3652   37.50

* size varies upward

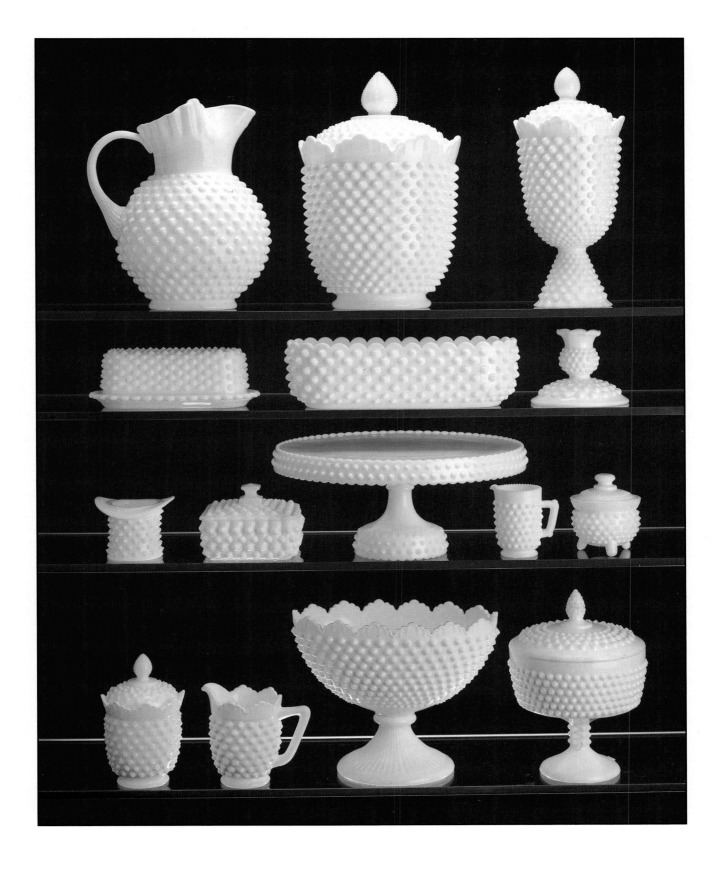

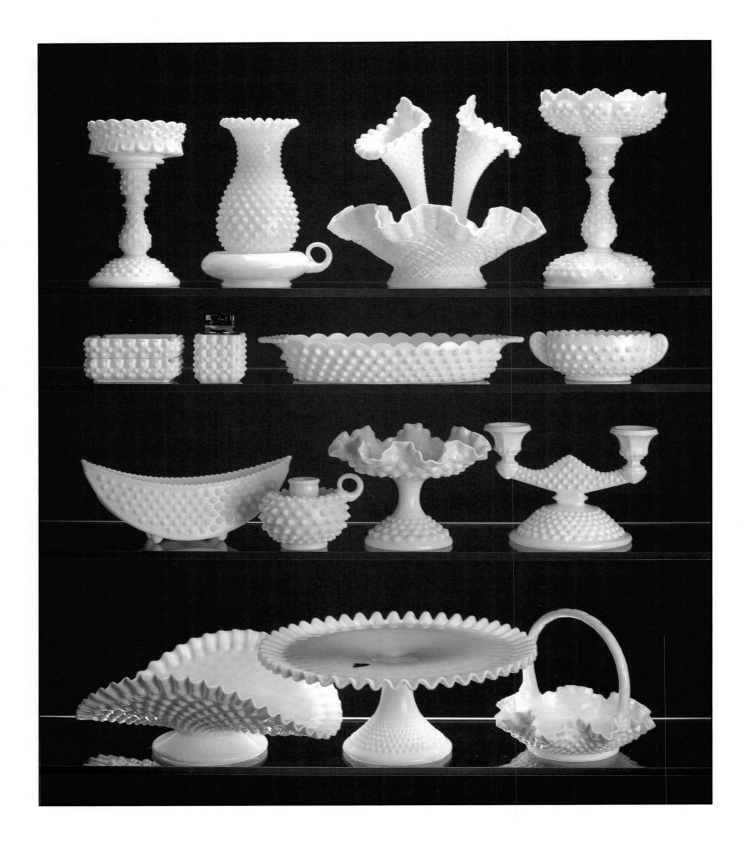

HOLIDAY, "BUTTONS AND BOWS," JEANNETTE GLASS COMPANY, 1947 – mid 1950s

Colors: Pink, iridescent; some Shell Pink and crystal

There are dissimilar styles of Holiday pieces which cause problems for beginning collectors. I have spent an extra page in the past picturing and explaining these differences. Unfortunately, the time has come for that space to be used to introduce new patterns.

Neophytes need to be conscious of three styles of cup and saucer sets. One style cup and saucer has plain centers. These are easy to match. Two other cup styles have a rayed center. You can not mix these since one cup's base size of 2" will only fit a 2⅛" cup ring and the 2⅜" cup base will fit a 2½" saucer ring.

Two styles of 10 ounce tumblers occur. One is flat bottomed and the other has a small raised foot and is narrower at the bottom. These are from different moulds, but untrained collectors sometimes get upset with differences on an equivalent item purchased from different places.

Two styles of sherbets exist. One has a rayed foot while the other is plain. Two dissimilar sherbet plates have 2¾" centers, but one has a "beads" effect in the center, while the other has a center ring with a "diamond" effect in the center. Mould variations occur in nearly all patterns, but Holiday is especially confusing. It's okay to mix styles, but some purists can not abide to do so.

I remember when $10.00 seemed like a high price for the 6" footed tumblers and now $155.00 is the asking price. (I know, parents walked uphill to school every day — both ways!) If we had invested in these tumblers instead of mutual funds..!

Holiday console bowls, candlesticks, and cake plates continue to be the most difficult pieces to find besides footed teas. If you are bewildered by how such a recently manufactured glassware could have so many hard-to-find pieces, welcome to the club. Apparently, there were few requests for pieces other than the basics. Maybe the serving pieces were premiums. So far, no facts have surfaced to elucidate these mysteries.

Iridescent pieces of Holiday are bought by some collectors to enhance their sets. Only four different pieces were made.

Holiday appears to have been a well-used pattern judging by the abundance of damaged pieces I have examined in numerous sets over the years. Be sure to look at the underside of the edges. Pointed edges are prone to chips, nicks, and "chigger bites," an auction term that varies from place to place. Remember, damaged glass cannot be almost mint. Prices listed here are for mint condition glassware!

	Pink	Crystal	Iridescent		Pink	Crystal	Iridescent
Bowl, 5⅛", berry	12.00			Plate, 9", dinner	16.00		
Bowl, 7¾", soup	50.00			Plate, 13¾", chop	100.00		
Bowl, 8½", large berry	27.50			Platter, 11⅜", oval	20.00		12.50
Bowl, 9½", oval vegetable	25.00			Sandwich tray, 10½"	17.50		15.00
*Bowl, 10¾", console	125.00			Saucer, 3 styles	4.00		
Butter dish and cover	40.00			Sherbet, 2 styles	6.00		
Butter dish bottom	10.00			Sugar	10.00		
Butter dish top	30.00			Sugar cover	15.00		
Cake plate, 10½", 3 legged	95.00			Tumbler, 4", 10 oz., flat	21.00		
Candlesticks, 3" pr.	100.00			Tumbler, 4", footed, 5 oz.	42.50		12.00
Creamer, footed	8.00			Tumbler, 4¼", footed, 5¼ oz.		7.50	
Cup, three sizes	8.00			Tumbler, 6", footed	155.00		
Pitcher, 4¾", 16 oz. milk	60.00	15.00	22.50				
Pitcher, 6¾", 52 oz.	35.00			* Shell Pink $40.00			
Plate, 6", sherbet	6.00						

IRIS, "IRIS AND HERRINGBONE," JEANNETTE GLASS COMPANY, 1928 – 1932; 1950s; 1970s

Colors: crystal, iridescent; some pink; recently bi-colored red/yellow and blue/green combinations, and white

Iridescent Iris belongs entirely within the time frame of this 50s book; and although crystal production goes back to 1928 for its start, some crystal was made in the late 1940s, and 1950s. Additionally, candy bottoms and vases were manufactured as late as the 1970s. Consequently, I have decided to include crystal Iris prices in this book as well.

Many serious collectors have had to "bite the bullet" and buy all pieces they could afford. Almost all rare pieces doubled (or more) in price in the last four years. That is remarkable! It even beats the stock market! It was not exceptional for a $5.00 item to double between books, but when $75.00 items surge to $165.00 and $40.00 items increase to $120.00, it makes quite an impact! I will say I have noticed many of these high priced pieces remaining on dealers' tables recently. Perhaps Iris prices are reaching a plateau, with some prices being resisted by average collectors. All major patterns have had pricing surges, but the one for Iris has lasted longer than any I have encountered. Still, at the Tulsa show, I heard one dealer saying he could sell all the Iris he could get his hands on!

Realize that those iridescent candy bottoms are a product of the 1970s when Jeannette made crystal and iridized or flashed bottoms with two-tone colors such as red/yellow or blue/green. Pictured in the lower half of 131 is a flashed blue candy bottom. These bases were sold as vases. Some of these colors have washed or peeled over time, again making crystal candy bottoms. Some have been stripped of their color to fool unknowing collectors. These newly made pieces have a non-rayed foot; no tops were ever made. Similarly, the regular 9" vases were made in white and sprayed green, red, and blue on the outside. Many of these vases have lost the colors on the outside and are now only white. White vases sell in the $12.00 – 15.00 range. No white vases were made before the early 1970s no matter what you are told!

The 8 ounce water goblet, 5¾", 4 ounce goblet, 4" sherbet, and the demitasse cup and saucer are the most difficult pieces to find in iridescent. The 5¾", 4 ounce goblet is displayed in *Very Rare Glassware of the Depression Era, 4th Series* and you can see the demitasse cup and saucer on the right as well as three other rarely seen colors of amethyst, blue, and red! I missed a couple of iridized water goblets over the last year. I still need one to show readers they do exist. The tall sherbet will be shown in the next book!

Decorated red and gold Iris that turns up on crystal was called "Corsage" and styled by Century in 1946. We know this because of a card attached to a 1946 "Corsage" wedding gift that a reader shared with me. I am still trying to find more information about this decoration; if you have any, let me know. If I could get even one percent of the mail regarding Corsage that I did on the "Badcock Furniture" bowl, I would be ecstatic!

That "Iris" plate on the bottom right of page 131 is plastic! Does anyone know any more about these?

	Crystal	Iridescent	Green/Pink		Crystal	Iridescent	Green/Pink
Bowl, 4½", berry, beaded edge	42.00	9.00		Goblet, 4¼", 4 oz., cocktail	27.50		
Bowl, 5", ruffled, sauce	9.00	27.50		Goblet, 4¼", 3 oz., wine	17.00		
Bowl, 5", cereal	120.00			Goblet, 5¾", 4 oz.	27.50	195.00	
Bowl, 7½", soup	160.00	60.00		Goblet, 5¾", 8 oz.	26.00	195.00	
Bowl, 8", berry, beaded edge	85.00	20.00		**Lamp shade, 11½"	85.00		
Bowl, 9½", ruffled, salad	12.50	13.00	125.00	Pitcher, 9½", footed	37.50	40.00	
Bowl, 11½", ruffled, fruit	15.00	14.00		Plate, 5½", sherbet	15.00	14.00	
Bowl, 11", fruit, straight edge	60.00			Plate, 8", luncheon	105.00		
Butter dish and cover	47.50	42.50		Plate, 9", dinner	55.00	42.50	
Butter dish bottom	13.50	12.50		Plate, 11¾", sandwich	32.00	32.00	
Butter dish top	34.00	30.00		Saucer	12.00	11.00	
Candlesticks, pr.	42.50	45.00		Sherbet, 2½", footed	27.50	15.00	
Candy jar and cover	155.00			Sherbet, 4", footed	25.00	195.00	
Coaster	100.00			Sugar	11.00	11.00	125.00
Creamer, footed	12.00	12.00	125.00	Sugar cover	12.00	12.00	
Cup	15.00	14.00		Tumbler, 4", flat	135.00		
*Demitasse cup	35.00	150.00		Tumbler, 6", footed	18.00	16.00	
*Demitasse saucer	135.00	225.00		Tumbler, 6½", footed	35.00		
Fruit or nut set	65.00			Vase, 9"	27.50	25.00	150.00
Goblet, 4", wine		30.00					

*Ruby, Blue, Amethyst priced as Iridescent

**Colors: $65.00

Please refer to Foreword for pricing information

JAMESTOWN, FOSTORIA GLASS COMPANY, 1958 – 1982

Colors: Amber, amethyst, blue, brown, crystal, green, pink, and red

Jamestown is yet another Fostoria pattern where pieces (other than stems) seem to be invisible! Serving items were not promoted by Fostoria for the duration of the stemware line; that leaves both collectors and dealers foraging for serving pieces! Not all pieces were made in each color. I have grouped colors into three pricing groups, though they are pictured in different groupings for artistic reasons.

Ruby Jamestown has always sold well, but there is not a complete line of Ruby. An unsavory note for collectors is that Ruby stemware is once again being made and sold in the Fostoria outlet stores. Those stems are selling for $16.00 each and that is causing prices to drop on older Ruby Jamestown. Unfortunately, there is virtually no difference in the old and the newly made items. Both the older stems and the new stems have three mould lines so that is not a differentiating factor. Originally, Viking made most of the Ruby for Fostoria and they are once again producing it. You cannot blame Viking, since they are only making what they are paid to make. Is there not enough marketing imagination left to come up with new colors or patterns to attract the public?

There is little demand for amber or brown at present and few dealers stock these colors. If you are looking for either color, ask for it. You should be able to find some exceptional bargains. In the middle price group, crystal is most in demand, but green is beginning to be accumulated in some quarters. I received a letter from a collector who thought they had found an entire set of unlisted pieces of Moroccan Amethyst. They were unlisted under Moroccan but were listed under Jamestown. There would actually be more buyers for Moroccan than Jamestown amethyst!

My listings came from two different Fostoria catalogs. The line numbers on each stem in those catalogs have two separate dimensions and capacities listed. That is only one of the many things that complicates writing a book. Which figure do you use? Thus, I have included both stem listings for the purist. Either someone measured incorrectly one year or the sizes were actually changed. I have referred to this problem in the measurements section in the *Collector's Encyclopedia of Depression Glass*. Thus, your measurements could differ from those I have listed!

	Amber/Brown	Amethyst/Crystal/Green	Blue/Pink/Ruby
Bowl, 4½", dessert #2719/421	8.50	13.50	16.00
Bowl, 10", salad #2719//211	21.00	37.50	45.00
Bowl, 10", two hndl. serving #2719/648	21.00	42.50	55.00
Butter w/cover, ¼ pound #2719/300	24.00	45.00	55.00
Cake plate, 9½", hndl. #2719/306	16.00	32.50	37.50
Celery, 9¼" #2719/360	18.00	32.50	37.50
Cream, 3½", ftd. #2719/681	11.00	17.50	25.00
Jelly w/cover, 6⅛" #2719/447	32.50	57.50	80.00
Pickle, 8⅜" #2719/540	21.00	35.00	40.00
Pitcher, 7⁵/₁₆", 48 oz., ice jug #2719/456	45.00	95.00	135.00
Plate, 8" #2719/550	8.50	16.00	20.00
Plate, 14", torte #2719/567	26.00	42.50	60.00
Relish, 9⅛", 2 part #2719/620	16.00	32.00	37.50
Salad set, 4 pc. (10" bowl, 14" plate w/wood fork & spoon) #2719/286	55.00	85.00	100.00
Salver, 7" high, 10" diameter #2719/630	60.00	120.00	120.00
Sauce dish w/cover, 4½" #2719/635	18.00	30.00	35.00
Shaker, 3½", w/chrome top. pr. #2719/653	26.00	40.00	50.00
Stem, 4⁵/₁₆", 4 oz., wine #2719/26	10.00	20.00	24.00
*Stem, 4¼", 6½ oz., sherbet #2719/7	6.50	12.50	16.00
*Stem, 4⅛", 7 oz., sherbet #2719/7	6.50	12.50	16.00
*Stem, 5¾", 9½ oz., goblet #2719/2	10.00	16.00	16.00
*Stem, 5⅞", 10 oz., goblet #2719/2	10.00	16.00	16.00
Sugar, 3½", ftd. #2719/679	11.00	17.50	25.00
Tray, 9⅜", hndl. muffin #2719/726	26.00	42.50	55.00
Tumbler, 4¼", 9 oz. #2719/73	9.00	21.00	25.00
Tumbler, 4¾", 5 oz., juice #2719/88	9.50	21.00	26.00
Tumbler, 5⅛", 12 oz. #2719/64	9.00	21.00	26.00
Tumbler, 6", 11 oz., ftd. tea #2719/63	10.00	21.00	24.00
Tumbler, 6", 12 oz., ftd. tea #2719/63	10.00	21.00	24.00

*being remade at present

Please refer to Foreword for pricing information

United States Glass Company
TIFFIN, OHIO
KINGS CROWN
Also known as No. 4016 Thumbprint

Sugar

Cream

5" Bread and Butter Plate

10" Dinner Plate

Cup and Saucer

AVAILABLE PLAIN CRYSTAL, DECORATED CRANBERRY OR RUBY

KING'S CROWN, THUMBPRINT LINE NO. 4016, U.S. GLASS (TIFFIN) COMPANY
late 1800s – 1960s; INDIANA GLASS COMPANY, 1970s

Colors: Crystal, crystal with ruby or cranberry flash, crystal with gold or platinum

King's Crown has become my latest "can of worms." Unfortunately, I knew it would be, but I opened it anyway. King's Crown was made for so many years and by so many different companies that I doubt a complete listing will never be seen! There is a finite number of pieces, but like counting stars, you'll never be finished. This pattern causes confusion among both old and new collectors. Originally issued as Thumbprint Line No. 4016 by U. S. Glass in the late 1800s, this glassware was also made by Tiffin into the early 1960s. The catalog reprint shown is from 1955. Confusing the issue, Indiana bought the moulds and changed the design somewhat. Not only does this lend confusion, but there were over 20 other glassware companies who made similar patterns.

For this book I am including both Indiana pieces as well as those made by Tiffin after 1940. You will find additional pieces, but please realize that many of those could be from an earlier time. The Tiffin plates seem to have starred designs in the center while the Indiana ones appear to be plain. I have discovered no hard, fast rules in researching this confounding pattern! One of the exhilarating things about King's Crown is that you never know what piece is available around the next corner.

Page 137 and 138 show two different shadings of ruby flashed. Most collectors prefer the deeper red shade, but others like the lighter shade called "cranberry." Page 135 (bottom) shows a variety of King's Crown items I have found in the last two years. The pitcher and other purple pieces are Tiffin's Mulberry. Remember that amber, cobalt blue, Avocado green, and iridized carnival colors are all Indiana's production of the late 1970s and 1980s. In 1976, they also made a Smoky Blue for the Bicentennial. A duplicate blue was used in the Tiara Sandwich line that year!

Page 143 shows some of the harder to find pieces. Note that the price on the punch bowl set has almost doubled. Demand for these is almost unbelievable. Everyone collecting King's Crown has to have the punch set! That listed 24" plate on the party server measures 22½" to 23" on the ones I have seen.

There are pieces flashed with gold, platinum, blue, green, yellow, cranberry, or ruby. The market for other flashed colors is being more clearly established. Most flashed colors are selling for less than ruby, although gold items are not far behind ruby. Demand makes ruby the desired color. For crystal, subtract fifty percent of the prices listed. Gold and platinum decorated products were also made at Indiana.

Elongated thumbprint designs are from the original Tiffin moulds. Some elongated style may have been made at Indiana before they changed the moulds; but if the pieces you have show circular thumbprints, you definitely have King's Crown made by Indiana. The Tiffin made tumblers are flared at the top while Indiana's are straight. Count on paying less than the prices below for the more recently issued Indiana tumblers.

	Ruby Flashed		Ruby Flashed
Ash tray, 5¼", square	18.00	Plate, 7⅜", mayonnaise liner	12.50
Bowl, 4", finger	17.50	Plate, 7⅜", salad	12.00
Bowl, 4", mayonnaise	40.00	Plate, 9¾", snack w/indent	15.00
Bowl 5¾"	20.00	Plate, 10", dinner	37.50
Bowl, 6", diameter, ftd., wedding or candy	30.00	Plate, 14½", torte	75.00
Bowl, 8¾", 2-hdld., crimped bon bon	75.00	Plate, 24", party	155.00
Bowl, 9¼", salad	85.00	Plate, 24", party server (w/punch ft.)	260.00
Bowl, 10½", ftd., wedding or candy, w/cover	155.00	Punch bowl foot	125.00
Bowl, 11½", 4½" high, crimped	95.00	Punch bowl, 2 styles	400.00
Bowl, 11¼" cone	75.00	Punch cup	15.00
Bowl, 12½", center edge, 3" high	85.00	Punch set, 15 pc. w/foot	750.00
Bowl, 12½", flower floater	80.00	Punch set, 15 pc. w/plate	700.00
Bowl, crimped, ftd.	85.00	Relish, 14", 5 part	95.00
Bowl, flared, ftd.	75.00	Saucer	8.00
Bowl, straight edge	80.00	Stem, 2 oz., wine	7.50
Cake salver, 12½", ftd.	75.00	Stem, 2¼ oz., cocktail	12.50
Candleholder, sherbet type	30.00	Stem, 4 oz., claret	12.00
Candleholder, 2-lite, 5½"	65.00	Stem, 4 oz., oyster cocktail	14.00
Candy box, 6", flat, w/cover	60.00	Stem, 5½ oz., sundae or sherbet	10.00
Cheese stand	25.00	Stem, 9 oz., water goblet	12.00
Compote, 7¼", 9¾" diameter	45.00	Sugar	25.00
Compote, 7½", 12" diameter, ftd., crimped	95.00	Tumbler, 4 oz., juice, ftd.	12.00
Compote, small, flat	22.00	Tumbler, 4½ oz., juice	14.00
Creamer	25.00	Tumbler, 8½ oz., water	13.00
Cup	8.00	Tumbler, 11 oz., ice tea	16.00
Lazy susan, 24", 8½" high, w/ball bearing spinner	225.00	Tumbler, 12 oz., ice tea, ftd.	20.00
Mayonnaise, 3 pc. set	65.00	Vase, 9", bud	75.00
Pitcher	175.00	Vase, 12¼", bud	90.00
Plate, 5", bread/butter	8.00		

Please refer to Foreword for pricing information

KINGS CROWN

Center Edge Bowl 12½″ Diameter 3″ High

2-Lite Candle Holder 5½″ High

Footed Fruit Compote 9¾″ Diameter 7¼″ High

Crimped Bowl 11½″ Diameter 4½″ High

Cone Bowl 11¼″ Diameter 4¾″ High

Page 2   AVAILABLE PLAIN CRYSTAL, DECORATED CRANBERRY OR RUBY

KING'S CROWN

KINGS CROWN

Goblet 9 oz.

Wine 2 oz.

Juice 4 oz.

Claret 4 oz.

Cocktail 2¼ oz.

Oyster Cocktail 4 oz.

Sundae 5½ oz.

Water Tumbler 8½ oz.

Juice Tumbler 4½ oz.

Footed Ice Tea 12 oz.

Ice Tea Tumbler 11 oz.

Finger Bowl 4" Diameter

7⅜" Salad Plate

AVAILABLE PLAIN CRYSTAL, DECORATED CRANBERRY OR RUBY

Page 3

KINGS CROWN

15 pc. Punch Set, with foot
Capacity 12 qts. Diameter 23"

15 pc. Punch Set Flared
Capacity 12 qts. Plate Diameter 23"

Party Server 24" Diameter 8" High

AVAILABLE PLAIN CRYSTAL, DECORATED CRANBERRY OR RUBY

KINGS CROWN

Wedding Bowl and Cover
6" Diameter 10½" High

Flower Floater 12½" Diameter

Torte Plate 14" Diameter

Ash Tray 5¼" Square

Footed Cake Salver
12½" Diameter 4¾" High

LIDO PLATE ETCHING #329, FOSTORIA GLASS COMPANY, 1937 – 1960

Color: Crystal, Azure

The famous Lido is a location of much merriment and amusement. Picture fireworks shooting overhead and you'll be able to remember this pattern.

Lido is a Fostoria pattern that was made in Azure blue as well as crystal. You can see an Azure tumbler as the pattern shot on page 145. We sold that tumbler right after photography, but I have had several collectors ask if I still owned it! (By the time you see a picture in the book, it has been a minimum of nine months since the picture was taken.) Azure was discontinued during World War II; you will not find much of this color. Blue will fetch up to 50 percent more than the prices for crystal on hard to find items; but basic pieces sell for only a little more than crystal since there are few collectors searching for it,.

I looked at that Lido pitcher on page 145 for several years before I pried the money loose to buy it. The dealer only carried it to a couple of shows each year. This pitcher is not commonly found!

All items without a line number listed below are found on #2496 commonly known as the Baroque blank. You should find other items with this etching.

Bowl, 4", one hdld., square	14.00	Plate, 9½"	32.50
Bowl, 4⅜", one hdld.	14.00	Plate, 10", hdld. cake	30.00
Bowl, 4⅝", one hdld., 3 cornered	14.00	Plate, 10¼", dinner	45.00
Bowl, 5", one hdld., flared	13.00	Plate, 11", cracker	22.50
Bowl, 6¼", 3 ftd., cupped	20.00	Plate, 14", torte	40.00
Bowl, 7⅜" 3 ftd., bon bon	17.00	Relish, 6", square, 2 part	17.50
Bowl, 8½", 2 hdld.	40.00	Relish, 10", 3 part	30.00
Bowl, 10½", 2 hdld.	45.00	Saucer	4.00
Bowl, 12", flared	50.00	Shaker, 2¾"	25.00
Bowl, 12½", oval, #2545 "Flame"	45.00	Stem, #6017, 3⅝", 4 oz., oyster cocktail	20.00
Bowl, finger, #766	22.00	Stem, #6017, 3⅞", ¾ oz. cordial	40.00
Candlestick, 4½", duo	35.00	Stem, #6017, 4½", 6 oz., low sherbet	14.00
Candlestick, 4"	20.00	Stem, #6017, 4⅞". 3½ oz., cocktail	18.00
Candlestick, 5½"	22.00	Stem, #6017, 5½", 3 oz., wine	27.50
Candlestick, 6¾", duo, #2545 "Flame"	40.00	Stem, #6017, 5½", 6 oz., high sherbet	17.50
Candy w/cover, 6¼", 3 part	65.00	Stem, #6017, 5⅞", 4 oz., claret	30.00
Celery, 11"	22.50	Stem, #6017, 7⅜", 9 oz., water	22.50
Comport, 3¼", ftd. cheese	17.50	Sugar	9.00
Comport, 4¾"	17.50	Sugar, individual	10.00
Comport, 5½"	22.50	Sweetmeat, 6", square, 2 hdld.	17.50
Comport, 5¾"	22.50	Tid bit, 8¼", 3 ftd., flat	20.00
Creamer	10.00	Tray, 6½" ind. sug/cr., #2496½	12.00
Creamer, individual	11.00	Tumbler, #4132, 2⅛", 1½ oz., whiskey	22.50
Cup, ftd.	15.00	Tumbler, #4132, 3½", 4 oz., sham	10.00
Ice bucket	65.00	Tumbler, #4132, 3⅛", 7½ oz., old fashioned	15.00
Jelly w/cover, 7½"	55.00	Tumbler, #4132, 3¾", 5 oz., sham	10.00
Mayonnaise, 3 pc. set, 2496½	35.00	Tumbler, #4132, 3¾", 9 oz., sham	13.00
Oil bottle w/stopper, 3½ oz.	85.00	Tumbler, #4132, 4⅛", 7 oz., sham	12.00
Pickle, 8"	17.50	Tumbler, #4132, 4⅞", 12 oz., sham	15.00
Pitcher, #6011, 8⅞", 53 oz., ftd.	135.00	Tumbler, #4132, 5⅜", 14 oz., sham	17.50
Plate, 6"	6.00	Tumbler, #6017, 4¾", 5 oz., ftd. juice	14.00
Plate, 7", #2337	9.00	Tumbler, #6017, 5½", 9 oz., ftd. water	18.00
Plate, 7½"	9.00	Tumbler, #6017, 6", 12 oz., ftd. ice tea	22.00
Plate, 8½"	12.50	Tumbler, #6017, 6½", 14 oz., ftd.	27.50

MAYFLOWER PLATE ETCHING #332, FOSTORIA GLASS COMPANY, 1938 – 1954

Color: Crystal

Mayflower pattern has a cornucopia of flowers as its principal design. Mayflower is sometimes mistaken for Fostoria's Corsage pattern. Refer to page 49 to see the cone-shaped nosegay of flowers that makes up the Corsage design so you can compare these two patterns.

Most Mayflower etchings are on Fostoria's #2560 blank which is commonly called Coronet. There are three wavy lines encircling the top of Coronet blanks. These are represented by the relish, comport, two-handled bowl, creamer, and sugar on page 147. Note the handles on the sugar and creamer. These are a dead give away to #2560. Do you like the shelf photographs on blue for some of the crystal patterns in this book?

The pitcher is the #4140 jug. This style is rarely found. I bought it from an antique mall in Florida for a little more than the price of the four repaired tumblers that were with it. The dealer may still have those tumblers! The large vase on the bottom right stands 8" tall, but looks much larger due to its wide mouth. This is the #2430 vase in the listing. The vase in the middle of that row is the #5100 blank. Vases are rarely seen in Fostoria crystal patterns, contrary to what you see here!

A "Flame" #2545 oval bowl and single candlestick represent the other blank on which you may find Mayflower. The cordial is on stemware line #6020. If you find additional pieces other than those listed, be sure to drop me a card!

Bowl, finger, #869	25.00	Plate, 7½", #2560	10.00
Bowl, 5", hdld., whip cream, #2560	22.50	Plate, 8½", #2560	15.00
Bowl, 5½", hdld., sweetmeat, #2560	17.50	Plate, 9½", #2560	37.50
Bowl, 5¾" x 6¼", hdld., bon bon, #2560	20.00	Plate, 10½", hdld. cake, #2560	32.50
Bowl, 7¼", 3 ftd., bon bon, #2560	22.50	Plate, 14", torte #2560	40.00
Bowl, 8½", hdld., #2560	37.50	Relish, 6½", hdld., 2 part, #2560	20.00
Bowl, 10", salad, #2560	45.00	Relish, 10" x 7¾", 3 part, #2560	32.50
Bowl, 10½", hdld., #2496	45.00	Salt & Pepper, pr	65.00
Bowl, 11", hdld., #2560	55.00	Saucer, #2560	5.00
Bowl, 11½", crimped, #2560	60.00	Stem, #6020, 3¾", 1 oz., cordial	40.00
Bowl, 12", flared, #2560	50.00	Stem, #6020, 3¾", 4 oz., oyster cocktail	20.00
Bowl, 12½", oval, #2545 "Flame"	50.00	Stem, #6020, 4⅝", 6 oz., low sherbet	15.00
Bowl, 13", fruit, #2560	55.00	Stem, #6020, 4⅞", 3½ oz., cocktail	18.00
Candlestick, 4", #2560½	27.50	Stem, #6020, 5⅜", 3½ oz., wine	30.00
Candlestick, 4½", #2545 "Flame"	25.00	Stem, #6020, 5½", 6 oz., saucer champagne	18.00
Candlestick, 4½", #2560	25.00	Stem, #6020, 5¾", 4½ oz., claret	35.00
Candlestick, 5", duo, #2496	35.00	Stem, #6020, 6⅛", 5½ oz., claret	35.00
Candlestick, 5⅛", duo, #2560	40.00	Stem, #6020, 7¼", 9 oz., water	25.00
Candlestick, 6¾", duo, #2545 "Flame"	42.00	Sugar, #2560	11.00
Celery, 11", #2560	35.00	Sugar, individual, #2560	12.00
Creamer, #2560	12.00	Tray, 7½", individual cr./sug #2560	15.00
Creamer, individual, #2560	12.50	Tray, 10" x 8¼", hdld., muffin, #2560	32.50
Cup, ftd., #2560	17.00	Tumbler, #6020, 4⅞", 5 oz., ftd. juice	17.50
Mayonnaise set, 3 pc., #2560	37.50	Tumbler, #6020, 5¾", 9 oz., ftd. water	20.00
Olive, 6¾", #2560	17.00	Tumbler, #6020, 6⅜", 12 oz., ftd. ice tea	25.00
Pickle, 8¾", #2560	20.00	Vase, 3¾", #2430	55.00
Pitcher, 7½,", 60 oz., flat, #4140	265.00	Vase, 8", #2430	110.00
Pitcher, 9¾", 48 oz., ftd. #5000	265.00	Vase, 10", ftd., #2545, "Flame"	125.00
Plate, 6", #2560	6.00	Vase, 10", ftd., #5100	110.00
Plate, 6¼", hdld., lemon, #2560	6.00		

MEADOW ROSE PLATE ETCHING #328, FOSTORIA GLASS COMPANY, 1936 – 1982

Colors: Crystal and Azure

Meadow Rose was added to this book in the last edition because I had so many requests to do so. Little did I know how confused some of the antique mall and part-time dealers would become. I mentioned that Meadow Rose was similar in design to Navarre, but I have never seen so many pieces mislabeled! Since Navarre is a little higher priced, no one has found any Meadow Rose. It is all Navarre! Please notice that there is an opening in the middle of the Meadow Rose medallion that is filled in Navarre. See the catalog reprint on page 175. That alone should keep you straight. Buying a mislabeled piece in a mall usually means you are stuck. It is your responsibility to know what you are buying!

You will find that pricing for Meadow Rose is similar to Navarre's, but most items sell for less due to a present lack of demand. Meadow Rose collectors are outnumbered dramatically by those searching for Navarre. That could change!

There is little Azure being found. That color was discontinued during World War II in all Fostoria patterns. Pieces found in Azure will fetch an additional 20% – 25% more than crystal. If you have Azure pieces, please send me a list or photo so we can document the pieces made in Azure.

Those pieces without a mould blank number in the listing below are #2496 or Baroque. Look for the raised fleur-de-lis on this line. Meadow Rose was sold alongside its sister pattern, Navarre, for over 40 years. Matching stemware service was obtainable until Fostoria's closing.

Bowl, 4", square, hdld.	11.00	Plate, 9½", dinner	45.00
Bowl, 4½", #869, finger	40.00	Plate, 10", hdld., cake	47.50
Bowl, 4⅝", tri-cornered	15.00	Plate, 11", cracker	30.00
Bowl, 5", hdld., flared	18.50	Plate, 14", torte	57.50
Bowl, 6", square, sweetmeat	17.50	Plate, 16", torte, #2364	85.00
Bowl, 7⅜", 3 ftd., bonbon	27.50	Relish, 6", 2 part, square	32.50
Bowl, 8½", hdld.	40.00	Relish, 10" x 7½", 3 part	45.00
Bowl, 10", oval, floating garden	50.00	Relish, 13¼", 5 part, #2419	85.00
Bowl, 10½", hdld.	55.00	Salad dressing bottle, #2083, 6½"	225.00
Bowl, 12", flared	62.50	Salt & pepper, #2375, 3½", ftd., pr.	95.00
Bowl, 12", hdld., ftd.	62.50	Sauce dish liner, 8", oval	30.00
Bowl, #2545, 12½", oval, "Flame"	55.00	Sauce dish, 6½" x 5¼"	125.00
Candlestick, 4"	25.00	Sauce dish, div. mayo., 6½"	37.50
Candlestick, 4½", double	35.00	Saucer	6.00
Candlestick, 5½"	32.00	Stem, #6016, ¾ oz., cordial, 3⅞"	47.50
Candlestick, 6", triple	50.00	Stem, #6016, 3¼ oz., wine, 5½"	40.00
Candlestick, #2545, 6¾", double, "Flame"	50.00	Stem, #6016, 3½ oz., cocktail, 5¼"	25.00
Candy, w/cover, 3 part	110.00	Stem, #6016, 4 oz., oyster cocktail, 3⅝"	27.50
Celery, 11"	37.50	Stem, #6016, 4½ oz., claret, 6"	40.00
Comport, 3¼", cheese	27.50	Stem, #6016, 6 oz., low sherbet, 4⅜"	24.00
Comport, 4¾"	30.00	Stem, #6016, 6 oz., saucer champagne, 5⅝"	24.00
Creamer, 4¾", ftd.	20.00	Stem, #6016, 10 oz., water, 7⅝"	30.00
Creamer, individual	17.50	Sugar, 3½", ftd.	18.00
Cup	20.00	Sugar, individual	16.00
Ice bucket, 4⅜" high	100.00	Tid bit, 8¼", 3 ftd., turned up edge	22.00
Jelly w/ cover, 7½"	65.00	Tray, #2375, 11", center hdld.	35.00
Mayonnaise, #2375, 3 piece	55.00	Tray, 6½", 2496½, for ind. sugar/creamer	22.00
Mayonnaise, 2496½, 3 piece	55.00	Tumbler, #6016, 5 oz., ftd., juice, 4⅝"	25.00
Pickle, 8"	30.00	Tumbler, #6016, 10 oz., ftd., water, 5⅜"	25.00
Pitcher, #2666, 32 oz.	225.00	Tumbler, #6016, 13 oz., ftd., tea, 5⅞"	30.00
Pitcher, #5000, 48 oz., ftd.	350.00	Vase, #4108, 5"	75.00
Plate, 6", bread/butter	11.00	Vase, #4121, 5"	75.00
Plate, 7½", salad	15.00	Vase, #4128, 5"	75.00
Plate, 8½", luncheon	20.00	Vase, #2470, 10", ftd.	165.00

Please refer to Foreword for pricing information

MODERNTONE PLATONITE, HAZEL ATLAS GLASS COMPANY, 1940 – early 1950s

Colors: Platonite pastel, white, and white decorated

Platonite Moderntone collectors are enthusiastically searching for white trimmed in red or blue. Display a piece of Blue or Red Willow or Deco-trimmed Moderntone (shown on page 151 – 152) and you will see collectors' eyes gleam! I have purchased as much Willow decorated Moderntone as I have had the opportunity to find. All the Deco decorated blue pieces on page 151 came out of one set found in Ohio. It is as scarce as hen's teeth!

Demand is minuscule for plain white. The first item in row 4 on page 151 is a cone-shaped tumbler found only in white. The lid states that this tumbler was given free with the purchase of "Lovely" cherry gelatin costing 10¢. Many tumblers of this era were obtained by acquiring some product.

Pastel colors are the lighter shades of blue, green, pink, and yellow. Pastel green is shown on the left atop page 153; pastel pink is on the bottom left of page 153. Pastel yellow is at the top right of page 154; and pastel blue is on the right of page 156.

At the bottom of page 153 you may notice that there are two dissimilar shades of pink. I have been guaranteed by Moderntone collectors that this difference in shade is of no significance to them. It vexes me to the point that I placed the lighter shades on the far right of the photograph to illustrate the variences in the shades of pink. I hope these show well in the printed copy!

Four tumblers are shown on the top of page 155. They are fired-on Moderntone tumblers in color shades I have never seen before and were unusual enough that I bought them. They are fired-on over crystal and not white Platonite. If you have any other pieces of this pattern fired-on over crystal, let me know. The dealer I bought them from had them labeled Swanky Swigs.

In pastel colors, there is an insignificant price difference on the pieces with white interiors as opposed to those with colored interiors. Over the years, I have found more demand for colored interiors than the white. Cathy, my wife, favors white interiors.

Each bowl comes with or without rims. Bowls without rims are more difficult to find, but bowls with rims tend to have more inner rim roughness which is a turn off to many collectors. Pastel pink 8" bowls with or without rims and yellow 12" platters are easier to find than other pastel colors. These must have been a premium at one time which would account for their abundance.

For discussions regarding the darker colors of Platonite, turn to page 155. Children's dishes have a section all their own starting on page 157.

	Pastel Colors	White or w/stripes	Deco/Red or Blue Willow		Pastel Colors	White or w/stripes	Deco/Red or Blue Willow
Bowl, 4¾", cream soup	6.50	4.00	20.00	Mug, 4", 8 oz.		8.00	
Bowl, 5", berry, w/rim	5.00	3.00	12.50	Plate, 6¾", sherbet	4.50	2.50	9.00
Bowl, 5", berry, wo/rim	6.00			Plate, 8⅞", dinner	6.50	3.50	25.00
Bowl, 5", deep cereal, w/white	7.50	4.00		Plate, 10½", sandwich	16.00	8.00	
Bowl, 5", deep cereal, wo/white	9.00			Platter, 11", oval		12.50	35.00
				Platter, 12", oval	**15.00	9.00	45.00
Bowl, 8", w/rim	*14.00	6.00	32.50	Salt and pepper, pr.	16.00	13.00	
Bowl, 8", wo/rim	*20.00			Saucer	1.00	1.50	5.00
Bowl, 8¾", large berry		7.00	32.50	Sherbet	4.50	2.50	15.00
Creamer	5.00	4.00	20.00	Sugar	5.00	4.00	20.00
Cup	3.50	2.50	20.00	Tumbler, 9 oz.	9.00		
				Tumbler, cone, ftd.		6.00	

*Pink $9.00
* *Yellow $9.00

Please refer to Foreword for pricing information

MODERNTONE PLATONITE, HAZEL ATLAS GLASS COMPANY, 1940 – early 1950s (cont.)

Colors: Dark Platonite fired-on colors

Collecting Moderntone in the darker, later colors will test your patience! When compared to the quantities of pastel, there is a minute amount of darker colors obtainable. You should be primed to buy it no matter when you discover it!

The price listing below divides colors into two price groups based upon availability. The first group consists of cobalt blue, turquoise green, lemon yellow, and orange. These can be found pictured as follows: cobalt (page 156 left), turquoise (top page 153 center), lemon (top page 154 left) and orange (bottom page 154). All of those colors can be collected in sets with difficulty, but they can be found in due time. This group can be found with white or colored interiors. White interiors appear to be more plentiful. It only matters if you do not wish to mix the different color treatments made by Hazel Atlas. Most collectors will take anything they can find!

Accumulating a set of any of the other colors, Chartreuse, Burgundy, Green, Gray, "rust," or "gold" is another matter. None of the preceding colors can be found with white interiors. These colors are shown at the top of page 157 except for Chartreuse that can only be seen on the right on page 153. Colors shown on the top of page 157 are as follows from left to right: Burgundy, Green, Gray, "rust," and "gold." Collectors have mistakenly called the Green "forest green" and the Burgundy "maroon." I have also heard the "gold" referred to as "butterscotch." As with pink, some collectors consider "gold" merely a variation of "lemon" yellow and not a separate color.

You will be challenged if you pick any of those final colors to collect! Several pieces listed under pastel are not to be found in the darker colors. So far, cream soups, bowls with rims, sandwich plates, and salt and pepper shakers have not been found in any of these colors! Green (dark) tumblers appear to be the only color found in the later colors. If you see others, please let me know!

	Cobalt Turquoise Lemon Orange	Burgundy Chartreuse Green/Gray Rust/Gold		Cobalt Turquoise Lemon Orange	Burgundy Chartreuse Green/Gray Rust/Gold
Bowl, 4¾", cream soup	10.00		Plate, 8⅞" dinner	12.00	13.00
Bowl, 5", berry, w/rim	11.00		Plate, 10½" sandwich	22.00	
Bowl, 5", berry, wo/rim	8.00	12.00	Platter, 12" oval	22.00	32.00
Bowl, 5", deep cereal, w/white	12.00		Salt and pepper, pr.	22.50	
Bowl, 5", deep cereal, wo/white		15.00	Saucer	4.00	5.00
Bowl, 8", w/rim	32.00		Sherbet	7.00	9.00
Bowl, 8", wo/rim	32.00	37.50	Sugar	8.00	11.00
Creamer	8.00	11.00	Tumbler, 9 oz.	12.50	*22.50
Cup	7.00	8.00			
Plate, 6¾", sherbet	6.00	8.00	*Green 16.00		

MODERNTONE "LITTLE HOSTESS PARTY DISHES"
HAZEL ATLAS GLASS COMPANY, early 1950s

Doll collectors and doll dish collectors have also joined the search for our "Little Hostess" sets. This causes prices to increase since more collectors are vying for these little sets. Demand is the driving force.

As a child, Cathy received a set as a gift premium from Big Top Peanut Butter. (See top page 159.)

You will notice a price escalation in the harder to find colors. An all white set has been found in an original box. It is pictured in *Very Rare Glassware of the Depression Years, Fourth Series.* Turquoise teapots continue to be more difficult to find than Burgundy. When buying Burgundy teapot tops or bottoms individually, you could have a problem matching the Burgundy shades!

A person in California called recently to ask where she could find a pink and black set. She had fallen in love with a set she had seen. Fortunately, I had recently found a set and she got a great birthday gift from her family. The picture at the top of page 158 contains two mixed sets. There is a pink and black set and an all white set. I was trying to show several pieces in one photo (in case you were confused by this).

LITTLE HOSTESS PARTY SET
Pink/Black/White (top 146)

Cup, ¾", bright pink, white	17.50
Saucer, 3⅞", black, white	12.00
Plate, 5¼", black, bright pink, white	15.00
Creamer, 1¾", bright pink	20.00
Sugar, 1¾", bright pink	20.00
Teapot, 3½", bright pink	80.00
Teapot lid, black	80.00
Set, 16 piece	370.00

LITTLE HOSTESS PARTY SET
Lemon/Beige/Pink/Aqua
(bottom 146)

Cup, ¾", bright pink/aqua/lemon	17.50
Saucer, 3⅞", same	12.00
Plate, 5¼", same	15.00
Creamer, 1¾", pink	20.00
Sugar, 1¾", pink	20.00
Teapot, 3½", brown	80.00

Teapot lid, lemon	80.00
Set, 16 piece	370.00

LITTLE HOSTESS PARTY SET
Gray/Rust/Gold
Turquoise (top 147)

Cup, ¾", Gray, rust	13.00
Cup, ¾", gold, turquoise	13.00
Saucer, 3⅞", all four colors	8.00
Plate, 5¼", same	8.00
Creamer, 1¾", rust	15.00
Sugar, 1¾", rust	15.00
Teapot, 3½", turquoise	62.50
Teapot lid, turquoise	62.50
Set, 16 piece	290.00

LITTLE HOSTESS PARTY SET
Green/Gray/Chartreuse/
Burgundy (bottom 147 left)

Cup, ¾", Green, Gray, Chartreuse	10.00

Cup, ¾", Burgundy	13.00
Saucer, 3⅞", Green, Gray & Burgundy, Chartreuse	7.00
Plate, 5¼", Burgundy	10.00
Plate, 5¼", Green, Gray, Chartreuse	8.00
Creamer, 1¾", Chartreuse	12.50
Sugar, 1¾", Chartreuse	12.50
Teapot, 3½", Burgundy	55.00
Teapot lid, Burgundy	60.00
Set, 16 piece	245.00

LITTLE HOSTESS PARTY SET
Pastel pink/green/blue
yellow (bottom 147 right)

Cup, ¾", all four colors	9.00
Saucer, 3⅞", same	7.00
Plate, 5¼", same	10.00
Creamer, 1¾", pink	15.00
Sugar, 1¾", pink	15.00
Set, 14 piece	110.00

MOONSTONE, ANCHOR HOCKING GLASS CORPORATION, 1941 – 1946

Colors: crystal with opalescent hobnails and some green with opalescent hobnails

Moonstone is truly 1940s glassware. This was predominately displayed in all the five and dime stores during the middle of the War. The photograph of a J. J. Newborn store window display on page 162 is one example of how well this glassware was promoted. I wish more records like this could be found!

There are quite a few experimental pieces showing up in Moonstone including a 9¼" dinner plate. Had that plate been a production item, this set would attract more collectors. Collectors tend to avoid sets without dinner plates. You can see the dinner plate, a tooth pick, and a 7¾" divided relish without a crimped edge in *Very Rare Glassware of the Depression Years*, *Fifth Series*. Yes, new items continue to surface! All the pieces pictured below (note dinner plate) are from Hocking's morgue. (Discontinued or experimental items were stored in some place appropriately called a morgue.) Some of these pieces may have found their way home with factory workers on the days they were produced. It happened!

The most troublesome normal production pieces to find today are 5½" berry bowls (top right foreground of page 161) listed as M2775 in the Hocking brochure on page 162. There are none of those in the store display photo either! Admittedly, goblets and cups and saucers are also excluded in that store window display; and they are easily found today.

Ruffled 5½" bowls are more available than their straight-side counterparts; but even they are not as abundant as once believed. The sandwich plate measures 10¾" instead of 10" as erroneously listed. I have seen very few of these of late. Moonstone is a pattern that has gently slipped away into collections. Little is seen at shows and there are fewer quantities appearing in the market place.

Green Moonstone was issued under the name "Ocean Green" and was made in sets containing goblets, cups, saucers, plates, creamer, and sugar. Notice the two pieces shown are slightly different from the standard line in the catalog pages on 162.

Fenton Opalescent Hobnail pitchers and tumblers are good companion pieces to go with Anchor Hocking Moonstone sets since there are no pitchers, flat tumblers, or shakers found in Moonstone. Those found are Fenton. There is also no Moonstone cologne bottle about which I must receive a dozen letters a year. The Fenton pieces look fine with Moonstone; and, if you would like additional pieces that are similar to your pattern, buy them! The hobs on the Fenton are more pointed than on Moonstone, but the colors match very well. Glass companies often mimicked contemporary wares. That still occurs.

	Opalescent Hobnail		Opalescent Hobnail
Bowl, 5½", berry	16.00	Cup	8.00
Bowl, 5½", crimped, dessert	9.50	Goblet, 10 oz.	18.00
Bowl, 6½", crimped, handled	10.00	Heart bonbon, one handle	14.00
Bowl, 7¾", flat	12.00	Plate, 6¼", sherbet	6.00
Bowl, 7¾", divided relish	12.00	Plate, 8⅜", luncheon	15.00
Bowl, 9½", crimped	22.50	Plate, 10¾", sandwich	27.50
Bowl, cloverleaf	13.00	Puff box and cover, 4¾", round	25.00
Candle holder, pr.	18.00	Saucer (same as sherbet plate)	6.00
Candy jar and cover, 6"	27.50	Sherbet, footed	7.00
Cigarette jar and cover	22.50	Sugar, footed	9.00
Creamer	9.00	Vase, 5½", bud	12.50

Please refer to Foreword for pricing information

Opalescent "MOONSTONE" Glassware

"MOONSTONE" Glassware

	DOZ. TO CTN.	WT. OF CTN.
Tableware		
M2779— 3⅞" Cup	6	32#
M2729— 6¼" Saucer	6	32#
M2713— 6 oz. Sherbet	6	32#
M2729— 6¼" Sherbet Plate	6	32#
M2775— 5½" Dessert	6	32#
M2716—10 oz. Goblet	4	36#
M2740— 8⅜" Luncheon Plate	4	44#
Gift Ware		
M2769— 7¾" Divided Relish	2	27#
M2766— 6½" Crimped Handled Bowl	2	19#
M2755— 6¾" Clover Leaf Dish	2	22#
M2772— 6½" Heart Bonbon	2	20#
M2767— 7¾" Flat Bowl	2	23#
M2753— 3¼" Sugar	2	13#
M2754— 3¼" Creamer	2	12½#
M2722— 4¾" Puff Box & Cover	2	22#
M2799— 5" Cigarette Jar & Cover	2	25#
M2782— 5½" Vase	2	16#
M2792— 6" Candy Jar & Cover	1	20#
M2760—10¾" Sandwich Plate	1	21#
M2768— 9½" Crimped Bowl	1	21#
M2765— 5½" Crimped Dessert	6	33#
M2781— 4¼" Candleholder	2	10#
Suggested Sets - Bulk Packed		
M2700/1—7 Pce. Dessert Set (Bulk Packed in 2 Cartons)	12 Sets	54#
M2700/2—4 Pce. Buffet Set (Bulk Packed in 3 Cartons)	12 Sets	52#

Now Available at Low Prices

MOROCCAN AMETHYST HAZEL WARE, DIVISION OF CONTINENTAL CAN, 1960s

Color: Amethyst

Moroccan Amethyst is a pleasant purple color found on several different moulds of Hazel Ware glass. As with Anchor Hocking's Forest Green and Royal Ruby, the color took precedence over the pattern, hence its "name" with collectors.

Square or rectangular based pieces (shown on page 164) are being called Colony. That amber tumbler has a Colony label on it. Page 165 shows mostly the Moroccan Swirl with some Octagonal and other assorted styles. All of these patterns occur in Capri which means that the color name will have to precede the pattern derivative. Also at the top of page 166 is a set of "Tulip"-like ash trays. These have been confused with Dell's Tulip pattern. Note the similarities in the two; remember there are no known ash trays in Dell's Tulip!

One of the most interesting pieces pictured on page 166 is the apple-shaped salad bowl set which was discovered south of Pittsburgh. Both bowls have an embossed apple blossom design in the bottom. You may find this salad set in fired-on Platonite, usually in Chartreuse or Green; however the apple blossom design is missing from the bottom of these bowls. There is also a floral design in the bottom of the 4½" square ash tray, but it is covered by an original Moroccan Amethyst sticker which I wouldn't let the photographer remove! The 4½", five-pointed star candlesticks are an additional find. All these items came from the grandson of a worker at the Hazel Atlas plant.

The top of page 167 reveals other colors being found with the swirled design. You will find swirled bowls in green, amber, and white! Bowls are usually reasonably priced in these colors. I imagine that they are a later production made to go with the 1970s Avocado and Harvest Gold colors. Somebody told me those colors were coming back into vogue. Crystal and white stemware are also being found that match the Moroccan designs.

An original box for the amethyst and white punch bowl set, called Alpine by the factory, is shown on page 167. The punch cups have open handles to hang onto the side of the punch bowl. I have seen some extreme prices on that set. A "Seashell" snack set in the same two colors was also labeled as "Alpine." The amethyst bowl pictured in the center of the punch bowls served not only as a bowl, but also as the punch bowl base. Many companies' punch bowl bases had additional functions that saved making another expensive mould.

"The Magic Hour" 4-piece cocktail set on page 169 features a clock showing six o'clock and says "yours" on one side and "mine" on the other. In this boxed set are two 2½", 4 ounce tumblers and a spouted cocktail mixer with a metal stirring spoon. You will find two and three tier tidbit trays made from assorted pieces (bowls, plates, ash trays).

Not much sprayed red over crystal is being found, but there is little demand for it at present. Crystal, amber, and green pieces may someday be desirable to own; but for now, that does not seem to be the case!

New pieces seem to turn up once or twice a year. Send me a picture and measurements of what you discover!

	Amethyst		Amethyst
Ash tray, 3¼", triangular	5.50	Goblet, 4¼", 7½ oz., sherbet	7.50
Ash tray, 3¼", round	5.50	Goblet, 4⅜", 5½ oz., juice	9.00
Ash tray, 6⅞", triangular	9.50	Goblet, 5½", 9 oz., water	10.00
Ash tray, 8", square	13.00	Ice bucket, 6"	35.00
Bowl, 4¾", fruit, octagonal	7.50	Plate, 5¾"	4.50
Bowl, 5¾", deep, square	10.00	Plate, 7¼", salad	7.00
Bowl, 6", round	11.00	Plate, 9¾", dinner	9.00
Bowl, 7¾", oval	16.00	Plate, 10", fan shaped, snack w/cup rest	8.00
Bowl. 7¾", rectangular	14.00	Plate, 12", round	15.00
Bowl. 7¾", rectangular w/ metal handle	17.50	Plate, 12", sandwich, w/metal /handle	17.50
Bowl, 10¾"	30.00	Saucer	1.00
Candy w/lid short	35.00	Tumbler, 4 oz., juice, 2½"	8.50
Candy w/lid tall	35.00	Tumbler, 8 oz., old fashion, 3¼"	14.00
Chip and dip, 10¾" & 5¾" bowls in metal holder	40.00	Tumbler, 9 oz., water	10.00
Cocktail w/stirrer, 6¼", 16 oz., w/lip	32.00	Tumbler, 11 oz., water, crinkled bottom, 4¼"	12.00
Cocktail shaker w/lid	30.00	Tumbler, 11 oz., water, 4⅝"	12.00
Cup	5.00	Tumbler, 16 oz., iced tea, 6½"	16.00
Goblet, 4", 4½ oz., wine	10.00	Vase, 8½", ruffled	37.50

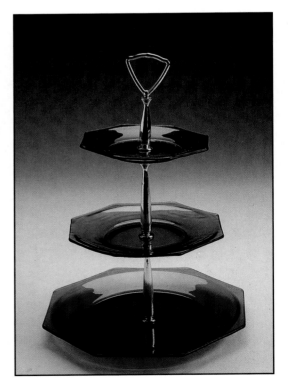

NATIONAL, JEANNETTE GLASS COMPANY, late 1940s – mid 1950s

Colors: Crystal, pink, and Shell Pink

National is a Jeannette pattern acknowledged by collectors, but rarely by name. Two pieces are more familiar to Shell Pink collectors than anyone else. The National candy bottom is seen frequently in Shell Pink, maybe even more so than in crystal. What I just realized is that the vase we have all called the "heavy bottomed Shell Pink 9" vase" is actually National pattern.

National is a bold pattern filled with accessory pieces, but weak in basic table ware. The Lazy Susan and the punch set are affordable items and are practical gifts! Both are pictured. In the top photo of page 171 is a bowl in the center that was bought with other National. However, it may not be a part of this pattern since it does not have the dotted pattern in the center that the other pieces do. It makes a great go-with piece if not. I am sure there are additional pieces. Adding new patterns is always a challenge to find as many pieces and get as many items listed as possible. I try to have a representative example to picture, but there seems to be no way to get a complete listing even with catalogs available in most patterns. This is why I am always appreciative of your help in adding to the listings!

Ash tray, small	3.00	Plate, 15", serving/punch liner	15.00
Ash tray, large	4.00	Punch bowl, 12"	25.00
Bowl, 4½", berry	4.00	Punch bowl stand	15.00
Bowl, 8½", large berry	12.00	Punch cup	3.00
Bowl, 12", flat	10.00	Punch set, 15 pc.	85.00
Candy, ftd., w/cover	22.50	Saucer	1.00
Cigarette box	12.50	Shakers, pr.	9.00
Creamer	5.00	Sugar	5.00
Cup	3.00	Tray, 8", hdld., sug/cr	5.00
Jar, relish	10.00	Tray, 12½", hdld	15.00
Pitcher, 20 oz., milk	17.50	Tumbler, 5⅛", ftd.	8.00
Pitcher, 64 oz.	27.50	Vase, 9"	17.50
Plate, 8", salad	5.00		

Please refer to Foreword for pricing information

NAVARRE PLATE ETCHING #327, FOSTORIA GLASS COMPANY, 1937 – 1982

Colors: crystal, blue, pink, and rare in green

Most Navarre was sold after 1940, although it was first introduced in 1937. I have included it in this book as well as my Elegant book. This is the only overlapping pattern of Elegant glassware in the *Collectible Glassware of the 40s, 50s, 60s....*

Numerous hard to find pieces were made near the end of Fostoria's reign (late 1970s and early 1980s). A majority of these pieces were signed "Fostoria" (acid etched on base) although a small number only had a sticker. Factory "seconds" sold through the outlet stores were rarely signed. Quality signed pieces were run through the outlets only when those stores ran short of seconds.

Shown on page 173 are a few of the later made pieces of Navarre. The top row shows water goblets, a magnum, and continental champagnes. The second row shows the large claret, regular claret, saucer champagnes, low sherbet, oyster cocktail, and bells. On the third row are footed teas, footed water, footed juice, double old fashioned, highball, and cordial. Some of the items pictured in the top three rows were made in blue and pink. Those colored items are priced separately in the listings. The fourth row shows a 10½" footed #2470½ bowl, a three-part candy, and a "Flame" oval bowl. The bottom shelf holds a #2482 triple candlestick, #2440 sugar and creamer, and the "Flame" double candlestick. Parts of several 1982 catalog sheets are reprinted on page 175. They also display many pieces made at the end of Fostoria's production. You will find that assembling a crystal set of Navarre will be a time-consuming chore, but it can still be done with patience and money! Prices for Navarre are certainly not standing still!

	Crystal	Blue/Pink		Crystal	Blue/Pink
Bell, dinner	60.00	85.00	Plate, #2440, 10½" oval cake	50.00	
Bowl, #2496, 4", square, hndl.	12.00		Plate, #2496, 14", torte	60.00	
Bowl, #2496, 4⅜", hndl.	12.00		Plate, #2464, 16", torte	90.00	
Bowl, #869, 4½", finger	65.00		Relish, #2496, 6", 2 part, square	32.50	
Bowl, #2496, 4⅝", tri-cornered	15.00		Relish, #2496, 10" x 7½", 3 part	47.50	
Bowl, #2496, 5", hndl., ftd.	18.50		Relish, #2496, 10", 4 part	52.50	
Bowl, #2496, 6", square, sweetmeat	17.50		Relish, #2419, 13¼", 5 part	87.50	
Bowl, #2496, 6¼", 3 ftd., nut	22.00		Salt & pepper, #2364, 3¼", flat, pr.	65.00	
Bowl, #2496, 7⅜", ftd., bonbon	27.50		Salt & pepper, #2375, 3½", ftd., pr.	110.00	
Bowl, #2496, 10", oval, floating garden	55.00		Salad dressing bottle, #2083, 6½"	350.00	
Bowl, #2496, 10½", hndl., ftd.	65.00		Sauce dish, #2496, div. mayo., 6½"	50.00	
Bowl, #2470½, 10½", ftd.	50.00		Sauce dish, #2496, 6½" x 5¼"	125.00	
Bowl, #2496, 12", flared	62.50		Sauce dish liner, #2496, 8", oval	30.00	
Bowl, #2545, 12½", oval, "Flame"	60.00		Saucer, #2440	5.00	
Candlestick, #2496, 4"	20.00		Stem, #6106, ¾ oz., cordial, 3⅞"	47.50	
Candlestick, #2496, 4½", double	35.00		Stem, #6106, 3¼ oz., wine, 5½"	37.50	
Candlestick, #2472, 5", double	42.50		Stem, #6106, 3½ oz., cocktail, 6"	25.00	
Candlestick, #2496, 5½"	30.00		Stem, #6106, 4 oz., oyster cocktail, 3⅝"	30.00	
Candlestick, #2496, 6", triple	60.00		Stem, #6106, 4½ oz., claret, 6"	55.00	85.00
Candlestick, #2545, 6¾", double, "Flame"	55.00		Stem, #6106, 5 oz., continental		
Candlestick, #2482, 6¾", triple	75.00		champagne, 8⅛"	75.00	95.00
Candy, w/cover, #2496, 3 part	125.00		Stem, #6106, 6 oz., cocktail/sherry, 6³⁄₁₆"	60.00	
Celery, #2440, 9"	30.00		Stem, #6106, 6 oz., low sherbet, 4⅜"	24.00	
Celery, #2496, 11"	40.00		Stem, #6106, 6 oz., saucer champagne, 5⅝"	24.00	40.00
Comport, #2496, 3¼", cheese	35.00		Stem, #6106, 6½ oz., large claret, 6½"	50.00	70.00
Comport, #2400, 4½"	35.00		Stem, #6106, 10 oz., water, 7⅝"	30.00	50.00
Comport, #2496, 4¾"	30.00		Stem, #6106, 15 oz., brandy inhaler, 5½"	75.00	
Cracker, #2496, 11" plate	42.50		Stem, #6106, 16 oz., magnum, 7¼"	125.00	140.00
Creamer, #2440, 4¼", ftd.	20.00		Sugar, #2440, 3⅝", ftd.	18.00	
Creamer, #2496, individual	17.50		Sugar, #2496, individual	16.00	
Cup, #2440	20.00		Syrup, #2586, Sani-cut, 5½"	365.00	
Ice bucket, #2496, 4⅜" high	120.00		Tid bit, #2496, 8¼", 3 ftd., turned up edge	22.00	
Ice bucket, #2375, 6" high	150.00		Tray, #2496½, for ind. sugar/creamer	22.00	
Mayonnaise, #2375, 3 piece	67.50		Tumbler, #6106, 5 oz., ftd., juice, 4⅝"	25.00	
Mayonnaise, #2496½, 3 piece	67.50		Tumbler, #6106, 10 oz., ftd., water, 5⅜"	25.00	
Pickle, #2496, 8"	27.50		Tumbler, #6106, 12 oz., flat, highball, 4⅞"	75.00	
Pickle, #2440, 8½"	30.00		Tumbler, #6106, 13 oz., flat,		
Pitcher, #5000, 48 oz., ftd.	345.00		double old fashioned, 3⅝"	75.00	
Plate, #2440, 6", bread/butter	11.00		Tumbler, #6106, 13 oz., ftd., tea, 5⅞"	32.00	60.00
Plate, #2440, 7½", salad	15.00		Vase, #4108, 5"	90.00	
Plate, #2440, 8½", luncheon	20.00		Vase, #4121, 5"	90.00	
Plate, #2440, 9½", dinner	47.50		Vase, #4128, 5"	90.00	
Plate, #2496, 10", hndl., cake	50.00		Vase, #2470, 10", ftd.	175.00	

Please refer to Foreword for pricing information

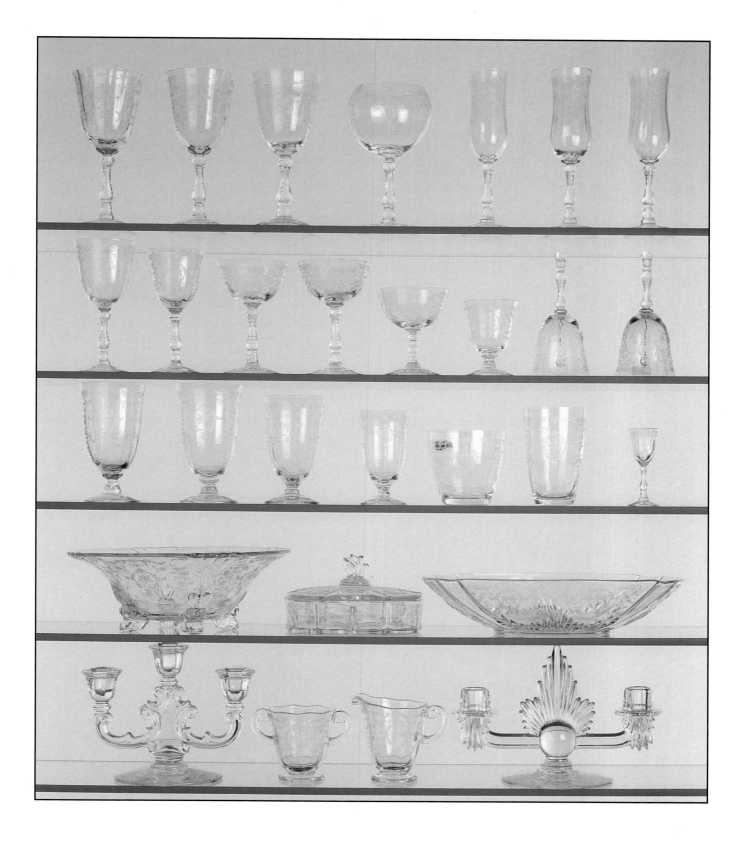

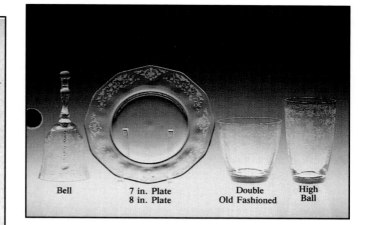

Bell | 7 in. Plate / 8 in. Plate | Double Old Fashioned | High Ball

Wilma Blue — Goblet | Wilma Crystal — Goblet | Navarre Crystal — Goblet | Low Dessert/ Champagne | High Dessert/ Champagne

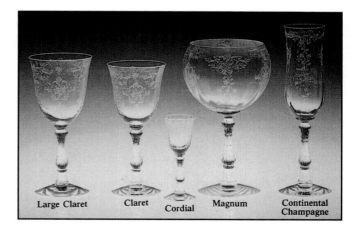

Large Claret | Claret | Cordial | Magnum | Continental Champagne

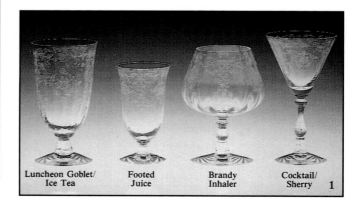

Luncheon Goblet/ Ice Tea | Footed Juice | Brandy Inhaler | Cocktail/ Sherry

1

NEW ERA #4044, A.H. HEISEY CO., 1934 – 1941; 1944 – 1957 (stems, celery tray, and candlesticks)

Colors: crystal, frosted crystal, some cobalt with crystal stem and foot

Production of New Era was launched in the 1930s; but the stemware repeatedly seen now fits the 50s setting of this book. New Era is popular with Art Deco collectors. The stems always attract new collectors! Little do they realize how difficult flat serving pieces are to find! However, stems can be used with a variety of patterns, old or new!

Note the cobalt items on the second row. Any New Era piece with a cobalt bowl will fetch $125.00 to $150.00. Keep that in the memory bank on your jaunts!

The double branched candelabra with the New Era bobeches is not hard to find, and very appealing. Dinner plates without scratches and after-dinner cups and saucers will keep you searching for a long time unless you are lucky!

I received an amusing letter from a person in New England wondering if that "flower pot saucer" might be one from a relative's estate sale where New Era plates were marked as such. I had no way of knowing, but I would have been surprised had someone hauled those to an antique mall in Evansville, Indiana, to sell for $7.50 each. If I had only thought to ask if they were monogrammed! A luncheon plate with that unusual label ("flower pot saucer") is shown on the right below!

	Crystal		Crystal
Ash tray or indiv. nut	30.00	Stem, 1 oz. cordial	45.00
Bottle, rye w/stopper	120.00	Stem, 3 oz. wine	35.00
Bowl, 11" floral	35.00	Stem, 3½ oz., high, cocktail	12.00
Candelabra, 2 lite w/2 #4044 bobeche & prisms	70.00	Stem, 3½ oz. oyster cocktail	12.00
Creamer	37.50	Stem, 4 oz. claret	18.00
Cup	10.00	Stem, 6 oz. sherbet, low	12.50
Cup, after dinner	62.50	Stem, 6 oz. champagne	12.50
Pilsner, 8 oz.	27.50	Stem, 10 oz. goblet	16.00
Pilsner, 12 oz.	32.50	Sugar	37.50
Plate, 5½" x 4½" bread & butter	15.00	Tray, 13" celery	30.00
Plate, 9"x 7", luncheon	25.00	Tumbler, 5 oz. ftd. soda	8.00
Plate, 10" x 8", dinner	45.00	Tumbler, 8 oz. ftd. soda	11.00
Relish, 13" 3-part	25.00	Tumbler, 10 oz., low, ftd.	11.00
Saucer	5.00	Tumbler, 12 oz. ftd. soda	14.00
Saucer, after dinner	12.50	Tumbler, 14 oz. ftd. soda	17.50

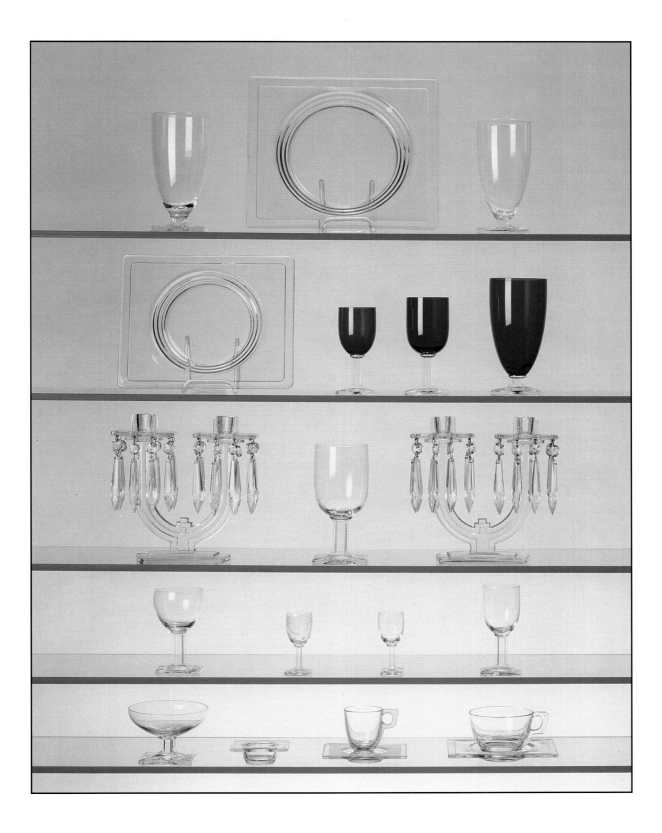

NEWPORT, "HAIRPIN," HAZEL ATLAS GLASS COMPANY, 1940 – early 1950s

Colors: Platonite white and fired-on colors

Newport is a pattern that Hazel Atlas made in the late 1930s in several transparent colors; afterward, they continued making it in Platonite until the early 1950s. Thus Newport pattern divides listings between this 50s book and *The Collector's Encyclopedia of Depression Glass*. The transparent colors were made before 1940; and Platonite white and white with fired on colors was a popular line for Hazel Atlas beginning in the 1940s.

Notice the white edge on the fired-on pink plate in the rear. The edges and back of this plate are white. The pink (or other pastel color) decorates only the top. On the other hand, the turquoise blue bowl and dark green plate have colors fired-on front and back.

As luck would have it, I had a call from California wanting to sell me nine tumblers in different colors right after the picture of Newport was made containing one pink tumbler. That photo is shown below. However, I arranged for a new photograph shown on page 179 with all nine tumblers illustrated. Have you any other color?

The white color comes in two distinct shades. One is very translucent and the other is a flat white similar to what many collectors know as milk glass. The white shaker is often used by Petalware collectors for their pattern since there are no shakers in the MacBeth-Evans set. It is not unprecedented for collectors to be fooled into thinking these shakers really are Petalware.

If you have unlisted Platonite pieces, please let me know! Do not assume I already have information you can not find listed. I very often learn from collectors — witness those tumblers!

	White	Fired-on colors
Bowl, 4¾", berry	3.50	5.50
Bowl, 4¾", cream soup	5.50	9.00
Bowl, 8¼, large berry	9.50	15.00
Cup	3.50	6.00
Creamer	4.50	7.50
Plate, 6", sherbet	1.00	1.50
Plate, 8½", luncheon	3.00	5.00
Plate, 11½", sandwich	10.00	15.00
Platter, 11¾", oval	12.00	17.50
Salt and pepper, pr.	18.00	22.50
Saucer	.75	1.00
Sherbet	3.50	6.00
Sugar	4.50	7.50
Tumbler		20.00

OVIDE, incorrectly dubbed "NEW CENTURY," HAZEL ATLAS GLASS COMPANY, 1930 – 1950s

Colors: green, black, white Platonite, and white with trimmed or fired-on colors in 1950s

Hazel Atlas's Ovide began production in the Depression era mostly in transparent colors; yet it continued well into the 1950s as opaque Platonite. Pattern names have surfaced for some of the pastel-banded Platonite that was used in restaurants, competing with Anchor Hocking's Jade-ite Restaurant Ware line. A full-page ad is shown on page 182 introducing Sierra Sunrise. The charcoal and pink combination shown below was named Informal as can be seen in the 1955 ad on page 183. This ad boldly states that pink and charcoal were popular color combinations in 1955. I have been unable to find a name for the chartreuse and darker green color combination. Have you any ads or boxed sets with names?

This economically priced glassware is being utilized as everyday dishes and works well in both the microwave and the dishwasher according to collectors! There is only a trickle of collector interest in this Platonite with pastel banded edges at the present time; but a few years ago, no one was interested in Jade-ite!

Colors shown on the bottom of page 181 have been interesting to discover. I have never found a platter in any color other than the one shown which I refer to as "Butterscotch." Platters in all Platonite patterns have a tendency to be found in one color only. Each of the other basic pieces should be found in all colors, but serving pieces may be only "Butterscotch." Let me known what you find!

One of the difficulties in ordering glass through the mail or Internet is miscommunication between buyer and seller. I ordered an 18 piece set of dark "Moderntone" colors through the mail years ago expecting to receive Moderntone pattern. I got Moderntone Ovide. Evidently, *Moderntone* referred to the colors and not the pattern. You will find Ovide pieces in the 50s Moderntone colors Burgundy, Chartreuse, Green, and Gray. That green is the actual color designation by Hazel Atlas for what collectors have always called forest or dark green. These colors were Hazel Atlas Glass Company's answer to the popular 50s Fiesta dinnerware.

Prices can be found on the top of page 181.

Please refer to Foreword for pricing information

OVIDE, incorrectly dubbed "NEW CENTURY" (cont.)

	White w/trims	Decorated White	Fired-on Colors	Art Deco
Ash tray, square			4.00	
Bowl, 4¾", berry	3.50	6.50	5.50	
Bowl, 5½", cereal, deep		15.00		
Bowl, 8", large berry			18.00	
Creamer	4.50	18.00	5.50	85.00
Cup	3.50	12.50	4.50	60.00
Plate, 6", sherbet	1.50	2.50		
Plate, 8", luncheon	2.50	13.00	4.00	45.00
Plate, 9", dinner	3.50			
Platter, 11"	7.50	25.00		
Refrigerator stacking set, 4 pc.		47.50		
Salt and pepper, pr.	13.00			
Saucer	1.00	2.50		20.00
Sherbet	5.50	2.00		50.00
Sugar, open	4.50	18.00	5.50	85.00
Tumbler		20.00		85.00

Please refer to Foreword for pricing information

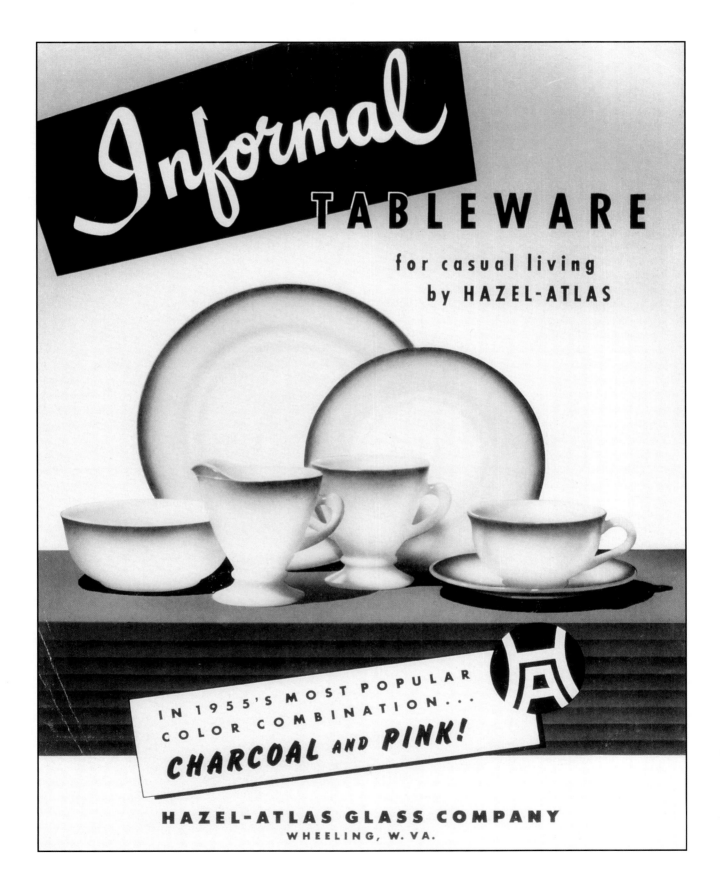

PANELED GRAPE, PATTERN #1881 WESTMORELAND GLASS COMPANY, 1950 – 1970s

Colors: white and white w/decorations, and some green

Paneled Grape is the most recognized Westmoreland pattern after English Hobnail. Introduced in 1950, Pattern #1881 (Paneled Grape) soon became a line that encompassed over a hundred pieces. Westmoreland listed this pattern with both appellations as you can see from the catalog pages that follow. (Pieces shown on the catalog sheets as line #1884 are called Beaded Grape and are not priced in the Paneled Grape listing below.)

Prices on some rarely found items have recently slowed while those for basic pieces are holding steady. Manufactured for so long, supply of #1881 has been able to keep up with demand. I have sold four punch sets and seen six more in the last year. I do not believe these to be as rare as once thought. The operative word is "sold," so there is a demand for them!

I am not sure how rare the green epergne pictured on the right actually is. I bought it to use for a photograph and sold it for $325.00. Many Westmoreland collectors are very close-mouthed about values on their glass and no one I asked wanted to share information on that epergne! The other individual photo is of a banana stand. Tall vases on page 185 and again at the top of page 187 are various sizes of swung vases. These vases are actually swung while hot to extend their shape!

1973 catalog pages are depicted on pages 188 – 198. Paneled Grape is either revered or detested. Some people can not abide white milk glass; others think it is the most beautiful glass on earth. Thankfully, there are enough different colors and patterns from this era to suit every collecting need.

	White, w/decorations		White, w/decorations
Appetizer or canapé set, 3 pc. (9" three-part relish/round fruit cocktail/ladle)	62.50	Candelabra, 3 lite, ea.	285.00
		Candle holder, 4", octagonal, pr.	27.50
Basket, 5½", ruffled	55.00	Candle holder, 5", w/colonial hdld.	35.00
Basket, 6½", oval	25.00	Candle holder, 8", 2 lite (4 of these	
Basket, 8"	77.50	form a circular center piece)	35.00
Basket, 8", ruffled	65.00	Candy jar, 3 ftd., w/cover	32.50
Bon bon, 8", ruffled w/metal handle	50.00	Candy jar, 6¼", w/cover	25.00
Bottle, 5 oz., toilet	62.50	Canister, 7"	135.00
Bottle, oil or vinegar, w/stopper, 2 oz.	22.00	Canister, 9½"	160.00
Bowl, pedestal base, 5" (used w/12"/12½"		Canister, 11"	195.00
lipped/10" rnd. bowls & epergne)	70.00	Celery or spooner, 6"	40.00
Bowl, 4", crimped	22.00	Cheese/old fashioned butter, 7", round w/cover	57.50
Bowl, 6", crimped, stemmed	30.00	Chocolate box, 6½", w/cover	52.50
Bowl, 6", ruffled edge, stemmed	30.00	Compote, 4½", crimped	30.00
Bowl, 6½" x 12½", 3⅛" high	115.00	Compote, 7" covered, ftd.	47.50
Bowl, 6½", oval	23.00	Compote, 9" ftd., crimped	77.50
Bowl, 8", cupped	38.00	Condiment set, 5 pc. (oil and vinegar, salt	
Bowl, 8½", shallow	55.00	and pepper on 9" oval tray)	110.00
Bowl, 9", ftd., 6" high, skirted base	47.50	Creamer, 6½ oz.	16.00
Bowl, 9", ftd., w/cover	67.50	Creamer, individual	11.00
Bowl, 9", lipped	110.00	Creamer, large (goes w/lacy edge sugar)	22.50
Bowl, 9", lipped, ftd.	115.00	Creamer, small	10.00
Bowl, 9", square, w/cover	35.00	Cup, coffee, flared	13.00
Bowl, 9½", bell shape	45.00	Cup, punch, cupped	12.00
Bowl, 9½", ftd., bell shaped	110.00	Decanter, wine	145.00
Bowl, 10", oval	37.50	Dresser set, 4 pc. (2)5 oz. toilet bottles, puff	
Bowl, 10½", round	77.50	box and 13½" oval tray	235.00
Bowl, 11", oval, lipped, ftd.	120.00	Egg plate, 12"	75.00
Bowl, 11½", oval, ruffled edge	80.00	Egg tray, 10", metal center handle	57.50
Bowl, 12", lipped	120.00	Epergne vase, 8½", bell	60.00
Bowl, 12" ftd., banana	150.00	Epergne vase, pattern at top	195.00
Bowl, 12½", bell shape	135.00	Epergne set, 2 pc. (9" lipped bowl/8½" epergne vase)	125.00
Bowl, 13", punch, bell or flared	325.00	Epergne set, 2 pc. (11½" epergne flared	
Bowl, 14", shallow, round	150.00	bowl/8½" epergne vase)	125.00
Bowl, ftd., ripple top	75.00	Epergne set, 2 pc. (12" epergne lipped	
Butter w/cover, ¼ pound	22.50	bowl/8½" epergne vase)	225.00
Cake salver, 10½"	65.00	Epergne set, 2 pc. (14" flared bowl/8½"	
Cake salver, 11", round ftd., w/skirt	70.00	epergne vase)	235.00
Canapé or set, 3 pc. (12½" canapé		Epergne set, 3 pc. (12" epergne lipped	
tray/3½" cocktail/ladle)	120.00	bowl/5" bowl base/8½" epergne vase)	325.00

PANELED GRAPE

	White, w/decorations		White, w/decorations
Epergne set, 3 pc. (14" flared bowl/5" bowl base/8½" epergne vase)	325.00	Salt and pepper, 4¼", small, ftd., pr.	22.50
Flower pot	47.50	*Salt and pepper, 4¼", small, ftd., pr.,	27.50
Fruit cocktail, 3½" w/6" sauce plate, bell shape	22.50	Salt and pepper, 4½", large, flat, pr.	52.50
Fruit cocktail, 4½" w/6" sauce plate, round	25.00	Sauce boat	30.00
Ivy ball	47.50	Sauce boat tray, 9"	30.00
Jardiniere, 5", cupped and ftd.	25.00	Saucer	8.50
Jardiniere, 5", straight sided	25.00	Sherbet, 3¾", low foot	16.00
Jardiniere, 6½", cupped and ftd.	35.00	Sherbet, 4¾", high foot	17.50
Jardiniere, 6½", straight sided	35.00	Soap dish	90.00
Jelly, 4½", covered	27.50	Stem, 2 oz. cordial or wine goblet	22.50
Ladle, small	10.00	Stem, 3 oz.	30.00
Ladle, punch	47.50	Stem, 5 oz., wine goblet	30.00
Lighter in 2 oz. goblet	30.00	Stem, 8 oz. water goblet	18.00
Lighter in tooth pick	33.00	Sugar w/cover, lacy edge on sugar to serve as spoon holder	32.50
Marmalade, w/ladle	57.50	Sugar, 6½"	14.00
Mayonnaise set, 3 pc. (round fruit cocktail/6" sauce plate/ladle)	35.00	Sugar, small w/cover	14.00
Mayonnaise, 4", ftd.	27.50	Tid-bit or snack server, 2 tier (dinner and breakfast plates)	65.00
Napkin ring	17.50	Tid-bit tray, metal handle on 8½" breakfast plate	27.50
Nappy, 4½", round	14.00	Tid-bit tray, metal handle on 10½" dinner plate	47.50
Nappy, 5", bell shape	22.00	Toothpick	24.00
Nappy, 5", round w/handle	30.00	Tray, 9", oval	45.00
Nappy, 7", round	30.00	Tray, 13½", oval	80.00
Nappy, 8½", round	30.00	Tumbler, 5 oz. juice	24.00
Nappy, 9", round, 2" high	40.00	Tumbler, 6 oz. old fashioned cocktail	27.50
Nappy, 10", bell	45.00	Tumbler, 8 oz.	22.50
Parfait, 6"	23.00	Tumbler, 12 oz. ice tea	25.00
Pedestal, base to punch bowl, skirted	140.00	Vase, 4", rose	20.00
Pickle, oval	21.00	Vase, 4½, rose, ftd., cupped, stemmed	35.00
Pitcher, 16 oz.	47.50	Vase, 6", bell shape	20.00
Pitcher, 32 oz.	37.50	Vase, 6½" or celery	35.00
Planter, 3" x 8½"	35.00	Vase, 8½", bell shape	25.00
Planter, 4½", square	40.00	Vase, 9", bell shape	25.00
Planter, 5" x 9"	38.00	Vase, 9", crimped top	32.00
Planter, 6", small, wall	75.00	Vase, 9½", straight	35.00
Planter, 8", large, wall	125.00	Vase, 10" bud (size may vary)	20.00
Plate, 6", bread	14.00	Vase, 11", rose (similar to bud vase but bulbous at bottom)	35.00
Plate, 7" salad, w/depressed center	25.00	Vase, 11½", bell shape	47.50
Plate, 8½", breakfast	22.00	Vase, 11½", straight	35.00
Plate, 10½", dinner	45.00	Vase, 12", hand blown	165.00
Plate, 14½"	120.00	Vase, 14", swung (size varies)	22.00
Plate, 18"	165.00	Vase, 15"	30.00
Puff box or jelly, w/cover	27.50	Vase, 16", swung (size varies)	22.00
Punch set, 15 pc. (13" bowl, 12 punch cups, pedestal and ladle)	595.00	Vase, 18", swung (size varies)	25.00
Punch set, 15 pc. (same as above w/11" bowl w/o scalloped bottom)	525.00		
Relish, 9", 3 part	40.00		

*All over pattern

"Panel Grape"

GIFT SUGGESTIONS TO PLEASE THE DISCRIMINATING

1881
Bowl, Crimp.

1881 Bowl,
Lip. Ftd.

1881 Bowl,
Shallow

1881
Basket, Hld.

1881
Bowl, Lip.

1881
Bowl, Oval

1881/6½"
Basket

1881
Appetizer Set

1881
Bowl, Bell

1881
Bowl, Rose

1881
Butter

1881
Bon Bon

3

FAMOUS *"Panel Grape"* THE COLLECTORS FAVORITE

1881 Plates, 14½", 10½" & 8½"

1881
3 pc. Canister Set

1881
Jug, Qt.

1881
Salver, Skirted

1881
Salver, Ftd.

1881 Snack Server

1881
Egg Tray

1881
Ice Tea

1881
Goblet

1881
Sauce Boat/Tray

1881
Mayonnaise

1881
Condiment Set

1881
Salt/Pepper,
Lg.

1881
Oil

1881
Salt/Pepper
(Min. 3 Sets)

1881
Candy

1881
Dish, 3 Ftd.

1881
Puff Box/
Jelly

1881
Chocolate Box

1881
Candy, Crimp.

1881
Pickle

1881
Starter Set

1881
Candlestick

1881
Mayo
Set

1881
Cup/Saucer

1881
Dish, Oval

4

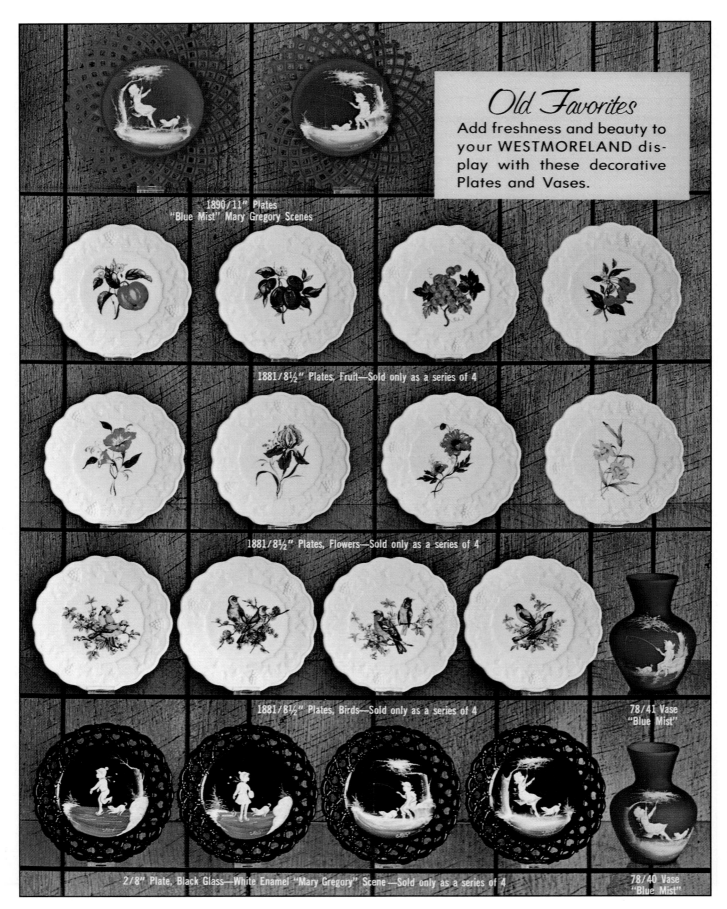

Old Favorites
Add freshness and beauty to your WESTMORELAND display with these decorative Plates and Vases.

1890/11" Plates
"Blue Mist" Mary Gregory Scenes

1881/8½" Plates, Fruit—Sold only as a series of 4

1881/8½" Plates, Flowers—Sold only as a series of 4

1881/8½" Plates, Birds—Sold only as a series of 4

78/41 Vase
"Blue Mist"

2/8" Plate, Black Glass—White Enamel "Mary Gregory" Scene—Sold only as a series of 4

78/40 Vase
"Blue Mist"

MGT0731
Plate, 14½"

MGT0730
Plate, 10½"

MGT0734
Sauce Boat

MGT0729
Plate, 8½"

MGT0737
Sugar & Cream, Small

MGT0724
Cup & Saucer

MGT0733
Salt & Pepper
Small, Height, 4¼"

MGT0721
Appetizer Set

MGT0726
Jug, 1 Qt.

MGT0725
Goblet

MGT0736
Sugar & Cream,
Large

MGT0722
Butter

MGT0732
Salt & Pepper
Large, Height, 4½"

MGT0739
Wine

MGT0738
Tid Bit Tray

Milk Glass Tableware

1881 Sauce Boat/Tray

1881 Goblet 8 oz.

1881 Sugar/Cream, Lg.

1881 Jug, Qt.

1881 Salt/Pepper

large

small

1881 Oil, 2 oz.

small

1881 Sugar/Cream

1881 Snack Server

1881 Tid Bit Tray

1881 Appetizer Set

1881 Marmalade W/Ladle

1881 Plate, 14½"

1881 Plate, 10½"

1881 Plate, 8½"

1881 Cheese

1881 Butter

1881 Cup/Saucer

109 Cookie Jar

29

...Kitchen & Table Accessories

Collector's items from the vast "Paneled Grape" pattern

1881/9"
Bowl, Sq.

1881/9"
Compote, Crimped

1881
Compote, Crimped

1881/7"
Compote

1881
Candy Jar

1881
Decanter

1881
Celery/Vase

1881
Dish, 3 Ftd.

1881
Chocolate Box

1881
Candleholder

1881
Cocktail, Fruit

1881
Cheese

1881/9"
Bowl, Bell

1881/¼ #
Butter

1881
Cup/Saucer

1881
Candle

1881
Dish

1881/12"
Bowl, Lipped

1881
Bowl, Banana

1881
Bowl, Oval Lpd.

PANELED GRAPE

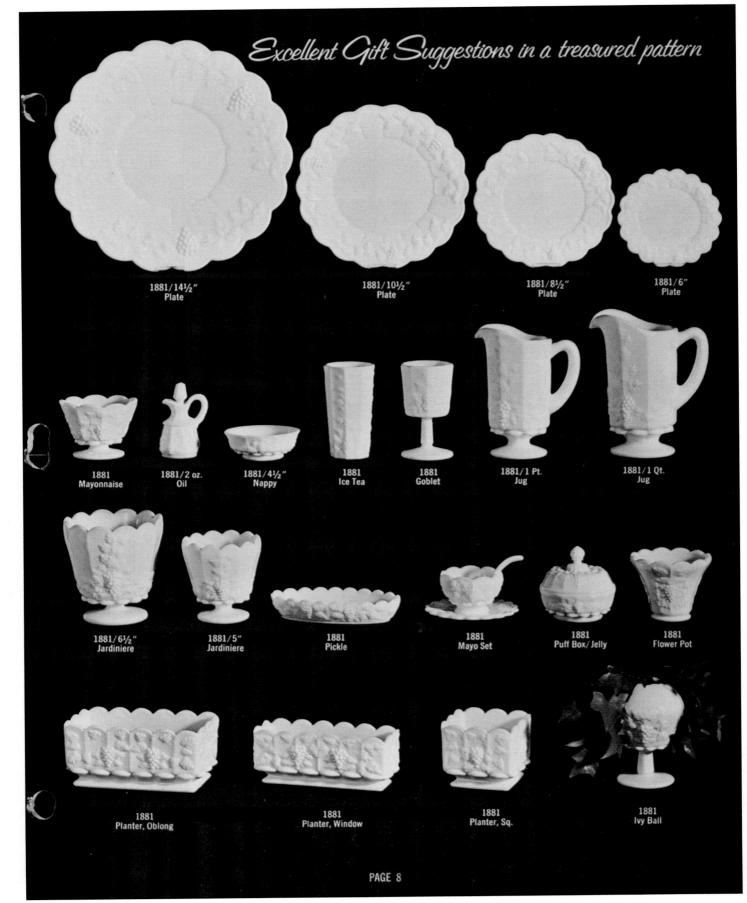

Excellent Gift Suggestions in a treasured pattern

1881/14½"
Plate

1881/10½"
Plate

1881/8½"
Plate

1881/6"
Plate

1881
Mayonnaise

1881/2 oz.
Oil

1881/4½"
Nappy

1881
Ice Tea

1881
Goblet

1881/1 Pt.
Jug

1881/1 Qt.
Jug

1881/6½"
Jardiniere

1881/5"
Jardiniere

1881
Pickle

1881
Mayo Set

1881
Puff Box/Jelly

1881
Flower Pot

1881
Planter, Oblong

1881
Planter, Window

1881
Planter, Sq.

1881
Ivy Ball

PAGE 8

194

Exquisite Reproductions from choice Originals

1881/15"
Vase

1881/2/11½"
Vase

1881/9"
Vase

1881/8½"
Vase

1881
Vase, Rose

1881
Vase, Blown

1881/18"
Vase

1881/6"
Vase

1881
Vase, Bud

1881
Sauce Boat/Tray

1881
Sugar/Cream

1881/1
Sugar/Cream

1881
Snack Server

1881/11"
Cake Salver

1881/10½"
Cake Salver

1881
Soap

1881
Salt/Pepper Set

1881
Wine

1881
Sherbet

1881
Sugar/Cream, Ind.

1881
Tumbler

1881
Toothpick

PAGE 9

PANELED GRAPE

FAMOUS PANELED GRAPE THE MILK GLASS COLLECTOR'S FAVORITE

1881
Decanter

1881
Jug, Pt.

1881
Jug, Qt.

1881
Dish, 3 Ftd.

1881/9"
Compote, Crimp.

1881/4½"
Compote, Crimp.

1881
Goblet

1881
Ice Tea

1881
Compote

1881
Candy

1881
Celery/Vase

1881
Flower Pot

1881
Candlestick

1881
Condiment Set

1881
Candy, Crimp.

1881
Canape Server

1881
Cheese

1881
Choc. Box

1881 Dish, Oval

1881 Wine

1881 Cup/Saucer

1881 Cocktail, Fruit

13

1881
15 Pc. Punch Set
(Ind. Boxed)

1881
Pickle

1881
Snack Server

1881
Sauce Boat/Tray

1881
Oil

1881
Salt/Pepper, Lg.

1881
Cake Salver
(Ind. Boxed)

1881
Planter, Obl.

1881
Puff Box/Jelly

1881
Salt/Pepper
(Packed 3 Sets Per Box)

1881
Mayonnaise

1881
Mayo Set

1881/10½″
Plate
14½″ Plate Also Available

1881/8½″
Plate

1881/6″
Plate

14

PANELED GRAPE

GIFT SUGGESTIONS TO PLEASE THE MOST DISCRIMINATING

1881/15"
Vase

1881/9"
Vase, Crimp.

1881/9"
Vase

1884/9"
Bowl, Fld.
(Ind. Boxed)

1881/6"
Vase

1881/8½"
Vase

1881
Vase, Bud

1881
Vase, Rose

1884/5"
Bowl, Fld.

1884/7"
Bowl, Sq.

1881
Sugar/Cream, Ind.

1881
Sugar/Cream

1881/1
Sugar/Cream

1881
Toothpick
(6 per box)

1884/6½"
Ash Tray

1884/5"
Ash Tray

1884/4"
Ash Tray

1884/4" Bowl, Sq.

15

PARK AVENUE, FEDERAL GLASS COMPANY, 1941 – early 1970s

Colors: amber, crystal, and crystal w/gold trim

Park Avenue's amber is being found infrequently as you can see by my one piece in the photo below. Gold-trimmed items are difficult to find with a strong gold decoration. Gold wears off easily since it is a very soft 22K. I just returned from a Depression glassware show in Sanford, Florida, where a couple of Park Avenue items were brought in for me to identify. Evidently, this line was distributed in the central Florida area. I found the bowl with the wire hanging vases in this area.

The Federal Glass Company trademark F within a shield is embossed on the bottom of most of the pieces. No Park Avenue pitchers, per se, were made as far as catalog records indicate. Star pitchers shown on page 230 were distributed with tumblers from this set.

The small whisky tumbler in Park Avenue may be found with jelly labels still affixed to them. Peach preserves were enclosed in the one pictured. Evidently, these small tumblers were used as samples or perhaps for jelly containers in gift sets.

All pieces listed were made into the early 1960s except the whisky glass that was in production until the early 1970s. The catalogue uses the British spelling of whisky without the "e," so I kept it. This pattern is one of the smaller sized sets shown in this book, and would make an ideal introductory pattern for someone wishing to keep expenses down.

	Amber/Crystal
Ash tray, 3½", square	5.00
Ash tray, 4½", square	7.00
Bowl, 5", dessert	5.00
Bowl, 8½", vegetable	12.00
Candleholder, 5"	15.00
Tumbler, 2⅛", 1¼ oz., whisky	4.00
Tumbler, 3½", 4½ oz., juice	5.00
Tumbler, 3⅞", 9 oz.	6.00
Tumbler, 4¾", 10 oz.	7.00
Tumbler, 5⅛", 12 oz., iced tea	9.00

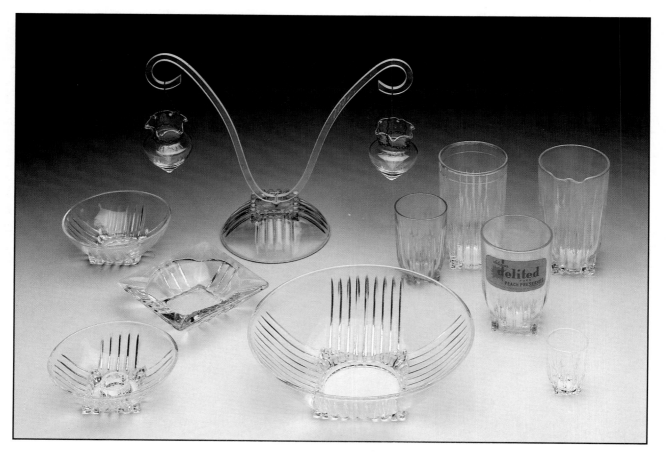

Please refer to Foreword for pricing information

PRESSED TUMBLERS

Matching lines . . . such as the famed Park Avenue on this page, or the Star Line on the next . . . new, unusual shapes, and standard staples, are shown here in Federal's selection of pressed tumblers. All are designed and engineered for eye-appeal, serviceability, and good value.

PARK AVENUE

TUMBLERS

1122 — 1¼ oz.
PARK AVENUE WHISKY
Ht. 2⅛"
Pkd. 12 doz. ctn. Wt. 16 lbs.

1122 — 4½ oz.
PARK AVENUE JUICE TUMBLER
Ht. 3½"
Pkd. 12 doz. ctn. Wt. 35 lbs.

1122 — 9 oz.
PARK AVENUE TUMBLER
Ht. 3⅞"
Pkd. 12 doz. ctn. Wt. 56 lbs.

1142 — 10 oz.
PARK AVENUE TUMBLER*
Ht. 4¾"
Pkd. 6 doz. ctn. Wt. 37 lbs.

1122 — 12 oz.
PARK AVENUE ICED TEA
Ht. 5⅛"
Pkd. 6 doz. ctn. Wt. 43 lbs.

*CK 1142—10 oz. PARK AVENUE TUMBLER IN CARRY-KITS
are available factory-packed: 6 tumblers to each
Carry-Kit, 12 kits to ctn. Wt. 40 lbs.

Own PRELUDE and be envied ... give PRELUDE and be proud

Choose Viking's beautifully etched Prelude pattern
for your home and your important gift-giving. See your
favorite good store's exciting display.
See the stemware especially.

VIKING
HAND MADE
Treasured American Glass

Hand made by
VIKING GLASS COMPANY
NEW MARTINSVILLE, WEST VIRGINIA

PRELUDE, NEW MARTINSVILLE & VIKING GLASS COMPANY, mid 1930s – 1950s

Color: Crystal

Originally introduced under the auspices of the New Martinsville Glass Company, Prelude production was continued by the Viking Glass Company when they took over the New Martinsville Glass factory in 1943. I have included a few pages from an early 1950s Viking Glass catalog. There are fewer records being found for the New Martinsville Prelude than for the Viking issues. You may notice that some pieces of Prelude are similar, but contrarily shaped. I believe the fancier edged pieces were New Martinsville and that the similar item made at Viking was less detailed to accommodate faster production! Let me know what you find that is not listed here.

Bonbon, 6", hdld.	18.00
Bonbon, 6", 3 ftd.	20.00
Bowl, 7", cupped	25.00
Bowl, 8", crimped	35.00
Bowl, 8", 3 part, shrimp	60.00
Bowl, 9", 3 ftd., crimped	50.00
Bowl, 9½", crimped, ftd.	50.00
Bowl, 10", crimped	45.00
Bowl, 10", 3 ftd.	40.00
Bowl, 10", shallow	35.00
Bowl, 10½', nut, center hdld.	37.50
Bowl, 11", 3 ftd.	50.00
Bowl, 12½", crimped	50.00
Bowl, 13", oval	42.00
Bowl, 13", shallow	45.00
Bowl, 15", 3 ftd.	70.00
Butter dish, 6½", oval w/cover	37.50
Butter dish, 8½", oval w/cover	32.50
Cake salver, 11", 5½" high	55.00
Cake salver, 11" w/metal base	50.00
Candlestick, 4",	17.50
Candlestick, 4½",	20.00
Candlestick, 5", double	32.00
Candlestick, 5½",	25.00
Candlestick, 6", double	38.00
Candy box, 6", w/cover, closed knob	60.00
Candy box, 6½", w/cover, open knob	65.00
Candy box, 7", w/cover, 3 ftd.	65.00
Celery, 10½"	30.00
Cocktail shaker, w/metal lid	175.00
Compote, cheese	15.00
Compote, 5½" diameter, 3" high	30.00
Compote, 6"	22.00
Compote, 7", crimped	32.00
Compote, 7½", flared	32.00
Creamer	12.50
Creamer, 4 ftd.	15.00
Creamer, individual	12.00
Cup	25.00
Ensemble set, 13" bowl w/candle holder	135.00
Ensemble set, 13" bowl w/flower epergne	150.00
Lazy susan, 18", 3 pc. set	150.00
Mayonnaise, 3 pc.	35.00
Mayonnaise, divided, 4 pc.	40.00
Nappy w/pc, 6" for candle	40.00
Oil bottle, 4 oz.	50.00

Pitcher, 78 oz.	235.00
Plate, 6", bread & butter	6.00
Plate, 6½", hdld.	12.50
Plate, 6½", lemon, 3 ftd.	12.50
Plate, 7"	8.00
Plate, 7", lemon, 3 ftd.	13.50
Plate, 8", salad	10.00
Plate, 9"	22.50
Plate, 10", dinner	37.50
Plate, 10", 3 ftd.	22.00
Plate, 11"	27.00
Plate, 11", 3 ftd., cake	35.00
Plate, 11", cracker	22.50
Plate, 13", hdld.	40.00
Plate, 14", flat or turned up edge	45.00
Plate, 16"	75.00
Plate, 16", 3 ftd.	65.00
Plate, 18"	75.00
Platter, 14½"	60.00
Relish, 6", 2 part	15.00
Relish, 6", 2 part, hdld.	15.00
Relish, 7", 2 part, hdld.	15.00
Relish, 7", 3 part, hdld.	15.00
Relish, 10", 3 part, hdld.	30.00
Relish, 13", 5 part	35.00
Salt and pepper, 3½" pr., 2 styles	40.00
Saucer	5.00

Stem, 1 oz., cordial	40.00
Stem, 1 oz., cordial, ball stem	42.50
Stem, 3 oz., wine	22.00
Stem, 3 oz., wine, ball stem	25.00
Stem, 3½ oz., cocktail	15.00
Stem, 4 oz., cocktail, ball stem	15.00
Stem, 6 oz., low sherbet	12.00
Stem, 6 oz., sherbet, ball stem	12.00
Stem, 6 oz., tall sherbet	15.00
Stem, 9 oz., water	25.00
Sugar	12.50
Sugar, 4 ftd.	15.00
Sugar, individual	12.00
Tid bit, 2 tier, chrome hdld.	40.00
Tray, 11", center handled	35.00
Tray, ind. cr./sug	10.00
Treasure jar, 8", w/cover	90.00
Tumbler, 5 oz., ftd. juice	16.00
Tumbler, 5 oz., juice, ball stem	17.50
Tumbler, 10 oz., water, ball stem	20.00
Tumbler, 12 oz., ftd. tea	20.00
Tumbler, 13 oz., tea, ball stem	25.00
Vase, 8"	40.00
Vase, 10", bud	30.00
Vase, 10", crimped	65.00
Vase, 11", crimped	70.00
Vase, 11", ftd.	75.00

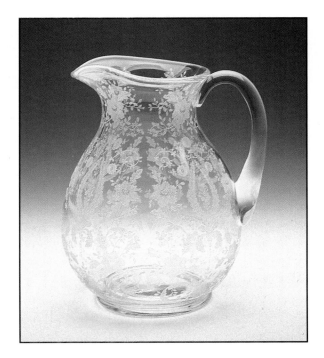

Prelude Etching

Magnificent expression of the designer's art in glass that is timeless and "right", with more than a touch of class.

5201
13" Bowl

5217
14" Plate

5287
13" 5-pt. Relish

7539
8" Vase

5226
11" Cake Salver

5223
13" 2-hdl. Plate

5238
10" 3-pt. Relish

13
Salt & Pepper

5247
Cream & Sugar

5217
14" RE. PLATE

5226
11" CAKE SALVER

13
3½" SALT & PEPPER
W/CHROME TOP

5249
CELERY TRAY

5247
SUGAR & CREAM

5201
SHALLOW BOWL

1010
LEMON PLATE

1091
3 TOED PLATE

1009
BONBON

7539
8" VASE

5287
OVAL RELISH

1003
10" CRIMPED BOWL

"PRETZEL," NO. 622 INDIANA GLASS COMPANY, late 1930s – 1980s

Colors: Crystal, teal, and avocado with recent issues in amber and blue

Indiana's No. 622 is better known by its collectors' name, "Pretzel." I have finally found juice and ice tea tumblers which can be seen in the photograph at the bottom of page 207. Actually, I also found a water tumbler, but after the photography was completed; now, all I need to locate is a pitcher to complete the set! The 4½" fruit cup is being found on a 6" plate that has a 1¼" tab handle.

A few ardent collectors are beginning to seek non-decorated "Pretzel." Have you seen any teal "Pretzel"? If so, I would like to know what you have found. The cup previously pictured is still the only piece that I have seen!

The photograph on page 207 shows fruit centered pieces, frosted crystal, and a green astrological bowl. Fruit embossed pieces of "Pretzel" are selling for 25% – 50% more than plain centered pieces. Astrological bowls are selling in the $3.00 to $6.00 range although some have been bought for as little as a quarter! Sets of 12 have been seen for as little as $25.00 and as highly priced as $75.00. Presumably, these were a special order or promotional ploy. Notice the Jack Daniel's whiskey advertisement pictured below. I have been told that bars used these for peanuts or chips.

One reader reported finding a calendar plate with "Pretzel" design around the sides. No picture was enclosed; so, I don't know more. If you have one, please send some details. Other dated pieces are being found which seem to indicate that Indiana also recommended this line for special events.

	Crystal		Crystal
Bowl, 4½", fruit cup	4.50	Plate, 7¼", square, indent 3-part	9.00
Bowl, 7½", soup	10.00	Plate, 8⅜", salad	6.00
Bowl, 9⅜", berry	18.00	Plate, 9⅜", dinner	10.00
Celery, 10¼", tray	1.50	Plate, 11½", sandwich	11.00
Creamer	4.50	**Saucer	1.00
* Cup	6.00	Sugar	4.50
Olive, 7", leaf shape	5.00	Tumbler, 5 oz., 3½"	40.00
Pickle, 8½", two hndl.	5.50	Tumbler, 9 oz., 4½"	35.00
Pitcher, 39 oz.	235.00	Tumbler, 12 oz., 5½"	60.00
Plate, 6"	2.50		
Plate, 6", tab hndl.	3.00	* Teal - $125.00	
Plate, 7¼", square, indent	9.00	** Teal - $35.00	

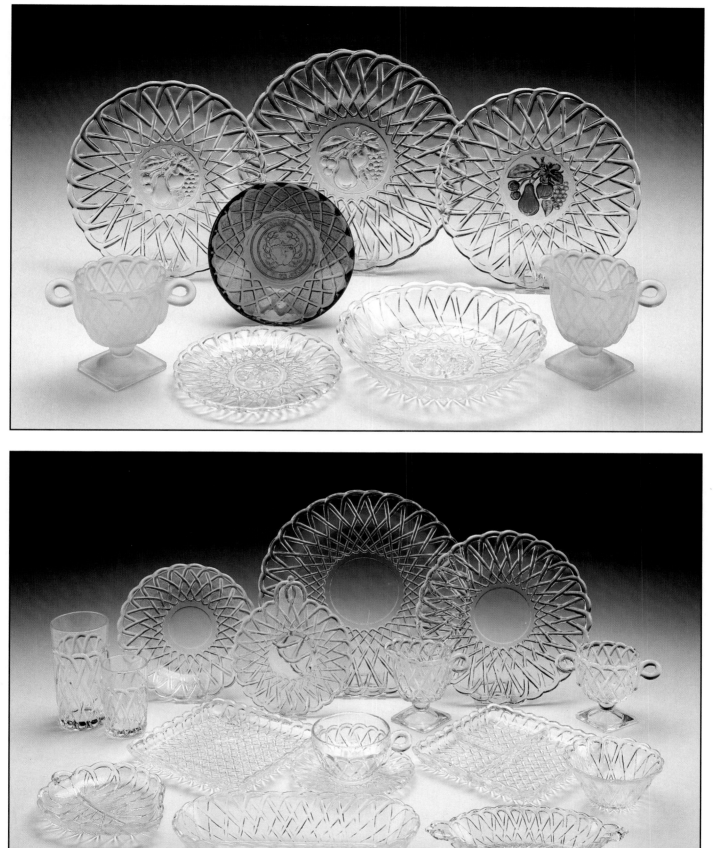

ROMANCE ETCHING #341, FOSTORIA GLASS COMPANY, 1942 – 1986

Color: crystal

Romance is often confused with Fostoria's June because of the "bow" in the design; be sure to compare the shapes of Romance to June which is found on the Fairfax blank. Romance is also a thicker, heavier glassware than the more delicate June. Since Romance is only found in crystal, the only confusion occurs with crystal June. By default, all Fostoria's colored pieces having a bow are June.

There are drastic regional pricing differences for Romance. Several dealers told me they couldn't give it away, while others considered it to sell as well for them as June. Using a few dealers' contributions for pricing information, I received as diverse a range of appraisals for Romance as for any pattern in this book! Remember, this pricing is to be taken only as a guide. You alone, must decide what any piece is worth — to you!

	Crystal		Crystal
Ash tray, 2⅝", indiv., #2364	12.50	Plate, 11", sandwich, #2364	37.50
Bowl, 6", baked apple #2364	15.00	Plate, 11¼", cracker, #2364	25.00
Bowl, 8", soup, rimmed, #2364	90.00	Plate, 14", torte, #2364	50.00
Bowl, 9", salad, #2364	37.50	Plate, 16", torte, #2364	90.00
Bowl, 9¼", ftd. blown, #6023	125.00	Plate, crescent salad, #2364	42.50
Bowl, 10", 2 hdld, #2594	45.00	Relish, 8", pickle, #2364	22.50
Bowl, 10½", salad, #2364	45.00	Relish, 10", 3 pt., #2364	25.00
Bowl, 11", shallow, oblong, #2596	47.50	Relish, 11", celery, #2364	27.50
Bowl, 12", ftd. #2364	55.00	Salt & pepper, 2⅝", pr., #2364	55.00
Bowl, 12", lily pond, #2364	45.00	Saucer, #2350	5.00
Bowl, 13", fruit, #2364	50.00	Stem, 3⅞", ¾ oz., cordial, #6017	42.50
Bowl, 13½", hdld., oval, #2594	55.00	Stem, 4½", 6 oz., low sherbet, #6017	15.00
Candlestick, 4", #2324	20.00	Stem, 4⅞", 3½ oz., cocktail, #6017	21.50
Candlestick, 5", #2596	27.00	Stem, 5½", 3 oz., wine, #6017	35.00
Candlestick, 5½", #2594	30.00	Stem, 5½", 6 oz., champagne, #6017	17.50
Candlestick, 5½", 2 lite, #6023	35.00	Stem, 5⅞", 4 oz., claret, #6017	35.00
Candlestick, 8", 3 lite, #2594	50.00	Stem, 7⅜", 9 oz., goblet, #6017	25.00
Candy w/lid, rnd., blown, #2364	95.00	Sugar, 3⅛", ftd., #2350½	16.50
Cigarette holder, 2", blown, #2364	37.50	Tray, 11⅛", ctr. hdld., #2364	32.50
Comport, 3¼", cheese, #2364	22.50	Tumbler, 3⅝", 4 oz., ftd., oyster cocktail, #6017	20.00
Comport, 5", #6030	22.50	Tumbler, 4¾", 5 oz., ftd., #6017	17.50
Comport, 8", #2364	40.00	Tumbler, 5½", 9 oz., ftd., #6017	21.00
Creamer, 3¼", ftd., #2350½	17.50	Tumbler, 6", 12 oz., ftd., #6017	27.50
Cup, ftd., #2350½	20.00	Vase, 5", #4121	40.00
Ice tub, 4¾", #4132	70.00	Vase, 6", ftd. bud, #6021	40.00
Ladle, mayonnaise, #2364	5.00	Vase, 6", ftd., #4143	55.00
Mayonnaise, 5", #2364	22.50	Vase, 6", grnd. bottom, #2619½	55.00
Pitcher, 8⅞", 53 oz., ftd., #6011	295.00	Vase, 7½", ftd., #4143	65.00
Plate, 6", #2337	8.00	Vase, 7½", grnd. bottom, #2619½	70.00
Plate, 6¾", mayonnaise liner, #2364	15.00	Vase, 9½", grnd. bottom, #2619½	95.00
Plate, 7", #2337	10.00	Vase, 10", #2614	85.00
Plate, 8", #2337	15.00	Vase, 10", ftd., #2470	105.00
Plate, 9", #2337	47.50		

ROYAL RUBY, ANCHOR HOCKING GLASS COMPANY, 1938 – 1960s; 1977

Color: Royal Ruby

Royal Ruby is the Anchor Hocking name for their red color. Only red glassware produced by Hocking or Anchor Hocking can be called by the patented name Royal Ruby. A sticker was attached to each red piece designating it as Royal Ruby, no matter what pattern it was. Red "Bubble" or Charm did not mean anything but Royal Ruby to the factory. So, if you find a red piece that belongs to some other Hocking pattern, do not be shocked by a Royal Ruby sticker.

Actual production of Royal Ruby was begun in 1938, but what most collectors recognize as Royal Ruby was made after 1940. A Royal Ruby section in my thirteenth edition of *Collector's Encyclopedia of Depression Glass* covers the pieces made in the late 1930s. Royal Ruby will continue to be shown in both books since it can be divided into pre-1940 and post 1940 eras.

I found an Anchor Hocking advertising page that shows the 6⅛"x4" "card holder" was cataloged as a cigarette box and sold with four Royal Ruby ash trays. The lid is Royal Ruby on a divided crystal bottom. It is one of the difficult pieces to find in Royal Ruby. The two styles of quart water bottles pictured at the bottom of page 211 are the most difficult pieces to find in this pattern. Note that the hard-to-find lids are the same. Bottles without a lid fetch about $75.00, but are hard to sell. What is hard to comprehend is that the lids themselves will not bring $150.00, but put them together and you can sell the completed bottle for $225.00. The mathematical rule about sum of its parts does not always work with glassware. Oval vegetable bowls remain elusive. Other items in short supply are the punch bowl base and the salad bowl with 13¾" underliner.

There are two styles of sherbets which seem to confuse new collectors. The non-stemmed version is shown in front of the stemmed sherbet on page 211.

Royal Ruby Charm became simply Royal Ruby after 1951 catalogs. Look under Charm for those pieces in Royal Ruby. That upright pitcher has been turning up more frequently than in the past. I am seeing reduced prices on it in many markets. At $45.00 you could not keep them in stock a few years ago, but at $35.00 there are few buyers now.

Also listed are the crystal stems with Royal Ruby tops called "Boopie" by collectors as well as the stems that go with Royal Ruby "Bubble." See a complete explanation under "Bubble" on page 16.

There were six or seven sizes of beer bottles made for Schlitz Beer Company in '49, '50, or '63. The date of manufacture is embossed on the bottom of each bottle. I have finally pictured a 7 ounce bottle with the Schlitz label still attached; and last week, I received a picture of a 12 ounce throw-away with an Old Milwaukee label. Millions of these bottles were made, but labeled ones are not often found. Bottle collectors find these more attractive than Royal Ruby collectors and prices are usually higher at bottle shows than at glass shows. The quart size is the most commonly seen. I do not consider these dinnerware items, although some beer drinkers do!

	Red		Red
Ash tray, 4½", leaf	5.00	Punch bowl base	37.50
Beer bottle, 7 oz.	20.00	Punch cup, 5 oz.	3.00
Beer bottle, 12 oz.	25.00	Saucer, round	2.50
Beer bottle, 16 oz.	35.00	Sherbet, ftd.	8.00
Beer bottle, 32 oz.	37.50	Sherbet, stemmed, 6½ oz.	8.00
Bowl, 4¼", round, fruit	5.50	*Stem, 3½ oz., cocktail	10.00
Bowl, 5¼", popcorn	13.00	*Stem, 4 oz., juice	10.00
Bowl, 7½", round, soup	12.50	Stem, 4½ oz., cocktail	10.00
Bowl, 8", oval, vegetable	30.00	Stem, 5½ oz., juice	12.50
Bowl, 8½", round, large berry	17.50	Stem, 6 oz., sherbet	8.00
Bowl, 10", deep, popcorn (same as punch)	40.00	*Stem, 6 oz., sherbet	8.00
Bowl, 11½", salad	33.00	*Stem, 9 oz., goblet	14.00
Cigarette box/"card holder," 6⅛" x 4"	60.00	Stem, 9½ oz., goblet	13.00
Creamer, flat	8.00	*Stem, 14 oz., iced tea	20.00
Creamer, ftd.	9.00	Sugar, flat	8.00
Cup, round	6.00	Sugar, ftd.	7.50
Goblet, ball stem	11.00	Sugar, lid	10.00
Ice bucket	35.00	Tumbler, 2½ oz., ftd. wine	14.00
Lamp	35.00	Tumbler, 3½ oz., cocktail	12.50
Pitcher, 3 qt., tilted	35.00	Tumbler, 5 oz., juice, ftd. or flat	7.50
Pitcher, 3 qt., upright	40.00	Tumbler, 9 oz., water	6.50
Pitcher, 42 oz., tilted or straight	30.00	Tumbler, 10 oz., 5", water, ftd.	6.50
Plate, 6¼", sherbet, round	4.00	Tumbler, 12 oz., 6" ftd., tea	15.00
Plate, 7", salad	5.00	Tumbler, 13 oz., iced tea	13.00
Plate, 7¾", salad, round	6.00	Vase, 4", ivy, ball-shaped	6.00
Plate, 9⅛", dinner, round	11.00	Vase, 6⅜", two styles	9.00
Plate, 13¾"	25.00	Vase, 9", two styles	17.50
Punch bowl	40.00	Water bottle (two styles)	225.00

* "Boopie"

SANDWICH COLORS, ANCHOR HOCKING GLASS COMPANY, 1939 – 1964

Colors: Desert Gold, 1961 – 1964; Forest Green, 1956 – 1960s; pink, 1939 – 1940; Royal Ruby, 1938 – 1939; White/Ivory (opaque), 1957 – 1960s

Forest Green Sandwich continues its pricing increases except for those five little pieces that were packed in Crystal Wedding Oats. Everyone ate hot oats; so there are realistically thousands of those five pieces (4⁵⁄₁₆" bowl, custard cup, custard liner, water and juice tumblers) available today. Prices for other Forest Green pieces have risen due to scarcity and demand! Demand is the key word! All known pieces of Forest Green are shown in the photograph. The rolled edge custard cup shown in the front has never been reported in any quantity. It may be more rare than the pitchers!

Pitchers in Forest Green are scarce. Everyone obtained the juice and water tumblers free in oats as explained above. Juice and water sets were offered for sale with a pitcher and six tumblers. Everyone already had more than enough tumblers, so they would not buy the complete sets. Most of these sets were returned to Anchor Hocking unsold.

Forest Green Sandwich sugar or cookie jar lids have never been found. Anchor Hocking employees remembered selling topless cookie jars as vases. They must have had a successful marketing promotion with them because so many are seen today!

I just had a report of a large pitcher selling to a dealer for the price listed below. It is the highest price I've heard of one selling; but if it were purchased for resale, I wonder at what it will be offered?

Even new collectors seem to be attracted to the green. Perhaps Forest Green Sandwich appears more desirable than plain Forest Green, although that has numerous fans! Dinner plates in Forest Green Sandwich are selling in the $100.00 range and this price does not seem to send collectors scurrying to do anything except buy them. I sell all I can find!

Cups are more available than saucers; therefore, the price of saucers is beginning to catch up to the price of cups.

I have priced Royal Ruby Sandwich here, but it is also found in *The Collector's Encyclopedia of Depression Glass* in the Royal Ruby section of that book.

I had thought only bowls were made in pink. A very light pink pitcher was found a few years ago. It is not a vivid pink, but none of the pink is! This pitcher is pictured in the *Very Rare Glassware of the Depression Years, Fifth Edition*.

Amber Sandwich is beginning to be noticed by a few new collectors. However, not even experienced glass hunters are finding footed amber tumblers. The rest of the set can be obtained with some work. That flashed-on blue cup and saucer may have been a special order and there should be other colors. I have not seen other Anchor Hocking patterns with this treatment.

Ivory punch sets were first offered in 1957, in plain and trimmed in 22K gold. There is little price distinction today; that set trimmed in gold seems to be less in demand because the gold has a tendency to wear when used! In 1964 Marathon gas stations in Ohio and Kentucky sold Ivory (with gold trim) punch bowl sets for $2.89 with an oil change and lubrication.

	Desert Gold	Royal Ruby	Forest Green	Pink	Ivory/White
Bowl, 4⁵⁄₁₆", smooth			3.50		
Bowl, 4⅞", smooth	3.00	16.00		4.00	
Bowl, 5¼", scalloped	6.00	20.00			
Bowl, 5¼", smooth				7.00	
Bowl, 6½", smooth	6.00				
Bowl, 6½", scalloped		27.50	45.00		
Bowl, 6¾", cereal	12.00				
Bowl, 7⅝", salad			60.00		
Bowl, 8¼", scalloped		40.00	75.00	17.50	
Bowl, 9", salad	30.00				
Cookie jar and cover	37.50		*17.50		
Creamer			30.00		
Cup, tea or coffee	3.50		20.00		
Custard cup			1.50		
Custard cup, crimped			25.00		
Custard cup liner			1.50		
Pitcher, 6", juice			165.00	225.00	
Pitcher, ½ gal., ice lip			450.00		
Plate, 9", dinner	9.00		110.00		
Plate, 12", sandwich	15.00				
Punch bowl, 9¾"					15.00
Punch bowl stand					15.00
Punch cup					2.00
Saucer	3.00		17.50		
Sugar, no cover			27.50		
Tumbler, 3⁹⁄₁₆", 5 oz., juice			4.00		
Tumbler, 9 oz., water			5.00		
Tumbler, 9 oz., footed	250.00				

* no cover

Please refer to Foreword for pricing information

SANDWICH CRYSTAL ANCHOR HOCKING GLASS COMPANY, 1939 – 1964; 1977

Color: Crystal, 1940 – 1960s

I have separated the crystal Anchor Hocking Sandwich from the colors to facilitate writing about each.

All four sizes of tumblers are shown in the top photograph on page 215. The footed tumbler has never been easy to find, but the 3⅜", 3 ounce juice is missing in many collections. I have been informed by several advanced collectors that this juice is not being offered for sale in any of the antique publications. I took a dozen of these juices to a show in the Midwest last year and a dealer who specializes in Anchor Hocking wares bought them. She informed me that she had never seen these!

Another recently discovered piece is the scalloped top, 6½" cereal bowl shown next to the regular cereal in the bottom photograph. A group of four were found in Ohio. Apparently, these scalloped edge pieces were a special order or a trial issue. This goes along with the scalloped-rim plate shown as a pattern shot below! The scalloped cereals have each sold for $125.00.

I might point out that the salad bowl that was listed at 9" in the catalogs is really the same bowl as the 9¾" punch bowl which is another reason why the punch bowl stands are harder to find than the punch bowls.

Other crystal pieces that are seldom found are the regular cereal, 5" crimped dessert bowl, and unblemished dinner plates. That 5" crimped dessert listed by Anchor Hocking only measures 4⅞" in most cases. Mould variation makes size listings a major problem! Both this and the crimped sherbets are listed as occasional Sandwich pieces only in the 1956 catalog. "Crimped" is their word used to describe these pieces. Listings for only one year means pieces in short supply today.

Collecting Anchor Hocking's Sandwich continues to flourish while Indiana's Sandwich does not do as well. Hocking went to some trouble to maintain the collectability of their older glassware; however, Indiana did not. Prices continue to increase in this popular Hocking pattern. In fact, Sandwich may be the most accumulated crystal pattern in this book except for Iris.

Remember that Anchor Hocking reintroduced a crystal cookie jar in the late 1970s that was larger than the old. For a comparison of these cookie jars see measurements below. The newer one sold in the $15.00 range. These are beginning to be seen in quantities at flea markets and even antique malls.

Pieces in short supply continue to be found, but demand keeps absorbing these. Cups, saucers, and 8" plates were premiums for buying $3.00 (about ten gallons) of gas at Marathon stations in 1964. The promotion took four weeks for cups and saucers and the next four weeks for the plates. You could have gotten the crystal punch bowl set for only $2.89 with an oil change and lube! Ah, the "good old days"! Most of these crystal punch sets were gold trimmed as were the Ivory ones.

COOKIE JARS	NEW	OLD
Height	10¼"	9¾"
Opening width	5½"	4⅞"
Circumference/largest part	22"	19"

	Crystal
Bowl, 4⁵⁄₁₆", smooth	5.00
Bowl, 4⅞"/5", crimped dessert	17.00
Bowl, 4⅞", smooth	6.00
Bowl, 5¼", scalloped	7.50
Bowl, 6½", smooth	7.50
Bowl, 6½", scalloped, deep	7.50
Bowl, 6¾", cereal	35.00
Bowl, 7", salad	7.00
Bowl, 7⅝", scalloped	8.00
Bowl, 8¼", scalloped	10.00
Bowl, 8¼", oval	7.00
Bowl, 9", salad	23.00
Butter dish, low	45.00
Butter dish bottom	25.00
Butter dish top	20.00
Cookie jar and cover	40.00
Creamer	6.00
Cup, tea or coffee	2.50
Custard cup	3.50
Custard cup, crimped, 5 oz.	13.00
Custard cup liner	17.50
Pitcher, 6", juice	65.00
Pitcher, ½ gal., ice lip	85.00
Plate, 7", dessert	11.00
Plate, 8"	4.00
Plate, 9", dinner	20.00
Plate, 9", indent for punch cup	5.00
Plate, 12", sandwich	14.00
Punch bowl, 9¾"	20.00
Punch bowl stand	30.00
Punch cup	2.25
Saucer	1.50
Sherbet, footed	8.00
Sugar	8.50

	Crystal
Sugar cover	15.00
Tumbler, 3⅜", 3 oz., juice	16.00
Tumbler, 3⁹⁄₁₆", 5 oz., juice	6.50
Tumbler, 9 oz., water	8.00
Tumbler, 9 oz., footed	30.00

Please refer to Foreword for pricing information

SANDWICH, INDIANA GLASS COMPANY, 1920s – 1980s

Colors: crystal late 1920s – 1980s; teal blue 1950s – 1980s; milk white, mid 1950s; amber, late 1920s – 1980s;
    Red, 1933/1969 – early 1970s; Smokey Blue, 1976 – 1977

Indiana's Sandwich pattern is adored by a few collectors, Cathy's friend among them. Still, many dealers and collectors avoid it due to this company's tendency in the past for reissuing glass patterns. This procedure never allows the older glassware to attain the status that other companies' glassware has. Pink and green Sandwich is priced in the twelfth edition of *Collector's Encyclopedia of Depression Glass* since they were made in the 1930s; and although green (now called Chantilly) has been made again, it is a different shade than the original. Perhaps they're learning from past errors. The older green will glow under an ultraviolet (black) light if you have one available! Chantilly green was made in dinnerware sets whereas the originally green was made only in occasional pieces. No dinner plates, cups, saucers, creamers, sugars, or water goblets were made in green until the 1980s!

Tiara Exclusives took over Sandwich from Indiana with an issue of red in 1969, amber in 1970, and crystal in 1978. Amber, Chantilly green, and crystal were made into the late 1980s.

Basically, the list below incorporates the original Sandwich line from the 1920s and the original Tiara listings from the late 1960s and early 1970s. Eventually, I may add all the Tiara listings throughout the 1970s and 1980s, but only if they become desirable. So far, I've seen little evidence of this. Some ex-Tiara dealers want you believe it is collectible. I've been told they are experiencing some difficulty unloading unwanted stock from the home party plans!

The mould for the old wine broke and a new one was designed. All the wines made in the last few years are fatter (like Iris cocktails) than the earlier ones that were shaped like Iris wines. These older wines are 4½" tall and hold 3 oz. The newer wines are shown in Tiara catalogs, but no measurements or capacities are given.

Teal blue and milk glass (white) are colors issued in the 1950s; but Tiara remade a teal butter dish as an exclusive hostess gift that unconditionally destroyed the $200.00 price tag on the 1950s butter dish. This new Tiara one originally sold for approximately $15.00. "New" Sandwich has been touted to prospective customers as glass that's going to be valuable based on its past performance; but the company is steadily undermining the collectability of the older glassware by selling new glass copies!

Six items in red Sandwich date from 1933, i.e., cups, saucers, luncheon plates, water goblets, creamers, and sugars. Many of these pieces are inscribed 1933 Chicago World's Fair. In 1969, Tiara Home Products produced red pitchers, 9 oz. goblets, cups, saucers, wines, wine decanters, 13" serving trays, creamers, sugars, salad, and dinner plates. There is virtually no difference in pricing unless you have some red Sandwich marked 1933 Chicago World's Fair. This older, marked glass will bring more due to its being a World's Fair collectible.

Amber and crystal prices are shown, but you must realize that most of the crystal and all the amber have been made since 1970. Prices below reflect the small amounts of these colors that I see at flea markets and malls.

	Amber Crystal	Teal Blue	Red		Amber Crystal	Teal Blue	Red
Ash trays (club, spade, heart, dmd. shapes, ea.)	3.50			Goblet, 9 oz.	13.00		45.00
Basket, 10", high	32.50			Mayonnaise, ftd.	13.00		
Bowl, 4¼", berry	3.50			Pitcher, 68 oz.	22.50		165.00
Bowl, 6"	4.00			Plate, 6", sherbet	3.00	7.00	
Bowl, 6", hexagonal	5.00	14.00		Plate, 7", bread and butter	4.00		
Bowl, 8½"	11.00			Plate, 8", oval, indent for sherbet		6.00	12.00
Bowl, 9", console	16.00			Plate, 8⅜", luncheon	5.00		20.00
Bowl, 11½", console	19.00			Plate, 10½", dinner	8.00		
Butter dish and cover, domed	22.50	*155.00		Plate, 13", sandwich	13.00	25.00	35.00
Butter dish bottom	6.00	42.50		Puff box	16.50		
Butter dish top	16.50	112.50		Salt and pepper, pr.	16.50		
Candlesticks, 3½", pr.	17.50			Sandwich server, center handle	18.00		47.50
Candlesticks 7", pr.	25.00			Saucer	2.25	6.00	7.00
Creamer	9.00		45.00	Sherbet, 3¼"	5.50	12.00	
Celery, 10½"	16.00			Sugar, large	9.00		45.00
Creamer and sugar on diamond shaped tray	16.00	32.00		Sugar lid for large size	13.00		
				Tumbler, 3 oz., footed cocktail	7.50		
Cruet, 6½ oz. and stopper		135.00		Tumbler, 8 oz., footed water	9.00		
Cup	3.50	8.00	27.50	Tumbler, 12 oz., footed tea	10.00		
Decanter and stopper	22.50		85.00	Wine, 3", 4 oz.	6.00		12.50

*Beware recent vintage sells for $25.00

SHELL PINK MILK GLASS, JEANNETTE GLASS CO., 1957 – 1959

Color: opaque pink

Those skyrocketing increases in prices for Shell Pink have slowed in the last two years. Yet, all pieces that were expensive have gotten even more so with all the new collectors searching for the pattern. The Lazy Susan and heavy bottomed, National vases are continuing to outdistance other pieces in price. This popular Jeannette pattern was made for only a short period in the late 1950s. It was called Shell Pink and included pieces from several popular Jeannette lines. It was marketed as "a delicate coloring that blends perfectly with all kinds of flowers. Its smooth satiny finish goes all the way through the glass — is not a spray or surface coating."

The quotations above are from a four page catalog from Jeannette. These pages also state "Shell Pink Milk Glass' lovely color and design make women admire it — and buy it!" Today, there may be as many male collectors searching for this colored glassware as women. My grammar dictionary on the computer now frowns upon gender specific references; so it may balk at this paragraph! It talked back when I used "lady," and I thought that was a complimentary term!

There are a couple of rarely seen Shell Pink pieces at the bottom of page 221. By the time you read this the advertising ash tray will be in the collection of the nuclear engineer who lent me Shell Pink for my photographs. The bird candle holder evidently was sold for a short time with the three-footed pheasant bowl. I assume the tail feathers were a problem and this mould was discontinued. The Anniversary cake plate has ferreted out no others to date. There are also Anniversary pin-up vases being found, but I haven't run across one to photograph.

The 9" heavy bottomed, National vase is shown in the back next to the oval, footed, Lombardi bowl at the top of page 219. The bowl was to be used with a pair of double candle holders like the one shown in front of it. These bowls are found plain or with a design inside. The plain one is found most often as you can tell by the price! Also pictured on the left are the covered wedding bowls. The honey jar is easy to spot with its beehive shape. No one could mistake the butterfly ash tray and cigarette box or the eagle candle, pheasant footed bowl, or the cookie jar. That cigarette box with the butterfly finial is rather hard to find in mint condition. The price below is for mint condition butterfly boxes. The compote in the back is Windsor and the open candy in front of it is Floragold. The only item not covered is the Venetian tray, which is 16½" and can't be missed because of its sheer size.

That Harp tray and cake stand at the bottom of page 219 are seen more often in crystal. The large, three-footed bowl is Holiday pattern; but the footed oval bowl on the left was called Florentine even though it has a similar pattern to Holiday. The Gondola fruit bowl by Jeannette is the long, handled bowl in front. The powder jar, sugar, creamer, and 7" vase round out that photograph.

A Vineyard 12" relish is pictured in the top photo on page 220. A three-part celery and relish tray is shown in the rear of that photo. All other pieces should be self-evident.

The punch set is shown at the bottom of page 220. Speaking of the punch bowl reminds me that the original ladle was pink plastic and not crystal. Cups for the punch set were the same as those used for the snack sets shown at the top of the page. "Hostess" snack sets were rather expensive at the time. A set of four was $1.75. These were a new fad for the TV trays in vogue then.

The elusive Lazy Susan is shown in the top photo on page 221; the base is the part that is almost non-existent, but original ball bearings to turn the trays are not easily found either. Some collectors have bought Dewdrop Lazy Susans just to get the ball bearings for their Shell Pink set. The Lazy Susan was packed one to a pink gift box similar to the blue one shown under Dewdrop on page 56. That photograph also shows the pieces made for "Napco Ceramics, Cleveland, Ohio." Each piece is marked thus with numbers (quoted in the price list) except for the piece with a sawtooth edge in the back that only has "Napco, Cleveland." The piece at left front is the candy bottom of a pattern Jeannette called National. It is a new pattern shown on pages 170 – 171. This Shell Pink candy bottom was promoted as a vase. The cake plate in the back is Anniversary. The reverse side is shown at the bottom of the page so you can see the pattern.

	Opaque Pink		Opaque Pink
Ash tray, butterfly shape	17.50	"Napco" #2255, ftd. bowl w/saw tooth top	25.00
Base, for lazy susan, w/ball bearings	150.00	"Napco" #2256, square comport	12.50
Bowl, 6½", wedding, w/cover	22.50	"National" candy bottom	10.00
Bowl, 8", Pheasant, ftd.	37.50	Pitcher, 24 oz., ftd., Thumbprint	27.50
Bowl, 8", wedding, w/cover	27.50	Powder jar, 4¾", w/cover	45.00
Bowl, 9", ftd., fruit stand, Floragold	25.00	Punch base, 3½", tall	35.00
Bowl, 10", Florentine, ftd.	27.50	Punch bowl, 7½ qt.	60.00
Bowl, 10½", ftd., Holiday	42.50	Punch cup, 5 oz. (also fits snack tray)	6.00
Bowl, 10⅞", 4 ftd., Lombardi, designed center	42.00	Punch ladle, pink plastic	20.00
Bowl, 10⅞", 4 ftd., Lombardi, plain center	27.00	Punch set, 15 pc. (bowl, base, 12 cups, ladle)	185.00
Bowl, 17½", Gondola fruit	40.00	Relish, 12", 4 part, octagonal, Vineyard design	40.00
Cake plate, Anniversary	195.00	Stem, 5 oz., sherbet, Thumbprint	10.00
Cake stand, 10", Harp	45.00	Stem, 8 oz., water goblet, Thumbprint	12.50
Candle holder, 2 light, pr.	37.50	Sugar cover	14.00
Candle holder, Eagle, 3 ftd., pr.	85.00	Sugar, ftd., Baltimore Pear design	11.00
Candy dish w/cover, 6½" high, square	30.00	Tray, 7¾" x 10", snack w/cup indent	9.00
Candy dish, 4 ftd., 5¼", Floragold	20.00	Tray, 12½" x 9¾", 2 hndl., Harp	60.00
Candy jar, 5½", 4 ftd., w/cover, grapes	20.00	Tray, 13½", lazy susan, 5 part	40.00
Celery and relish, 12½", 3 part	45.00	Tray, 15¾", 5 part, 2 hndl.	65.00
Cigarette box, butterfly finial	200.00	Tray, 16½", 6 part, Venetian	35.00
Compote, 6", Windsor	20.00	Tray, lazy susan complete w/base	190.00
Cookie jar w/cover, 6½" high	90.00	Tumbler, 5 oz., juice, ftd., Thumbprint	8.00
Creamer, Baltimore Pear design	15.00	Vase, 5", cornucopia	15.00
Honey jar, beehive shape, notched cover	40.00	Vase, 7"	35.00
"Napco" #2249, cross hatch design pot	15.00	Vase, 9", heavy bottom, National	95.00
"Napco" #2250, ftd. bowl w/berries	15.00		

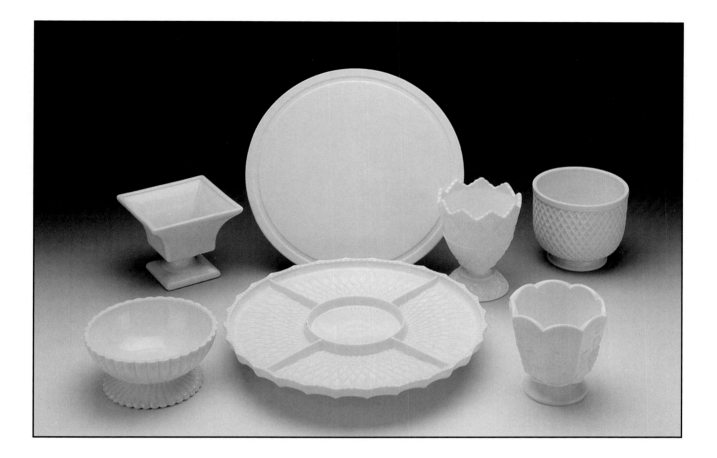

SILVER CREST, FENTON ART GLASS COMPANY, 1943 – present

Color: white with crystal edge

Silver Crest continues to be one of Fenton's longest production patterns. Every time they have discontinued it, requests force them to reissue. There are ways to help date your pieces. Before 1958, the white was called opal and had an opalescence to it when held up to the light. In 1958, a formula change to milk glass made the glass look very white without "fire" in the white. Any pieces reintroduced after 1973 will be signed Fenton. Fenton began signing carnival pieces in 1971, and in 1973 they continued this practice with all pieces. If you run into items that have white edging outside the crystal, this was called Crystal Crest and dates from 1942.

The pitcher, punch bowl set, and the hurricane lamps are very troublesome to acquire, but deliriously welcomed when found regardless of the price. Tumbler prices are edging upward; latch on to a few before they become exorbitantly expensive also. As with Emerald Crest, you will find several styles of tid-bits using bowls and plates or a combination of both.

A rarely seen Silver Crest shaker is pictured in the *Very Rare Glassware of the Depression Years, Fifth Edition*. This shaker was supposed to be Spanish Lace, but the overlay pattern was not applied, leaving it Silver Crest!

Some pieces of Silver Crest have two different line numbers. Originally, this line was #36 and all pieces carried that designation. In July 1952, Fenton began issuing a Ware Number for each piece. That is why you see two different numbers for some of the items below.

See page 60 for prices on Emerald Crest. Aqua Crest has a blue edge and prices run between those of Silver Crest and Emerald Crest.

	White		White
Basket, 5" hndl., (top hat) #1924	40.00	Candle holder, low, ruffled, pr. #7271	22.00
Basket, 5", hndl. #680	40.00	Candle holder, ruffled comport style, pr. #7272	55.00
Basket, 6½", hndl. #7336	40.00	Candy box #7280	70.00
Basket, 7" #7237	35.00	Candy box, ftd., tall stem #7274	120.00
Basket, 12" #7234	65.00	Chip and dip (low bowl w/mayo in center) #7303	65.00
Basket, 13" #7233	85.00	Comport, ftd. #7228	11.00
Basket, hndl. #7339	65.00	Comport, ftd., low #7329	18.00
Bon bon, 5½" #7225	12.00	Creamer, reeded hndl. #680	16.00
Bon bon, 8" #7428	12.00	Creamer, reeded hndl. (same as #680) #7201	16.00
Bonbon, 5½" #36	12.00	Creamer, ruffled top	50.00
Bowl, 5½", soup #680	35.00	Creamer, straight side #1924	32.50
Bowl, 5", finger or deep dessert #680	27.50	Creamer, threaded hndl. #680	17.50
Bowl, 7" #7227	18.00	Cup, reeded hndl. #680, #7209	22.50
Bowl, 8½" #7338	32.50	Cup, threaded look hndl. #680	22.50
Bowl, 8½" flared #680	32.50	Epergne set, 2 pc. (vase in ftd. bowl) #7202	55.00
Bowl, 9½" #682	46.00	Epergne set, 3 pc. #7200	125.00
Bowl, 10" #7224	46.00	Epergne set, 6 pc. #1522/951	125.00
Bowl, 10" salad #680	46.00	Epergne, 2 pc. set #7301	77.50
Bowl, 11" #5823	46.00	Epergne, 4 pc. bowl w/3 horn epergnes #7308	125.00
Bowl, 13" #7223	46.00	Epergne, 5 pc. bowl w/4 horn epergnes #7305	135.00
Bowl, 14" #7323	46.00	Lamp, hurricane #7398	175.00
Bowl, banana, high ft. w/upturned sides #7324	75.00	Mayonnaise bowl #7203	11.00
Bowl, banana, low ftd. #5824	60.00	Mayonnaise ladle #7203	5.00
Bowl, deep dessert #7221	32.50	Mayonnaise liner #7203	27.50
Bowl, dessert, shallow #680	32.50	Mayonnaise set, 3 pc. #7203	45.00
Bowl, finger or dessert #202	18.00	Nut, ftd. #7229	10.00
Bowl, ftd., (like large, tall comport) #7427	67.50	Nut, ftd. (flattened sherbet) #680	10.00
Bowl, ftd., tall, square #7330	67.50	Oil bottle #680	80.00
Bowl, low dessert #7222	26.00	Pitcher, 70 oz. jug #7467	185.00
Bowl, shallow #7316	46.00	Plate, 5½" #680	6.00
Cake plate, 13" high, ftd. #7213	50.00	Plate, 5½", finger bowl liner #7218	6.00
Cake plate, low ftd. #5813	40.00	Plate, 6" #680	6.50
Candle holder, 6" tall w/crest on bottom, pr. #7474	75.00	Plate, 6½" #680, #7219	14.00
Candle holder, bulbous base, pr. #1523	30.00	Plate, 8½" #680, #7217	27.50
Candle holder, cornucopia, pr. #951	60.00	Plate, 10" #680	37.50
Candle holder, cornucopia (same as #951), pr. #7274	57.50	Plate, 10½" #7210	37.50
		Plate, 11½" #7212	37.50
Candle holder, flat saucer base, pr. #680	25.00	Plate, 12" #680	47.50
		Plate, 12" #682	47.50

Please refer to Foreword for pricing information

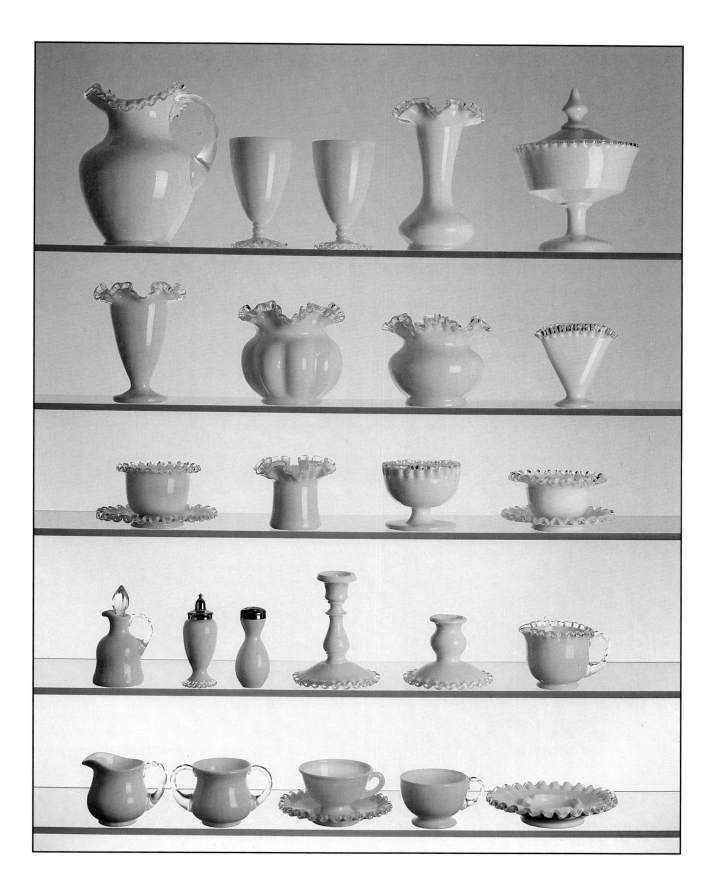

SILVER CREST (cont.)

	White
Plate, 12½" #7211	50.00
Plate, 16", torte 7216	60.00
Punch bowl #7306	275.00
Punch bowl base #7306	85.00
Punch cup #7306	13.50
Punch ladle (clear) #7306	22.50
Punch set, 15 pc. #7306	550.00
Relish, divided #7334	32.50
Relish, heart, hndl. #7333	22.50
Saucer #680, #7209	5.00
Shaker, pr. #7206	110.00
Shaker, pr (bowling pin shape)	150.00
Sherbert #680	10.00
Sherbet #7226	10.00
Sugar, reeded hndl. #680	17.50
Sugar, reeded hndl. (same as #680) #7201	17.50
Sugar, ruffled top	45.00
Sugar, sans hndls. #680	32.50
Tid-bit, 2 tier (luncheon/dessert plates) #7296	47.50
Tid-bit, 2 tier (luncheon/dinner plates) #7294	47.50
Tid-bit, 2 tier plates #680	47.50
Tid-bit, 2 tier, ruffled bowl #7394	75.00
Tid-bit, 3 tier (luncheon/dinner/dessert plates) #7295	47.50

	White
Tid-bit, 3 tier plates #680	47.50
Tid-bit, 3 tier, ruffled bowl #7397	85.00
Top hat, 5" #1924	47.50
Tray, sandwich #7291	27.50
Tumbler, ftd. #7342	57.50
Vase, 4½" #203	11.00
Vase, 4½" #7254	11.00
Vase, 4½", double crimped #36, #7354	11.00
Vase, 4½", fan #36	11.00
Vase, 5" (top hat) #1924	50.00
Vase, 6" #7451	16.00
Vase, 6", doubled crimped #7156	19.00
Vase, 6¼", double crimped #36, #7356	17.50
Vase, 6¼", fan #36	17.50
Vase, 7" #7455	17.50
Vase, 8" #7453	17.50
Vase, 8", bulbous base #186	50.00
Vase, 8", doubled crimped #7258	22.00
Vase, 8", wheat #5859	42.50
Vase, 8½" #7458	47.50
Vase, 9" #7454	47.50
Vase, 9" #7459	47.50
Vase, 10" #7450	115.00
Vase, 12" (fan topped) #7262	110.00

SQUARE, NO. 3797, CAMBRIDGE GLASS COMPANY, 1952 – mid 1950s

Colors: crystal, some red and black

Cambridge Square was first pictured in the 1949 Cambridge catalog, but was listed as "patent pending." You may find Square pieces with "patent pending" labels. In the past I pictured a cordial with such a sticker. This is one of the few patterns made by Cambridge that wholly falls into the time span of this book.

You can see a punch bowl set pictured at bottom of page 228. I sold it and the collector was very ecstatic at buying it for its $250.00 price!

A few pieces of Square were made in color (Carmen and Ebony); however, some Ruby (Imperial name) pieces were also made at Imperial in the late 1960s. Carmen pieces by Cambridge are rarely seen, but the red (Ruby) from Imperial can be found with some work. Four red pieces are pictured on the bottom of 227. The crackle tumbler shown on the right of the top photograph (page 227) sells for $55.00. There were several sizes of Square tumblers made in crackle.

	Crystal		Crystal
Ash tray, 3½" #3797/151	8.00	Plate, 9½", tidbit #3797/24	20.00
Ash tray, 6½" #3797/150	11.00	Plate, 11½" #3797/26	25.00
Bon bon, 7" #3797/164	13.50	Plate, 13½" #3797/28	30.00
Bon bon, 8" #3797/47	24.00	Relish, 6½", 2 part #3797/120	17.50
Bowl, 4½", dessert #3797/16	11.00	Relish, 8", 3 part #3797/125	22.50
Bowl, 6½", individual salad #3797/27	13.50	Relish, 10", 3 part #3797/126	25.00
Bowl, 9", salad #3797/49	22.50	Salt and pepper, pr. #3797/76	22.50
Bowl, 10", oval #3797/48	25.00	Saucer, coffee #3797/17	5.00
Bowl, 10", shallow #3797/81	30.00	Saucer, tea #3797/15	5.00
Bowl, 11", salad #3797/57	40.00	Stem, #3798, 5 oz., juice	10.00
Bowl, 12", oval #3797/65	30.00	Stem, #3798, 12 oz., iced tea	12.00
Bowl, 12", shallow #3797/82	35.00	Stem, #3798, cocktail	17.50
Buffet set, 4 pc. (plate, div. bowl, 2 ladles)		Stem, #3798, cordial	25.00
#3797/29	50.00	Stem, #3798, sherbet	11.00
Candle holder, 1¾", block #3797/492, pr.	25.00	Stem, #3798, water goblet	12.00
Candle holder, 2¾", block #3797/493, pr.	27.50	Stem, #3798, wine	20.00
Candle holder, 3¾", block #3797/495, pr.	27.50	Sugar #3797/41	10.00
Candle holder, cupped #3797/67, pr.	27.50	Sugar, individual #3797/40	10.00
Candy box and cover #3797/165	30.00	Tray, 8", oval, for individual sug/cr #3797/37	17.50
Celery, 11" #3797/103	23.00	Tumbler, #3797, 5 oz., juice	12.50
Comport, 6" #3797/54	25.00	Tumbler, #3797, 14 oz., iced tea	17.50
Creamer #3797/41	10.00	Tumbler, #3797, low cocktail	12.00
Creamer, individual #3797/40	10.00	Tumbler, #3797, low cordial	20.00
Cup, coffee, open handle #3797/17	10.00	Tumbler, #3797, low sherbet	10.00
Cup, tea, open handle #3797/15	10.00	Tumbler, #3797, low wine	15.00
Decanter, 32 oz. #3797/85	90.00	Tumbler, #3797, water goblet	13.50
Ice tub, 7½" #3797/34	35.00	Vase, 5", belled #3797/92	22.50
Icer, cocktail w/liner #3797/18	35.00	Vase, 5½", belled #3797/91	25.00
Lamp, hurricane, 2 pc. #3797/68	45.00	Vase, 6" #3797/90	22.50
Mayonnaise set, 3 pc. (bowl, plate, ladle)		Vase, 7½", ftd. #3797/77	22.50
#3797/129	30.00	Vase, 7½", rose bowl #3797/35	35.00
Oil bottle, 4½ oz. #3797/100	22.00	Vase, 8", ftd. #3797/80	20.00
Plate, 6", bread and butter #3797/20	8.00	Vase, 9½", ftd. #3797/78	27.50
Plate, 7", dessert or salad #3797/23	12.00	Vase, 9½", rose bowl #3797/36	45.00
Plate, 7", salad #3797/27	11.00	Vase, 11", ftd. #3797/79	40.00
Plate, 9½", dinner or luncheon #3797/25	28.00		

STAR, FEDERAL GLASS COMPANY, 1950s

Colors: amber, crystal, and crystal w/gold trim

Federal's Star pattern caused me to have to respond to several letters due to an omission in the last book. There was a creamer and sugar pictured, but not priced. Sorry! Apparently, I did not have a copy of the transparency in front of me as I wrote due to a multitude of dumb reasons that are not worth listing! At the time pricing was done, the photos were being separated or copied or whatever. Then, when proofing the final book, pictures were on bluelines; everything is blue and hard to see. Generally, I tried to see if the proper pattern was pictured rather than checking all pieces against the price listing. In any case, that omission is now corrected.

Amber Star is found in two different shades not unlike Hocking's Princess pattern. Most Star I have seen is yellow, but there are darker, more amber pieces found.

Although there were few pieces made, you can put together a set inexpensively. Notice the "star" shaped design on each piece. Cathy remembers pitchers marketed with small colored soaps for the bath. Pitchers were also sold with Park Avenue tumblers.

Note the frosted, decorated juice pitcher in the photo below. These pitchers (with several designs) are found with matching tumblers. Watch for a similar pitcher matching the red trimmed, Mountain Flowers Petalware (Depression glass book). The one I saw was frosted, but not for sale. I would like to find one to photograph!

That whisky tumbler is pictured with two different labels indicating jelly was contained in them. Does anyone remember if these were samples or individual servings?

	Amber/Crystal		Amber/Crystal
Bowl, 4⅝", dessert	4.00	Plate, 9⅜", dinner	5.00
Bowl, 8⅜", vegetable	10.00	Sugar	5.00
Creamer	8.00	Sugar lid	5.00
Pitcher, 5¾", 36 oz., juice	9.00	Tumbler, 2¼", 1½ oz., whisky	3.00
Pitcher, 7", 60 oz.	12.00	Tumbler, 3⅜" 4½ oz., juice	4.00
Pitcher, 9¼", 85 oz., ice lip	15.00	Tumbler, 3⅞", 9 oz., water	5.50
Plate, 6³⁄₁₆" salad	3.00	Tumbler, 5⅛", 12 oz., iced tea	8.00

STAR

1123 — 1½ oz.
STAR WHISKY
Ht. 2¼"
Pkd. 12 doz. ctn. Wt. 17 lbs.

1123 — 4½ oz.
STAR JUICE TUMBLER
Ht. 3⅜"
Pkd. 12 doz. ctn. Wt. 37 lbs.

1123 — 9 oz.
STAR TUMBLER
Ht. 3⅞"
Pkd. 12 doz. ctn. Wt. 56 lbs.

1123 — 12 oz.
STAR ICED TEA
Ht. 5⅛"
Pkd. 6 doz. ctn. Wt. 42 lbs.

2844 — 36 oz.
STAR JUICE JUG
Ht. 5¾"
Pkd. 2 doz. ctn. Wt. 37 lbs.

(Also available — 2845-60 oz. JUG
Ht. 7" Pkd. 1 doz. ctn. Wt. 26 lbs.)

2846 — 85 oz.
STAR ICE LIP JUG
Ht. 9¼"
Pkd. 1 doz. ctn. Wt. 38 lbs.

1116 — 5 oz.
PANEL JUICE TUMBLER
Ht. 3⅜"
Pkd. 12 doz. ctn. Wt. 38 lbs.

1116 — 9 oz.
PANEL TUMBLER
Ht. 4"
Pkd. 12 doz. ctn. Wt. 59 lbs.

1116 — 12 oz.
PANEL ICED TEA
Ht. 5⅜"
Pkd. 6 doz. ctn. Wt. 43 lbs.

1131 — 9 oz.
CATHEDRAL TUMBLER
Ht. 4"
Pkd. 12 doz. ctn. Wt. 58 lbs.

STARS and STRIPES, ANCHOR HOCKING GLASS GLASS COMPANY, 1942

Color: crystal

I considered retiring Stars and Stripes from the book, but there are some ardent fans who would utter unprintable expressions to me! While writing the first edition of *Collectible Glassware of the 40s, 50s, 60s...*, we were in the middle of Desert Storm and the 40s Stars and Stripes seemed to fit the nationalistic passion of the time. When penning the second, we dropped bombs on Iraq again. Russia was bomb dropping while working on the third. As I compose this fourth, the world seems much quieter. May it continue!

I had been questioned about this little pattern for years. Most collectors seemed to think that these pieces were Queen Mary; but this catalog page proved conclusively that it was a completely separate pattern called Stars and Stripes. Tumblers seem to be almost non-existent while sherbets are fairly common. Plates cost twice as much as other pieces originally; that has certainly changed in today's market.

	Crystal
Plate, 8"	14.00
Sherbet	15.00
Tumbler, 5", 10 oz.	35.00

SWANKY SWIGS, 1930s – 1950s

Swanky Swigs were originally sold with a Kraft cheese product in them. Pictured here are the Swigs marketed from the late 1930s into the 1950s with a collectible 1976 Bicentennial also displayed. Smaller size glasses (3¼") and the larger (4½") seem to have been distributed only in Canada. The limited availability of these sizes in the States makes their prices increase more than those regularly found! Tulip No. 2 only turns up on the West Coast and prices are a little less there. Earlier Swanky Swigs can be found in *The Collector's Encyclopedia of Depression Glass* if you become hooked on collecting these. Some original lids from these tumblers are shown on page 236. The two jars on row 2 of page 233 are store display Swankys (painted to look full of cheese). Lids fetch $5.00 up depending upon condition and the advertisement! Those with Kraft caramels, Miracle Whip, and TV show ads run $10.00 up. The most sought lid is pictured at the bottom of page 235. Bing is a popular guy and his Swanky lid will fetch $15.00 to 20.00 depending upon condition!

Page 233:

Row 1: Tulip No. 1

black, blue, red, green	3½"	3.00 – 4.00
black w/label	3½"	10.00 – 12.00
Blue, red, green	4½"	15.00 – 17.50
green	3¼"	15.00 – 17.50

Row 2: Tulip No. 3

lt. blue, yellow display jars	3¾"	25.00 – 30.00
lt. blue, red, yellow	3¾"	2.50 – 3.50
lt. blue, yellow	3¼"	15.00 – 17.50
red	4½"	15.00 – 17.50

Cornflower No. 1

lt. blue	4½"	15.00 – 17.50
lt. blue	3½"	4.00 – 5.00
lt. blue	3¼"	15.00 – 17.50

Row 3: Tulip No. 2

black, green, red	3½"	27.50 – 30.00
Carnival blue, green, red, yellow	3½"	5.00 – 7.00

Tulip No. 3

dk. blue	4½"	15.00 – 17.50
dk. blue	3¾"	2.50 – 3.50
Dk. blue	3¼"	15.00 – 17.50

Row 4: Posy Jonquil

yellow	4½"	17.50 – 20.00
yellow	3½"	5.00 – 6.00
yellow	3¼"	17.50 – 20.00

Posy: Tulip

red	4½"	15.00 – 17.50
red	3½"	4.00 – 5.00
red	3¼"	15.00 – 17.50

Posy: Violet

purple	4½"	17.50 – 20.00
purple	3½"	5.00 – 6.00
purple	3¼"	15.00 – 17.50

Row 5: Cornflower No. 2

dk. blue, lt. blue, red, yellow	3½"	2.50 – 3.50
dk. blue, lt. blue, yellow	3¼"	15.00 – 17.50

Forget-Me-Not

dk. blue,	3½"	2.50 – 3.50
dk. blue or yellow w/label		
(yel p 220)	3½"	10.00 – 12.50
dk. blue	3¼"	15.00 – 17.50

Page 234:

Row 1: Forget-Me-Not

lt. blue, red, yellow	3½"	2.50 – 3.50
lt. blue, red, yellow	3¼"	15.00 – 17.50

Daisy

red & white	3¾"	25.00 – 30.00
red & white	3¼"	35.00 – 40.00

Rows 2 – 5: Daisy

red, white & green	4½"	15.00 – 17.50
red, white & green	3¾"	2.00 – 3.00
red, white & green	3¼"	15.00 – 17.50

Bustling Betsy:

all colors	3¼"	15.00 – 17.50
all colors	3¾"	4.00 – 5.00

Antique Pattern:

all designs	3¼"	15.00 – 17.50
all designs	3¾"	4.00 – 500

clock & coal scuttle brown;
lamp & kettle blue;
coffee grinder & plate green;
spinning wheel & bellows red;
coffee pot & trivet black;
churn & cradle orange

Kiddie Cup:

all designs	4½"	20.00 – 25.00
	3¾"	4.00 – 5.00
	3¼"	15.00 – 17.50

bird & elephant red;
bear & pig blue;
squirrel & deer brown;
duck & horse black;
dog & rooster orange,
cat and rabbit green

bird & elephant w/label	3¾"	10.00 – 12.50
dog & rooster **w/cheese**	3¾"	25.00 – 30.00

Bicentennial issued in 1975;

yellow, red, green	3¾"	3.00 – 5.00

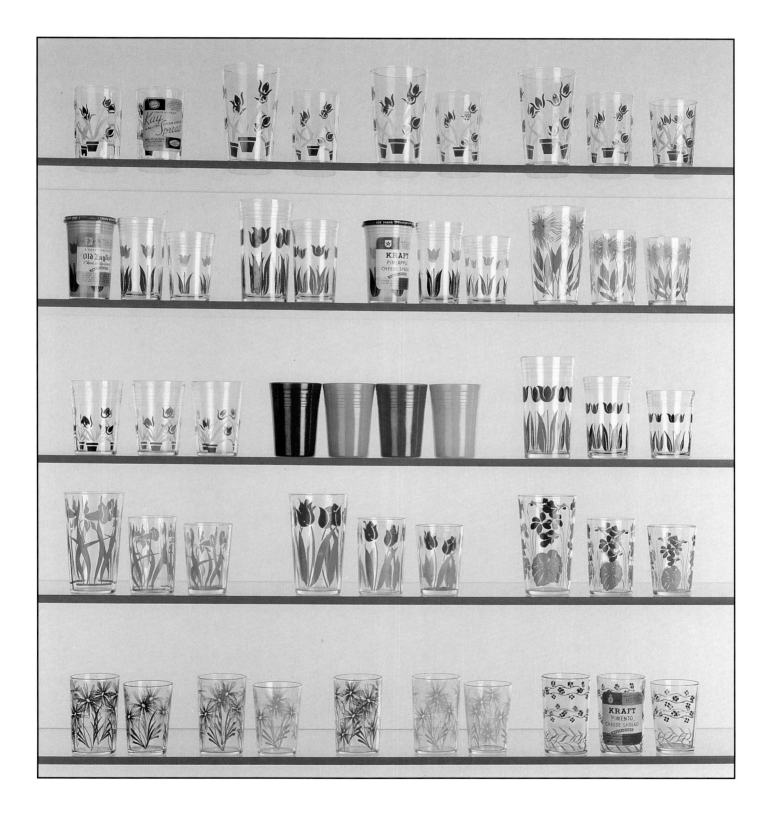

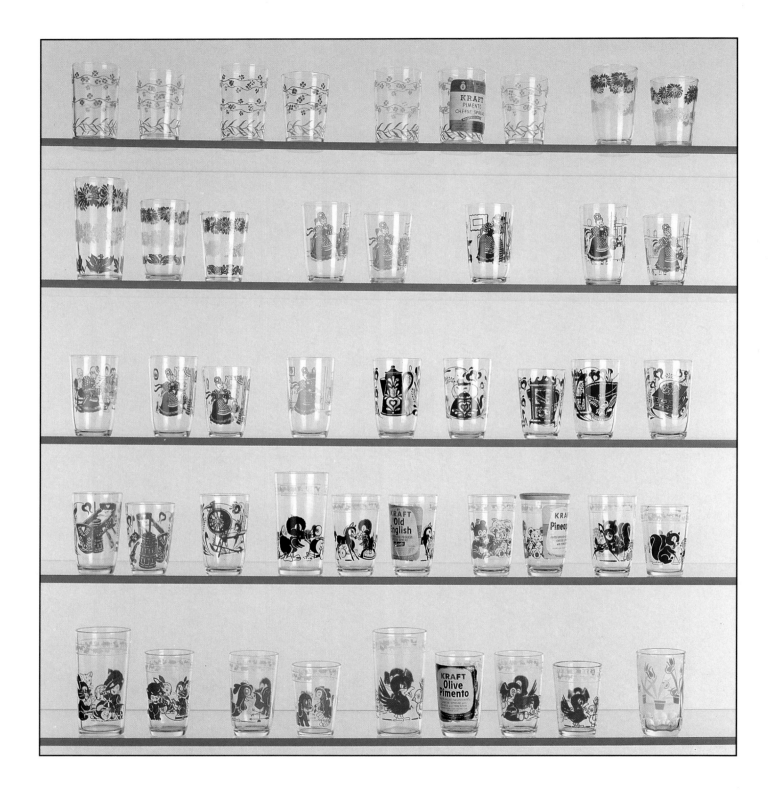

YORKTOWN, FEDERAL GLASS COMPANY, mid 1950s

Colors: crystal, white, and amber

Federal's Yorktown was a contemporary of Heritage and Golden Glory, but distribution of Yorktown seems to have outdistanced those two patterns combined. Since I was slated to write about this pattern today, I decided to see how many pieces I could see at the Webster, Florida, flea market this morning as an exercise in its availability in this area. I saw 11 different pieces. Considering I left a little after eight, and dealers were still unpacking, I felt encouraged that a set could be gathered within a short time if you really pursued it. Crystal is all I saw today, although there is enough amber around to collect a set. I am pricing both colors the same for now based strictly upon what I have paid or seen priced. Personally, I have not paid any more for amber than crystal; time will tell if there is to be a difference.

	Crystal/amber		Crystal/amber
Bowl, 5½", berry #2905	3.50	Plate, 11½" #2904	8.50
Bowl, 9½", large berry #2906	10.00	Punch set, 7 qt., base, 12 cups	40.00
Bowl, 10", ftd., fruit #2902	17.50	Saucer #2911	.50
Celery tray, 10" #2907	9.00	Sherbet, 2½", 7 oz. #1744	3.00
Creamer #2908	4.00	Sugar w/lid #2909	7.50
Cup #2910	3.00	Tumbler, 3⅞", 6 oz., juice #1741	4.00
Cup, snack/punch, 6 oz.	2.00	Tumbler, 4¾", 10 oz., water #1742	5.50
Mug, 5 1/16"	15.00	Tumbler, 5¼", 13 oz., iced tea #1743	7.00
Plate, 8¼" #2903	4.00	Vase, 8"	15.00
Plate, 10½" x 6¾", snack w/indent	3.00		

Please refer to Foreword for pricing information

A Publication I recommend:

DEPRESSION GLASS **DAZE**

THE ORIGINAL NATIONAL DEPRESSION GLASS NEWSPAPER

Depression Glass Daze, the original, national monthly newspaper dedicated to the buying, selling and collecting of colored glassware of the 20s and 30s. We average 60 pages each month, filled with feature articles by top-notch columnists, readers' "finds," club happenings, show news, a china corner, a current listing of new glass issues to be aware of and a multitude of ads! You can find it in the **DAZE**! Keep up with what's happening in the dee gee world with a subscription to the **DAZE**. Buy, sell or trade from the convenience of your easy chair.

Name _____ Street _____

City _____ State _____ Zip _____

☐1 Year - $21.00 ☐Check Enclosed ☐Please bill me

☐Mastercard ☐Visa (Foreign subscribers - Please add $1.00 per year)

Card No. _____ Exp. Date _____

Signature _____

Send to: D.G.D., Box 57GF, Otisville, MI 48463-0008 - Please allow 30 days

Other Books by Gene Florence

Kitchen Glassware of the Depression Years, 5th Edition $19.95
Pocket Guide to Depression Glass, 10th Edition...........................$9.95
Collector's Encyclopedia of Depression Glass, 13th Edition...........$19.95
Collector's Encyclopedia of Occupied Japan I $14.95
Collector's Encyclopedia of Occupied Japan II.............................$14.95
Collector's Encyclopedia of Occupied Japan III............................$14.95
Collector's Encyclopedia of Occupied Japan IV............................$14.95
Collector's Encyclopedia of Occupied Japan V $14.95
Collector's Encyclopedia of Occupied Japan Price Guide I – V $9.95
Elegant Glassware of the Depression Era, VII..............................$19.95
Very Rare Glassware of the Depression Years, 3rd Series $24.95
Very Rare Glassware of the Depression Years, 4th Series $24.95
Very Rare Glassware of the Depression Years, 5th Series $24.95
Stemware Identification $24.95

Collector's Encyclopedia of Depression Glass, 13th edition
by Gene Florence

Since the first edition of *Collector's Encyclopedia of Depression Glass* was released in 1972, it has been America's #1 bestselling glass book. Gene Florence now presents the completely revised 13th edition, introducing newly discovered pieces — verified and confirmed. Dealing primarily with the glass made from the 1920s through the end of the 1930s, it is a complete reference to the most popular glassware collected. Prices have soared over the years and anything that is Depression glass, whether it is a known pattern or not, has added value and collectibility. With the assistance of several nationally-known dealers, this book illustrates, as well as realistically prices, those items in demand. It also has many old catalog reprints, updated values, stunning color photos, and a special section on reissues and fakes. This information comes from years of research, experience, fellow dealers and collectors, and millions of miles of travel.

#4938 • 8½ x 11 • 240 Pgs. • HB $19.95

Stemware Identification Featuring Cordials with Values, 1920s – 1960s
by Gene Florence

Gene Florence has compiled an extraordinary book to help identify the hundreds of stemware patterns made during the Depression era. An overwhelming amount of information is presented in a very easy-to-use format. Companies and patterns are listed alphabetically within the major sections which are divided by color. More than 600 different pattern variations are illustrated by a full-color photograph of a cordial for each listing. Many famous glassmakers are included such as Tiffin, Cambridge, and Heisey. It makes a great companion volume to Florence's other glassware books. The descriptive text for each cordial includes pattern, maker, color, height, as well as a current value. This deluxe, hardcover book, the first of its kind, will long be considered the ideal reference book for glassware collectors and dealers.

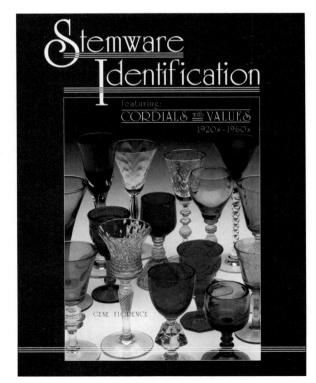

#4731 • 8½ x 11 • 160 Pgs. • HB. $24.95